PERSPECTIVES ON INTERNATIONAL TRADE

PERSPECTIVES ON INTERNATIONAL TRADE

ELTON V. SMITH (EDITOR)

Nova Science Publishers, Inc.
New York

Senior Editors: Susan Boriotti and Donna Dennis
Coordinating Editor: Tatiana Shohov
Office Manager: Annette Hellinger
Graphics: Wanda Serrano
Editorial Production: Vladimir Klestov, Matthew Kozlowski and Maya Columbus
Circulation: Ave Maria Gonzalez, Vera Popovic, Luis Aviles, Raymond Davis,
      Melissa Diaz and Jeannie Pappas
Communications and Acquisitions: Serge P. Shohov
Marketing: Cathy DeGregory

Library of Congress Cataloging-in-Publication Data
Available Upon Request

ISBN 1-59033-493-0.

CONTENTS

PREFACE

While some may dispute that economics is the driving force behind much of history, nobody can argue that trade is not a significant factor in international relations. In an increasingly globalized world, products are perpetually crossing borders, leading to both political and fiscal conflicts. Businesses have to face diverse markets and regions while worrying about protectionist government initiatives that hamper free trade. Even the ostensible champion of free markets, America, has its own streak of inhibiting the flow of goods; witness the recent steel tariffs which have angered European partners. No society, therefore, is immune to the pressures of world trade and the need to balance the free movement of products with the desire to preserve domestic industries.

This book assembles a collection of articles examining some of the most current and divisive issues in the international trade arena. They range from the tensions between the United States and Mexico in NAFTA to the war-fueled trade in diamonds in Africa. With such a broad range of issues discussed, this book serves as a needed tool for understanding the most important contemporary economic subjects.

Chapter 1

CONFLICT AND TRADE IN DIAMONDS

Nicolas Cook

ISSUE

The mining and sale of diamonds by parties involved in armed conflicts, notably in certain African countries, are regarded as a significant factor fueling hostilities. Such diamonds have been labeled "conflict diamonds" or "blood diamonds" because they fund purchases of arms and military materiel by belligerent forces. Trade in diamonds is a contributing factor to conflicts in Angola and the Democratic Republic of Congo (DRC). In Sierra Leone, where a fragile peace is taking hold, contention over control of diamond resources continues to generate political tensions and could potentially lead to renewed armed conflict. Diamonds have also contributed to the internationalization of all three civil conflicts. The possibility of gaining access to diamond wealth appears to have motivated foreign actors - including governments, private security-cum-mining firms, and mercenaries - to become party to each of these conflicts, reportedly in exchange for diamond mining rights.

BACKGROUND

Non-governmental organizations (NGOs) have campaigned to halt trade in conflict diamonds. As public knowledge of the problem has grown, and due to the persistence of diamond-related conflicts, international governmental organizations (IGOs) and national governments have undertaken legal, diplomatic, and military actions to halt the conflict diamond trade. The United Nations (U.N.) Security Council has prohibited trade in conflict diamonds and arms in Sierra Leone and Angola and has created several sanctions monitoring committees that have investigated and publicly documented developments relating to trade in conflict diamonds. An on-going, multilateral forum known as the Kimberley Process is focusing on legal and technical methods of controlling trade in conflict diamonds and is slated to present its findings to the 56th Session of the U.N. General Assembly (UNGA).

Controlling Conflict Diamonds

Effective policing of trade in conflict diamonds faces difficult challenges. The world diamond market is large. World diamond production in 2000 was estimated at about $7.86 billion, and U.S. diamond imports in 2000 totaled $12.093 billion. Diamonds are a highly fungible and concentrated form of wealth, and the legitimate international diamond industry is historically insular, self-regulating, and lacks transparency. Illicit trade in diamonds - of which the trade in conflict diamonds is a part, comprising between 3.7% and 8% of the international diamond trade by some estimates, and up to 15% by others - exploits these factors. Recent press reports have tied trade in conflict diamonds and other gems to several international terrorist organizations, including the Al Qaeda Organization of Osama bin Laden.

Policy Proposals

Most proposals to curtail trade in conflict diamonds seek to create systems to identify the origin of diamonds and to track trade in such gems in order to ensure that illicit diamonds do not enter into legitimate international commerce. Three primary approaches for determining or documenting the origin and provenance (place of purchase or import) of diamonds have been proposed.

- Structure-related, "geo-chemical," and other physical identification of diamonds based on analysis of trace elements and impurities within diamonds. Technologies to achieve these ends have not yet been perfected and are reportedly likely to remain prohibitively expensive in the near future.

- Tagging of diamonds, using laser and micro-etching technologies, to microscopically inscribe on individual diamonds identifying information, which can then be used to register and track them. High cost barriers prevent the widespread use of this approach in diamond commerce, and identifying marks may be subject to tampering.

- Certificate of origin laws. This approach seeks to create a legally-binding chain of warranties establishing the legitimate origin of diamonds and forming the basis for findings of legal fact in efforts to track and monitor trade in diamonds. Such an approach is likely to form a key part of any future international diamond trade regime. The effectiveness of certification regimes may be limited by weak administrative and regulatory systems in some poor diamond exporting states.

Industry Policy Initiatives

The Diamond High Council (HRD) is a formal trade organization representing the Belgian diamond industry. HRD has participated in the Kimberley Process, and has entered into bilateral agreements with the governments of Angola and Sierra Leone that employ certificate of origin export documentation systems, which HRD has helped to design.

The World Diamond Council (WDC) is an international diamond industry body representing the interests of large diamond trading firms and producing countries. Its stated aim is to develop and implement a tracking system for trade in rough diamonds to prevent the use of diamonds for illicit purposes. The WDC has proposed policies and model legislation to prevent illicit diamond trading, and its members are active in international forums focused on the issue, including the Kimberley Process.

De Beers, a large diamond production and trading business group, guarantees that it does not purchase or sell diamonds from "any area in Africa controlled by forces rebelling against the legitimate and internationally recognized government of the relevant country." It has also threatened to end business dealings with clients who trade in conflict diamonds. De Beers has participated in the Kimberley Process.

United Nations Policy

In addition to actions taken by the U.N. Security Council, the U.N. General Assembly (UNGA) has addressed the issue of conflict diamonds. In December 2000, UNGA adopted a resolution, A/RES/55/56, that sought to highlight the link between the illicit trade in diamonds and armed conflict and called for action to end such trade. The resolution was sponsored by 50 countries, including the United States, and is referenced in several congressional legislative proposals. UNGA is slated to consider the findings of the Kimberley Process.

U.S. Policy

U.S. efforts to curtail the trade in conflict diamonds were initiated by the Clinton Administration and centered on the creation of a multilateral diamond trade regime and the implementation of U.N. Security Council resolutions prohibiting trade in conflict diamonds. The Administration promoted this goal in multilateral forums, such as the G-8 and the Kimberley Process and took unilateral action to isolate and penalize governments that abet the illicit trade. It also sponsored diamond trade policy forums and contributed technical assistance to African diamond producing nations to enable them to develop diamond export regulatory systems. The Clinton Administration also sought to ensure that legitimate diamond-producing, democratic African states would not be harmed by efforts to end illicit diamond trading. Some Members of Congress criticized the Clinton Administration for not taking effective, concrete, and rapid action to prevent trade in conflict diamonds. The Administration countered that it had actively worked to curtail the conflict diamond trade, but did not believe that a firm international consensus - which it viewed as an essential prerequisite for successful policy formulation - had yet developed.

Bush Administration policies seek to end trade in conflict diamonds appear to share many of the same goals and approaches as those of the Clinton Administration. The Bush Administration has supported the passage of resolutions by the U.N. Security Council that prohibit the importation of diamonds from Liberia, as well as diamonds from Angola and Sierra Leone that are not certified by the governments of those countries. It has enforced such sanctions by executive order. It has also continued U.S. participation in the Kimberley

Process, as well as periodic meetings of an inter-agency group working on conflict diamond policy. Administration representatives have stated that congressional legislative initiatives have motivated an international unity of purpose within the Kimberley Process and that any final agreements relating to the Kimberley Process will likely require congressional legislative action.

Congressional Role

Congressional interest in ending the armed hostilities associated with the conflict diamond trade has generated several legislative initiatives. These proposals have generally aimed at curtailing the ability of rebel groups fighting internationally recognized governments to fund their armed activities through diamond sales. Several hearings in both the House and Senate have addressed the issue of conflict diamonds and related U.S. policies on Sierra Leone, Liberia, Angola, and U.N. activities in Africa. On October 10, 2001, the Subcommittee on Trade of the Committee on Ways and Means held a hearing entitled "Conflict Diamonds."

LEGISLATION

As in the 106th Congress, several conflict diamond-related bills have been introduced during the 107th Congress. *H.R. 918* (Hall) and *S. 1084* (Durbin), both entitled the Clean Diamonds Act and H.R. 2722(Houghton), entitled the Clean Diamond Trade Act, would prohibit diamond imports into the United States unless the exporting country is implementing rough diamond import and export controls that meet certain criteria. H.R. 918 and S. 1084 would prohibit the Overseas Private Investment Corporation (OPIC) and the Export-Import Bank (Ex-Im Bank) from engaging in certain transactions that assist countries violating the Act's requirements. On November 28, *H.R. 2722* as amended, was passed by 408 to 6 under a motion to suspend the rules (Roll no. 453). On November 29, the measure was received in the Senate, read the first time, read the second time on November 30 and placed on the Senate Legislative Calendar under General Orders, Calendar No. 248.

S. 787 (Gregg), the Conflict Diamonds Act of 2001, would prohibit the importation, or abetment thereof, of diamonds exported from Sierra Leone, Angola, or Liberia, except for diamonds certified by the internationally recognized governments of Sierra Leone or Angola. It would prohibit imports into the United States of diamonds from countries that are not signatories to an international rough diamond import and export certification agreement, that are not implementing such an agreement, or that are not acting unilaterally to establish and enforce a similar certification system. *S. 787* would authorize the President to prohibit imports of diamonds from Angola or Sierra Leone doing so is reasonably necessary to uphold conflict diamond-related UN Security Council resolutions. *H.R. 918, S. 1084, H.R. 2722*, and *S. 787* urge the President to negotiate an international agreement to eliminate the trade in conflict diamonds. Section 404 of *S.1215* (Hollings) would have enacted into law *S. 787* of the 107th Congress (as introduced on April 26, 2001), but *S. 1215* was indefinitely postponed in the Senate by unanimous consent after *H.R. 2500* a House alternative to *S. 1215* became law.

H.R. 2506 (Kolbe) would prohibit certain OPIC and Ex-Im Bank diamond-related projects in countries that are not implementing a system of rough diamond export and import controls, as defined in the Act. It would also prohibit the use of funds appropriated by the Act to assist countries that the Secretary of State determines, according to criteria outlined in the Act, to have actively destabilized the democratically elected government of Sierra Leone or aided or abetted illicit trade in Sierra Leonean diamonds.

Chapter 2

STEEL INDUSTRY AND TRADE ISSUES

Stephen Cooney

SUMMARY

The U.S. steel industry has faced increasing difficulties since the late 1990s, owing to a wide range of domestic and international problems, including intensified competition from imports since 1997. Imports increased from less than 20% in the early 1990s, to a pea share of 28% of apparent consumption in 1998. Import levels have fallen from this pea, but domestic producers in 2000-01 were further affected by rising energy prices, a general economic slowdown and a rising dollar exchange rate that has favored foreign-based competitors. More than 20 U.S. steel producers, including such famous names as Bethlehem, LTV, Republic and Wheeling Pittsburgh, have gone into bankruptcy and some mills have ceased operating. While different companies and parts of the industry have been affected in different degrees, active and retired steelworkers and their union representatives have become particularly concerned about the industry's possible inability to continue to fund pension and healthcare benefit commitments.

U.S. policymakers responded with a variety of measures, the House of Representatives in early 1999 approved a bill that would have required the President to set strict import quotas, or take other measures that would have rolled back imports to a level prevailing before the 1998-98 import surge. This measure did not pass the Senate, but the Clinton Administration responded with a "Steel Action Program" that included expedited enforcement of U.S. antidumping and countervailing duty laws, as well as a Section 201 trade case focused on wire rod and line pipe products. The 106th Congress approved and President Clinton signed laws to establish an Emergency Steel Loan Guarantee program and to distribute penalty duties from trade remedy cases, which frequently involve the steel industry, to plaintiffs.

These measures did not prevent a new downturn in the industry in 2001. The problems of the steel industry remain a major concern in the 107th Congress. A broader version of the 1999 import quota law was reintroduced and gained a majority of the House as co-sponsors. Pressed to act by Members of Congress, steel companies and labor representatives, President Bush on June 5, 2001, announced that he would request the U.S. International Trade

Commission to undertake a broad Section 201 trade case on the steel industry. On the other hand, some Members of Congress and economists are concerned that measures to aid the steel industry will have a negative impact on the competitiveness of a broad range of U.S. steel-consuming businesses. President Bush also indicated that as a major component of his strategy he would seek multilateral international negotiations on global overcapacity in the steel industry and future rules for world steel trade.

This report examines the recent performance of the U.S. steel industry and related policy issues, including the Bush Administration Section 201 initiative and measures in Congress addressing other aspects of problems in the steel industry. The report concludes with a review of the possible courses of action that the Administration and Congress may take, especially if there is no short-term recovery in the domestic steel industry.

BACKGROUND AND ISSUES

Since the late 1990s, the U.S. steel industry has experience increasing difficulties. Much of the industry has been in serious trouble since the financial crises of 1997-98 in Asia, Russia, and Latin America contributed to a rise in U.S. steel imports. After reactions from the Clinton Administration and Congress, imports fell in 1999 and the domestic steel industry staged a partial recovery by early 2000. However, this recovery was undermined by a renewed rise in imports, by a suddenly slowing domestic U.S. economy, and by the big rise in energy prices that affected the energy-intensive steel industry in 2000. The exchange rate of the U.S. dollar also increased nearly 30% in value against a range of other currencies after early 1997, making U.S.-produced steel less price-competitive.

Some commentators also say that there are still too many older, inefficient domestic mills that are not competitive with newer, more productive plants here and abroad, and that contracted wage and benefit costs are obstacles to restricting, consolidation, and modernization. Whatever the reasons, by October, 2001, more than 20 steel companies were in bankruptcy. Companies operating under Chapter 11 included LTV, Republic and Wheeling Pittsburgh, joined on October 15, 2001, by Bethlehem Steel, another large and historic integrated producer. Without improved economic prospects, the industry is finding it difficult to raise the financing necessary for further restructuring and modernization. Meanwhile, some companies are unable to fund the pension and healthcare packages for steelworkers and retirees to which they agreed in the 1980s, at the time of a major industry restructuring, an issue known as "legacy costs."

U.S. policymakers have responded to the problems of the industry with a variety of measures. The industry and the Commerce Department have filed dozens of antidumping and countervailing duty (AD/CVD) cases against foreign producers in recent years.[1] The 106th Congress passed and the President signed two laws specifically designed to assist the industry, the Emergency Steel Loan Guarantee Act of 1999 (P.L. 106-51) and the Continued dumping and Subsidy Offset Act, the latter added as a rider to the FY 2001 Agriculture appropriations bill (P.L. 106-387). Moreover, the House overwhelmingly approved a steel

---

[1] Antidumping is relief to remedy the adverse price impact of imports sold on the U.S. market at unfairly low prices...Countervailing duty is relief from the adverse price impact of imports that receive foreign government subsidies." In both cases, the form of relief is extra duties on imports. CRS Report RL30461, *Trade Remedy Law in the 107th Congress*, by William H. Cooper, p. 3.

import quota bill, which did not pass the Senate, but to which the Clinton Administration responded with a "Steel Action Program" in August, 1999.[2]

The continuing difficulties of the industry have ensured that steel-related issues remain a preoccupation in the 107th Congress. A new and more far-reaching mandatory quotas bill (H.R. 808), which would also establish a steel sales tax to pay for legacy costs, has been introduced and has gained 225 co-sponsors in the House. Legacy cost issues are also addressed in a bill that would reauthorize, revamp and expand the Trade Adjustment Assistance program (S. 1209). Legislation to strengthen the steel loan guarantee program has passed the Senate, as a rider to the Interior appropriations bill (July 12, 2001). Bills have been introduced in each body to make it easier for domestic plaintiffs to win trade remedy cases (H.R. 1988 and S. 979) and to enact relief for the upstream iron ore industry (H.R. 837 and S. 422).

Under increasing pressure from Congress, industry and workers' representatives, and after consultations with all three groups, the Bush Administration initiated an investigation of the steel industry under Section 201 of U.S. trade law on June 5, 2001. Such action, in conformity with the "safeguard" provisions of World Trade Organization (WTO) rules, allows a WTO ember country to implement temporary trade relief for a domestic industry after finding that it has been injured by suddenly higher levels of imports. Under U.S. law, the presidential request has gone to the U.S. International Trade Commission (ITC), for an investigation to determine if high import levels are a substantial cause of injury to the U.S. industry. The ITC has six months to investigate, report its findings and make recommendations, if any, for industry relief. President Bush may apply or support the ITC recommendations for action, take other measures on his own, or decide to take no action at all. In addition to this Section 201 case, the President also announced that his administration would inaugurate multilateral negotiations with other steel producing nations. The goals of these discussions would be to address the overcapacity in global steel markets and to consider the rules governing international trade in steel and subsidization of domestic industries.

Although Congress may await the outcome of these White House initiatives before taking any steel trade policy measures on its own, it may well act on some of the other initiatives noted above. Such steps could have an impact on U.S. industry, trade policy and the global steel trade environment. Moreover, the terrorist attacks of September 11 have added new concerns regarding national security to congressional considerations of steel-related issues. Some of these views were expressed by Members of Congress during the ITC's Section 201 case hearings later that month. And United Steelworkers union president Leo Gerard in his statement at the hearings directly quoted the words of President Bush from his visit to a US Steel plant's company picnic on August 26:

> If you're worried about the security of the country and you become over-reliant on foreign sources of steel, it can easily affect the capacity of our military to be well-supplied. Steel is an important job issue; it's also an important national security issue.[3]

---

[2] The Clinton Administration's views and response to the industry's trade difficulties are summarized in a special report. U.S. Department of Commerce. *Global Steel Trade: Structural Problems and Future* Solutions: Report to the President, *(July 26, 2000), www.ita.doc.gov/media/steelreport726.html.*

[3] Quoted in Leo W. Gerard, Statement before ITC Hearing on Steel, Investigation no. TA-201-73 (September 17, 2001), p. 4.

Also, Rep. Stephanie Tubbs Jones on September 21, 2001, introduced H.Con. Res. 234, with the support of 13 co-sponsors. It linked the September 11 attacks to the national security importance of the U.S. steel industry. No action has been taken on this measure. In terms of the direct impact of the attacks on the steel industry, the destruction of the World Trade Center included an estimated 300,000 tons of structural steel.[4] But the timing and nature of any rebuilding are probably too far in the future to have any immediate stimulative effects on demand.

The Bush Administration during the next several months will also be following up on other initiatives already in place before it announced its decision to pursue the Section 201 case. The Customs Service is implementing the 2000 Continued Dumping and Subsidy Offset Act, under which proceeds of penalty duties are to be paid to successful plaintiffs in AD/CVD cases. Nine U.S. trading partners have already begun the process of challenging this law before the WTO. The Bush Administration must also complete the investigation under Section 232 of U.S. trade law into the national security implications of high levels of imports of iron ore and semi-finished steel, which it initiated in February, 2001, following a request from some Members of Congress.

This chapter will review each of these issues in more detail.

- It will first review recent industry developments and the current economic situation of the steel industry.
- Second, the report will review the Section 201 case inaugurated by the Bush Administration.
- Third, the report will review other policy measures initiated by Congress with respect to the steel industry.
- In conclusion, the report will review dome possible courses of action that the Administration and Congress may consider, especially if no recovery in the steel industry is forthcoming in the near future.

THE U.S. STEEL INDUSTRY AND ITS COMPETITORS

The Asian financial crisis began in Thailand in 1997 and quickly spread across that region. It dampened demand for steel in that previously fast-growing region, and led Asian steelmakers to seek markets in the United States and Europe. By mid-1998, the financial crisis had spread to Russia and Brazil. These countries also sought to maintain steel production, in the face of domestic recessions and global oversupply of steel, by selling a larger share of their output to the United States. The result was a 33 percent increase in steel imports in 1998 over imports that were already at a record level in 1997. Japan, Korea, and Russia accounted for the largest share of increased imports (76%). Exacerbating the problem was the rising dollar that made low-priced foreign-produced steel even more competitive against U.S. products.

According to the Department of Commerce study, *Global Steel Trade: Structural Problems and Future Solutions,* the heavy volume of low-cost steel entering the U.S. market

---

[4] *American Metal Market (AMM),* October 2 and 4, 2001.

drove prices below levels at which U.S. producers could continue to make steel at a profit.[5]
Figure 1 shows the evolution of market supply in the 1990s. It indicates the total apparent
U.S. consumption of steel (finished and semi-finished) for each year, and the share that was
provided by imports.[6] Through 1992, the U.S. steel industry was still protected by voluntary
trade restraint agreements negotiated in the 1980s. These were allowed to lapse after failure to
negotiate a multilateral steel trade agreement.[7] Apparent consumption grew strongly in the
mid-1990s. But imports accounted for more than half of the increase between 1990-93
average levels and the 1998 peak – and surging imports accounted for all of the net one-year
growth in 1998.

Figure 1. U.S. Steel Consumption and Imports, 1990-2001

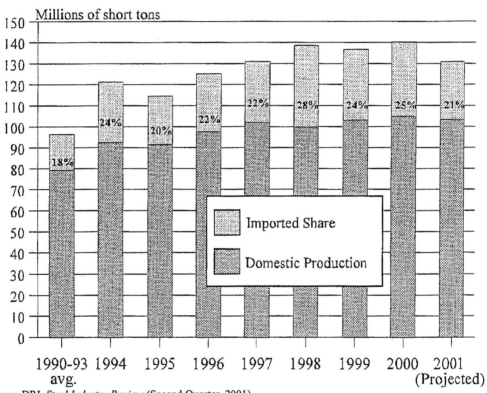

Source: DRI. *Steel Industry Review* (Second Quarter, 2001)

Some stakeholders have stated that part of the steel crisis is attributable to inefficient
domestic mills ("unproductive domestic capacity"[8]). But a 1999 report by the ITC suggests
that such an explanation in 1998 told only part of the story:

---

[5] *Global Steel Trade,* p. 27. An exhaustive, detailed and updated analysis of the industry's economic condition and
the developments that led to the present situation is the publicly released version of the ITC staff report, *Steel:
Prehearing Report to the Commission on Investigation No. TA-201-73* (September 4, 2001).

[6] "Apparent domestic consumption" equals total domestic product shipments plus imports, minus exports.

[7] Gary Clyde Hufbauer and Ben Goodrich, *Steel: Big Problems, Better Solutions* Washington, DC: Institute for
International Economics, International Economics Policy Brief no. PB01-9, July 2001, p. 1.

[8] Joseph B. Francois and Laura Baughman. *Costs to American Consuming Industries of Steel Quotas and Taxes.*
Washington, DC. The Consuming Industries Trade Action Coalition. April 30, 2001. P. 1.

Indeed, the same trends for the industry as a whole are also apparent in the separate results of both integrated mills and mini-mills. ... In fact, mini-mills fared even worse than integrated mills from 1997 to 1998. ... The worse financial performance of [mini-mill] producers reflects in part their greater dependence on the merchant market, where imports are concentrated.[9]

By mid-1998, U.S. companies were losing substantial market share to imports of cheaper foreign steel. Many previously profitable domestic steelmakers experienced a decline in sales revenue, operating income, and profit in 1998 and 1999. Some small companies experienced a loss of access to capital and liquidity problems, which forced more than a few companies into bankruptcy.[10] Confronted with a crisis in the industry, U.S. steel companies, steelworkers, and many Members of Congress argued that federal support for the steel industry and its workers was necessary. A number of measures were adopted to bolster the industry and to reduce the adverse impact of imports. But these measures have not averted a further worsening of conditions in parts of the industry since then.

In September 1998, the steel industry filed antidumping cases with the ITC against hot-rolled steel from Brazil, Japan, and Russia and a countervailing duty case against Brazil. As the situation worsened in other product areas, additional petitions were filed. In response to the import surge, the Clinton Administration responded by conducting more than 100 AD/CVD investigations on steel products, a number of which were expedited to provide faster relief to industry. According to Robert LaRussa, then-Under Secretary for International Trade, "these helped turn back massive import surges seen during the 1998 crisis."[11]

The Clinton Administration issued a Steel Action Program on August 5, 1999, which had three main elements that included: (1) vigorous enforcement of U.S. trade laws, including expedited investigations; (2) bilateral efforts to address the underlying problems that led to the crisis, including consultations with Japan and Korea, and an agreement with Russia to limit steel imports; and (3) improved import monitoring mechanisms to detect potential import surges. Moreover, the Congress passed, and the President signed, the Emergency Steel Loan Guarantee Act (August 17, 1999), which was designed to assist financing of troubled steel companies unable to obtain commercial loans at reasonable rates.[12]

---

[9] U.S. International Trade Commission. *Certain Hot-rolled Steel Products from Japan,* Publication no. 3202 (June 1999), p. 19. Cited in *Global Steel Trade,* p. 27.

[10] *Global Steel Trade.* P. 34.

[11] U.S. Department of Commerce. International Trade Administration. *Testimony of Undersecretary Robert S. LaRussa before the Senate and House Steel Caucus.* December 12, 2000. (http://www/ita/doc/gov/media/larussa121200.htm).

[12] Section 101(b) of that Act contained a number of congressional findings, including –
  1) the United States steel industry has been severely harmed by a record surge of more than 40,000,000 tons of steel imports into the United States in 1998, caused by the world financial crisis;
  2) this surge in imports resulted in the loss of more than 10,000 steel worker jobs in 1998, and was the imminent cause of three bankruptcies by medium-sized steel companies, Acme Steel, Laclede Steel, and Geneva Steel;
  3) the crisis also forced almost all United States steel companies into –
   A) reduced volume, lower prices, and financial losses; and
   B) an inability to obtain credit for continued operations and reinvestment in facilities;
  4) the crisis also has affected the willingness of private banks and investment institutions to make loans to the United States steel industry for continued operation and reinvestment in facilities;
  5) these steel bankruptcies, job losses, and financial losses are also having serious negative effects on the tax base of cities, counties, and States, and on the essential health, education, and municipal services that these government entities provide to their citizens; and

Despite these measures, large parts of the U.S. steel industry have never fully recovered from the 1997-98 import surge. Steel imports initially fell in 1999 as a share of U.S. consumption, as shown in Figure 1. However, the import share rose again in 2000 to 25%, substantially above the average 18% level of the early '90's. With penetration levels at 25% or higher, imported steel captured much of the increase in demand for steel that accompanied the strong growth in the U.S. economy in the late 1990s. According to another data source, many product areas experienced double-digit, or even triple-digit, one-year import percentage increases in 2000. And the increases were registered from a wide range of foreign sources.[13] But the same data source notes the substantial disagreement between domestic producers and users over the causes and nature of the problems of the U.S. industry. "Almost universally, U.S. steel producers blame the second-highest import year on record for their late-2000 financial losses. Steel importers disagree, saying the problems can be traced to early-2000 domestic price increases that made cheaper foreign-made steel more attractive."[14]

In its early 2001 forecasts, the economics consulting firm DRI projected a good-news, bad-news outlook for the steel industry. It stated that under most likely scenarios, imports may level off or fall – but partly because prices in the U.S. market are likely to remain depressed, and therefore, the market will be relatively less attractive to foreign exporters. Demand could pick up modestly in the latter part of the year, as excess inventories from 2000 are worked off and because widespread bankruptcies could leave a number of U.S. steelmakers permanently shuttered.[15] Through the first half of 2001, import tonnage levels were almost 30% lower than in early 2000.[16] The American Iron and Steel Institute (AISI), however, emphasized that second-quarter finished steel imports were on the rise again, 13% higher than in the first quarter, and import prices were lower than in 1998 in many import product lines.[17] Neither domestic production nor prices had launched a sustained recovery by mid-2001. Average steel industry capacity utilization for 2001 through early August was 79%, down about 10 points from the same period in 2000, according to weekly AISI figures.[18]

Figure 2 illustrates a point made frequently in the policy sections of this report that follow. The impact of trade and industry problems for steel has not been even across the sector. The production of the large integrated mills using mostly basic oxygen furnaces (the last U.S. open hearth plant closed in 1991) has been essentially flat since 1990, around 60 million short tons per year. Mini-mills employing electric-arc furnaces and reprocessing steel from scrap have steadily increased production since the recession of 1991. Their market share is almost 50% of domestic raw steel production, up from 37% at the beginning of the 1990s. In fact, DRI estimates that in the second quarter of 2001 production from mini-mills was virtually even with the output of domestic integrated plants in a slowing market. DRI further

---

6)   A strong steel industry is necessary to the adequate defense preparedness of the United States in order to have sufficient steel available to build the ships, tanks, planes, and armaments necessary for the national defense.

[13] "Steel Imports the Second-Highest Ever in 2000," *Purchasing.com* (March 2001).

[14] *Ibid.*

[15] DRI-WEFA. *Steel Industry Review,* summary forecasts at p. 1 for the 1st and 2nd quarter editions, 2001.

[16] According to the final June 2001 steel import data released by the U.S. Census Bureau Foreign Trade Division on August 17, 2001.

[17] American Iron and Steel Institute, "Finished Steel Imports in Second Quarter Up 13 percent from First Quarter..l.AISI Renews Calls for Effective 201 Trade Remedy" (press release), July 31, 2001 (www.steel.org/news/pr/2001/pr010731_imp.htm).

[18] *AMM,* August 8, 2001.

projects that mini-mills will slowly pull ahead over the coming decade.[19] Figure 2 also shows the source of supply from imports increasing, so that the integrated mills are under competitive pressure for some products from two different sources. Hence, the integrated mills and mini-mills have conflicting views on some policy issues, though both types of producers have supported President Bush's call for the Section 201 investigation of the industry.[20]

Figure 2. Sources of U.S. Steel

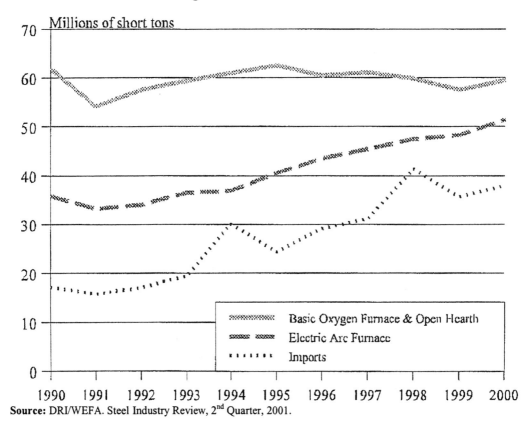

Source: DRI/WEFA. Steel Industry Review, 2nd Quarter, 2001.

But this U.S. industry call for a Section 201 case conflicts with the interests of a wide range of U.S. trading partners. **Figure 3** lists all trading partners that exported at least 500,000 tons of steel to the United States in 2000. It shows that significant exporters of steel to the United States form a geographically and economically diverse group. Almost every world region has at least one representative country in the group, although about a third of all imported steel, more than 11 million metric tons (MT), is from eastern and western Europe.

---

[19] DRI-WEFA. *Steel Industry Review* (2nd qtr., 2001), Tables 2 and 4.
[20] A recent letter from Andrew Sharkey, President of AISI, however, notes that "eight of the 18 U.S. steel producers that have declared bankruptcies have been electric-arc-furnace producers," and that electric furnaces account for more than half of closed capacity; *Industry Week,* August 13, 2001.

Figure 3. Sources of U.S. Steel Imports, 2000 (% Shares of Total Tonnage Imports)

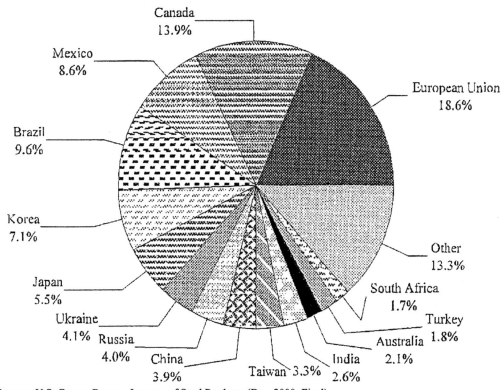

Source: U.S. Census Bureau. Imports of Steel Products (Dec. 2000, Final).

The European Union is a high-wage trading area with a mature steel industry facing some of the same problems as parts of the U.S. industry. Yet, the EU is actually the largest source of U.S. imported steel, some 6.4 million MT in 2000. Within the EU, most member countries export steel to the U.S. market. The leader is Germany (1.8 million MT), more than twice the total of any other EU member. France, Netherlands, and the U.K. and Spain follow in order, all above 500,000 MT, while Belgium and Italy each exported more than 400,000 MT to the United States in 2000. The U.S. market is thus an important one for this European industry that has been as troubled as ours in recent decades. The EU has been one of the toughest critics of U.S. steel trade policy and has begun to file WTO cases against the United States, in response to U.S. trade remedy measures.

Our North American Free Trade Area (NAFTA) partners, Canada (4.8 million MT) and Mexico (nearly 3.0 million MT), ranked second and fourth among steel exporters to the United States. They were exempted by the Clinton Administration from the limited Section 201 trade actions in 2000. (See next section of this report.) Their steel industries and economies will continue to rely heavily on unrestricted access to the U.S. market, and U.S. industry stakeholders are divided in their views on how to deal with them. AISI has called for NAFTA trading partners to be excluded from U.S. trade remedies, emphasizing that North

America has less capacity than actual consumption, unlike the rest of the world.[21] The United Steelworkers union would exempt Canada, but include Mexico in the Section 201 case.[22]

Brazil ranked third in 2000 with 3.3 million MT in steel exports to the United States. Brazil relies more heavily now on the U.S. market as it and its regional trading partners feel the trade and financial effects of the recession in Argentina and the general slowdown in world economic growth. Korea at 2.4 million MT is the leading Asian supplier, followed by Japan (1.9 million MT) and Taiwan, farther down the list at 1.1 million MT. Current and former centrally planned economies are represented by Ukraine, Russia and China, each with around 1.3-1.4 million MT of exports to the United States in 2000. In Russia, Ukraine and perhaps other former Soviet republics such as Moldova, the collapse of the Soviet Union has left major domestic industries without big government-financed projects that provided major markets for their steel. So now they look to the global market, including the United States.[23] Imports from former Soviet republics benefit from duty-free treatment under the Generalized System of Preferences (GSP) that the United States accords many developing countries, although the U.S. Trade Representative has suspended this status for the Ukraine in a dispute over intellectual property rights issues unrelated to trade in steel.[24] India exported nearly 1 million MT of steel to the United States in 2000, and Australia, Turkey and South Africa exported well over a half-million MT each. Even this long list of countries leaves an additional 13% of U.S. import supply in 2000 coming from other well-known producers, such as Venezuela, Argentina and Poland.

The big decline in imports in the first half of 2001 was not evenly distributed. Tonnage imports from the EU fell only by 11%, and from Germany and France only by single-digit margins, as compared to the first half of 2000. NAFTA imports, from Canada and Mexico, were down by 18% in each case. The biggest declines proportionally were from India (83%), Ukraine (79%) and Taiwan (68%), while imports actually increased from Turkey (up 31%) and Russia (up 17%).[25] A major determinant of gains and losses is product mix, with demand for steel used in construction holding up well compared to other products.

There are many reasons for the attractiveness of the U.S. market for international steel producers. In a period of slow global growth and a strong dollar, the U.S. market has become a safety valve for a systemic overcapacity that is distinctive for this industry. Gary Hufbauer and Ben Goodrich of the Institute for International Economics note that integrated steel mills have high fixed costs, so that "it makes sense for struggling steel firms to continue running their plants so long as the margi9nal revenues from extra production at least cover variable costs...economic logic differs somewhat for mini-mills...but while [they] account for a big share of U.S. steel production...their share of global production is much smaller. The world steel industry is still characterized by integrated steel producers and their overcapacity problems."[26]

Using data from the International Iron and Steel Institute and the Clinton Administration report, Global Steel Trade, Hufbauer and Goodrich calculate that global overcapacity at the

---

[21] "AISI Chairman Says Section 201 Relief Should Exclude NAFTA Partners," BNA, *Daily Report for Executives (DER)*, May 15, 2001.

[22] *AMM*, June 27, 2001.

[23] See, for example, Section 3.1 of *Global Steel Trade*.

[24] Office of the U.S. Trade Representative, press release, August 24, 2001 (www.ustr.gov).

[25] U.S. Bureau of the Census, Foreign Trade Division, "U.S. Imports for Consumption of Steel Products from Selected Countries and Areas," (June 2001 Final), Exhibit 2.

[26] Hufbauer and Goodrich, p. 3.

height of the 1998 steel import surge was 275 million MT, out of total world production of 776 million MT.[27] Using 1999 OECD figures, the Canadian Steel Producers Association reported that the U.S. steel industry was the only one whose production level was substantially below domestic consumption (about 15%). The Canadian steel industry's production was about equal to consumption, and only the U.S. and Canada were major net steel importers. Using this production/consumption ratio, the Canadian producers reckoned that the EUU overcapacity level was about 14%, Korea and Japan, 30-40%, Mexico 66% and Russia 191%.[28] Clearly, any plan to address steel trade issues would have major diplomatic implications. But U.S. steelmakers have cited job losses, past industry closures and capacity levels below current consumption to argue that they should not be required to participate in global capacity downsizing.[29] On the other hand, the European Commission has also argued that their producers have restructured, eliminated jobs, capacity and a net steel trade surplus, and that the U.S. industry should get its own domestic house in order before seeking further trade remedies.[30]

RELIEF UNDER SECTION 201 OF U.S. TRADE LAW

On June 5, 2001, responding to many requests from Congress, union representatives and steel companies, President Bush announced that his Administration would call upon the ITC to begin an investigation under Section 201 of U.S. trade law. He also announced that he would seek multilateral negotiations with U.S. trading partners on fundamental issues of overcapacity and subsidies.[31] Congress may defer action on further trade remedy measures until it sees the outcome of the Section 201 initiative.

Section 201 relief, often referred to as "safeguard" or "escape clause" relief, is defined in sections 201-204 of the Trade Act of 1974, as amended (19 U.S.C. 2251-2254). In conformity with WTO rules, safeguard relief provides for temporary duties, quotas, or other restrictions on imports that may be traded fairly, but that enter in such quantities as to cause or threaten to cause serious injury to a domestic industry. The relief is intended to give the domestic industry an opportunity to adjust to the new competition and remain competitive. Within six months, the ITC must conduct an investigation, determine if relief is warranted, and recommend appropriate remedial action from a specified range of options. The President then decides whether to implement the recommended measure, apply an alternative measure, or take no action at all.[32]

The steel industry already received limited import relief under Section 201 safeguard actions undertaken by the Clinton Administration in 1999-2000, but these measures are controversial. They focused specifically on steel wire rod and line pipe products. Although

---

[27] *Ibid.*
[28] Canadian Steel Producers Association, "Addressing World Steel Overcapacity" (May 1, 2001), reproduced in *Inside US Trade,* May 11, 2001.
[29] *AMM,* July 20, 2001.
[30] Letter of EU Ambassador Gunter Burghardt to USTR Robert Zoellick, May 3, 2001 (reproduced in *Inside US Trade,* May 11, 2001), and European Commission press release, June 5, 2001.
[31] President George W. Bush. *Statement by the President Regarding a Multilateral Initiative on Steel.* (June 5, 2001), http://www.whitehousereleases/2001/0605-4.html.
[32] CRS Trade Briefing Book, *Section 201 of the Trade Act of 1974* by Jeanne J. Grimmett (http://www.congress. gov/brbk/html/ebtra68.html)

relief was granted for a three-year period in accordance with WTO safeguard rules, the remedies have been questioned under WTO procedures and formal challenges from Korea and the EU are proceeding. The basis of the challenge is that the U.S. included Canadian and Mexican imports into the calculation when assessing the impact of imports on domestic steel producers, but did not subsequently apply remedy measures to these NAFTA imports.[33] At the same time, U.S. wire rod producers were also disappointed that the remedies did not apply to NAFTA competitors, and succeeded in gaining a subsequent ruling from the ITC that imports from these sources are indeed a substantial cause to injury to the industry.[34]

On June 22, 2001, U.S. Trade Representative Robert Zoellick forwarded the formal Bush Administration Section 201 request to the ITC. More than 500 steel mill products were covered in the request, including carbon and alloy flat, long, and pipe and tube products (wire rod and line pipe products are in the separate 201 case mentioned above), as well as some stainless and tool steel products. Most semi-finished steel products were included, but not the upstream inputs (iron ore, pig iron and coke), which some Members of Congress had urged be included.[35] The ITC held a series of hearings on the issue of injury to the steel industry from imports starting on September 17, 2001. Should the ITC finding be affirmative, which could be announced before the end of October, the hearings on possible remedies would begin on November 5, 2001.[36]

Senator Jay Rockefeller separately pursued a Senate Finance Committee resolution that would independently call for an ITC investigation, in addition to the presidential action. Sen. Rockefeller had originally considered including upstream inputs in a committee-sponsored request of its own to the ITC, but the final committee resolution endorsed the Administration action and product list, as well as the effort to seek a multilateral agreement. Accordingly, the ITC consolidated the Section 201 case requests from the Administration and Congress.[37]

United Steelworkers of America (USWA) President Leo Gerard called the Administration's 201 case "reasonably comprehensive," though he expressed disappointment regarding exclusion of the upstream inputs.[38] The reaction of steel industry producer associations, including the American Iron and Steel Institute and the Steel Manufacturers Association (the latter primarily representing mini-mills), has been almost uniformly favorable to the Section 201 case.[39] The American Institute for International Steel, representing importers, indicated that it would oppose "protectionist" actions or subsidization of the domestic industry, but supported the President's intention to address global

---

[33] "Korea Asks for WTO Ruling on U.S. Line Pipe Safeguard," *Inside U.S. Trade* (Sept. 29, 2000). European Commission Communication to Chairman of WTO Dispute Settlement Body (WT/DS214/4), August 10, 2001.

[34] *AMM*, August 23, 2001; *DER*, "ITC Says Import Surge of Wire rod from Canada, Mexico Is Undermining Relief," August 24, 2001.

[35] Letter from U.S. Trade representative Robert B. Zoellick to Chairman Stephen Koplan, U.S. International Trade Commission (June 22, 2001) with attachments. See also *Inside US Trade*, "Steel Section 201 Request to Include Semi-Finished Steel," June 22, 2001; *AMM*, June 26, 2001; and *DER*, "USTR Zoellick Asks ITC to Launch Probe on Steel Imports' Impact on U.S. Industry," June 26, 2001.

[36] U.S. International Trade Commission, "Investigation No. TA-201-73 (Steel)," announcement of June 28, 2001 ([http://www.usitc.gov/10629Y2.htm]).

[37] *AMM*, July 18 and 31, 2001; the Finance Committee resolution was forwarded by letter to the chairman of the ITC on July 26, 2001. U.S. International Trade Commission, revised announcement on consolidation of Senate Finance Committee request with USTR request of June 22, 2001, for a Section 201 investigation on steel, August 16, 2001.

[38] *DER, loc. cit.*

[39] *AMM*, June 7, 2001.

overcapacity and foreign governments' subsidization of the steel industry.[40] The International Iron and Steel Institute (IISI), the Brussels-based international industry organization, has called "for a rapid and positive response of the major steel-producing nations" to the Bush proposal on multilateral negotiations.[41]

The Consuming Industries Trade Action Coalition (CITAC) responded negatively to the 201 case and pointed out that their earlier study had found that steel import quotas could cost "as much as $2.34 billion annually or up to $565,000 per steel job"[42] Hufbauer and Goodrich calculated the total cost of quota protection at $3.5 billion or $363,000 per job, and emphasized that most of the benefits would go to creditors, investors and competitors, not directly to steelworkers.[43] Jon Jensen, President of CITAC, was quoted as saying that the problem of legacy costs was due to bad decisions made by the heads of integrated steel mills. "They made promises they can't keep. Why should the taxpayers and the steel users be made to feel guilty over promises they can't keep?" In the event of an ITC finding of injury, import quotas, he claimed, would add 15 to 20% to steel prices.[44]

International Reaction

The international reaction to the Section 201 case can best be described as guarded. The EU quickly announced its "disappointment" with the Bush decision to proceed with a broad 201 investigation.[45] But an EU representative testified at the ITC hearings on Section 201, showing a willingness to participate in the ITC deliberative process. Representatives of the Canadian and Mexican governments, as well as individual producers, also appeared at the ITC hearings. They argued that as North American producers, they have also been affected by import competition.[46] Indeed, under its own safeguard action Mexico has raised duties for non-NAFTA steel imports to 29% for one year.[47]

In recognition of the global nature of steel industry issues, other governments agreed to join representatives of the Bush Administration in discussing overcapacity and trade issues. Despite the disruptions of the September 11 terrorist attacks, the initial discussions took place on September 17-18 at the meeting in Paris of the steel committee of the Organization for Economic Cooperation and Development (OECD). The U.S. team was led by Commerce Under Secretary for International Trade Grant Aldonas. He reported some success in achieving the "modest goals" of the first meeting in a process that the U.S. government hopes will lead to international agreements on steel capacity being taken off line and on future disciplines over steel trade. The participants agreed to return in December, 2001, to indicate

---

[40] *Ibid.*

[41] IISI press release, July 18, 2001 ([http://www.worldsteel.org/cgi-bin]).

[42] CITAC press release, June 5, 2001.

[43] Hufbauer and Goodrich, pp. 8-10.

[43] *AMM,* August 27, 2001. The industry response is that the benefits commitments were made in good faith, but no one anticipated the surge of cheap imported steel into the U.S. market in the late 1990s because of global overcapacity (see above, pp. 5-6 and 11); for the union position, see below, pp. 22-23.

[44] *AMM,* August 27, 2001. The industry response is that the benefits commitments were made in good faith, but no one anticipated the surge of cheap imported steel into the U.S. market in the late 1990s because of global overcapacity (see above, pp. 5-6 and 11); for the union position, see below, pp. 22-23.

[45] Press release of the European Commission, June 5, 2001.

[46] *AMM,* October 2, 2001.

[47] *DER,* "Mexico Hikes Tariffs on Broad Range of Products Due to Import Surge." (September 6, 2001).

how they would identify steel production overcapacity in their own markets and to offer measures that they could take to reduce capacity on a voluntary basis, possibly over two to four years. But the chairman of the talks was quoted as saying, "We don't see on the horizon yet any kind of multilateral agreement. That's not on our radar screen." Alan Wolff, an attorney representing plaintiffs in the Section 201 case, commented, "We're talking about a quarter of a billion tons of excess capacity worldwide. Even if there were some miraculous agreement in Paris, there would still be an overhang in the near-to-medium term."[48]

ITC Hearings on Injury

Meanwhile, the ITC in September and early October, 2001, conducted its planned program of hearings on the injury phase of the Section 201 case. The structure of the case and hearings were themselves an issue. These were based on an extensive prehearing report on the industry by the ITC staff.[49] The report classified the subject products into 33 different categories, grouped under four general product headings:

- Carbon and alloy flat products;
- Carbon and alloy long products;
- Carbon and alloy tubular products;
- Stainless and tool steel products.

After opening with a general overview session on September 17, 2001, the ITC moved to a consideration of each of the broad product categories, before concluding with an unusual field hearing, held on October 5 in Merrillville (near Gary) Indiana. The Indiana hearing particularly focused on steelworker and community representatives, who provided evidence on how the industry downturn had economically affected their work, their lives and their regions.

The domestic plaintiffs were especially concerned that the ITC's planned approach could subdivide the industry artificially. The ITC could conclude that domestic producers might suffer from import competition in some lines, but in many others they do not. This could lead to a hit-and-miss or checkerboard pattern of trade relief across the product categories. Merchant suppliers of imported steel might then shift their focus to those product lines that had escaped trade relief action. Appearing on behalf of four large integrated steel mill companies, Alan Wolff presented a schematic diagram, which showed how semi-finished slabs were subsequently finished into hot-rolled steel and plate, and in the form case, then into cold-rolled steel, corrosion-resistant steel or tin products. But semi-finished slabs, which themselves are listed as a separate product under investigation, comp5rise 75-85% of the cost of hot rolled steel, and 65-70% of the cost of downstream cold-rolled products. Wolff further stated that domestic integrated mills and mini-mills are both "integrated" for the purposes of this case, because both basic oxygen and electric arc furnaces (EAFs) produce slab products for a subsequent industry processing. In subsequent testimony and questioning, however, it

---

[48] "Countries Agree to Voluntary Reviews in OECD Steel Talks," *Inside US Trade* (September 21, 2001) and public remarks by Grant Aldonas, Global Business Dialogue, Washington, DC (September 28, 2001).

[49] U.S. International Trade Commission. *Steel: Prehearing Report to the Commission on Investigation No. TA-201-73* (September 4, 2001).

was noted that intermediate EAF "thin slabs" are different as an intermediate output from the thicker slabs produced in fully integrated mills.[50]

Respondents rejoined that hot-rolled and slab imports were critical inputs for their businesses to remain competitive. They had developed essentially as finishing mills using expensive and sophisticated technology to manufacture and shape a wide range of cold-rolled or formed downstream products. They provided evidence that not only were their mills major investors and employers in their own right, but that the jobs in steel consuming industries in the United States were far more numerous and more widely dispersed than U.S. steelmaking jobs.[51] Some witnesses also testified that for their businesses steel of sufficient quality or quantity is not available in the domestic market, yet the subject products were included in the investigation.[52]

Another major subject of the hearings was whether imports were the "substantial" cause of injury, as the ITC must find in order to propose relief. For example, representatives of domestic flat and long producers relied heavily on an econometric analysis, which showed imports as the chief cause of declining prices for a wide range of products. With respect to the recent import decline, the analysis stated that the entire five-year period of investigation is the proper focus, as price impacts will have a lag effect for 12-18 months after import surges.[53] Thomas Usher, President and CEO of U.S. Steel, was asked why competition from Nucor, also a plaintiff, was any different from competition from overseas. Usher stated that when Nucor won an order with a lower price, he could make judgements based on knowledge of their U.S. capacity and whether they could subsequently compete at that level on future bids. When lower price bids came from many foreign mills, he had no ability to make such judgements, since the status of their capacity, the conditions of competition and government support in their domestic market, were frequently unknown or unknowable for him.[54]

In presenting their case, respondents also argued that their approach represented a move to reorganize the U.s. industry into its most profitable segments, as opposed to the investment mistakes made by domestic producers who expanded capacity despite declining prices and increasing competition. Respondents propounded a new model of the U.S. steel industry, based on segmented producers, integrating inputs from various market sources, including imports, while applying new technologies in specialized market niches. High levels of debt and over-leveraging to cover expansion and high costs (including legacy costs) were represented as the most substantial causes of the financial difficulties of the existing domestic industry.[55]

Finally, the hearings were especially notable for the injection of a strong sense of the political impact of this case. The first witness at the first hearing, testifying in support of

---

[50] Alan Wm. Wolff, Testimony Before ITC Steel Investigation no. TA-201-73 (September 19, 2001). Nucor CEO Dan DiMicco discussed the different processes, but also noted that steel rolled at mini-mills from "thin slabs" competed directly against steel rolled from imported slabs and that all long-rolled products should be considered as "like" products under the Section 201 statute; ITC Steel hearing testimony of September 19.

[51] See especially testimony of Lourenco Goncalves, California Steel Industries, ITC Steel hearings (September 19, 2001), and table prepared by CITAC on relative employment levels of steel and steel consuming industries.

[52] Testimony of W. Fergus Porter of Connecticut Steel (a steel "re-roller"), ITC Steel hearing (September 19, 2001) and William C. Lane, Caterpillar Inc., ITC Steel hearing (September 24, 2001).

[53] Testimony of Prof. Jerry Hausman, ITC Steel hearing (September 19, 2001).

[54] Answer to a question from ITC commissioner Jennifer Hillman, ITC Steel hearing (September 19, 2001).

[55] See esp. Testimony of Thomas J. Prusa, ITC Steel hearings (September 19, 2001). Professors Hausman and Prusa sharply criticized each other's analyses and rejected their fundamental premises. Witness Julie C. Mendoza on the same date made the most systematic critique of the financial management of the domestic industry.

relief, was Senator Robert Byrd of West Virginia. He was followed through the course of the hearings by 40 other political leaders, including members of both parties, both Houses of Congress, and several governors. All testified in support of relief. In view of the recent terrorist attacks on New York and Washington, DC, these political representatives frequently included in their remarks references of the importance of a domestic steel industry to U.S. national security. And President Bush's comments on steel and national security, noted earlier in this report and made even before the terrorist attacks, were widely referenced. This theme was sounded so frequently that the commissioners on September 24 asked steel industry representatives whether the increase in imports presented any national security implications. In response, the mini-mills' coalition provided a post-hearing brief "that a more compelling argument than national defense requirements were the national economic security needs of the country."[56]

OTHER STEEL TRADE AND INDUSTRY MEASURES

As noted above, the U.S. steel industry haws filed numerous petitions under existing U.S. trade law. Most of these petitions relate to antidumping and countervailing duty measures. CITAC has calculated that, "through 1999, 95 steel-product related AD/CVD orders were in effect, constituting 42% of all AD/CVD orders outstanding. Another 38 steel product cases are pending."[57] Earlier in 2001, the American Iron and Steel Institute counted 15 U.S. steel trade cases pending or recently resolved, the majority seeking AD/CVD relief.[58]

AD/CVD cases are still being filed while the Section 201 process goes on. For example, furnace coke producers, whose product was not covered in the Bush Administration 201 case, instead filed an antidumping case against products from Japan and China. In this case the ITC in early August voted 3-2 against an injury determination. The domestic plaintiffs have indicated that they will appeal the negative determination in the U.S. Court of International Trade.[59] On September 28, 2001, four major U.S. integrated steel producers (Bethlehem, U.S. Steel, LTV and National Steel) that supply the majority of domestically produced cold-rolled steel filed an antidumping case against cold-rolled imports from 20 countries. According to a Bethlehem Steel statement, "Imports from these countries now represent over 80% of all imports of cold-rolled steel products." The plaintiffs also filed a subsidy case against four of the countries (Argentina, Brazil, France and Korea).[60] Meanwhile, on September 24, the Department of Commerce found that nine countries are dumping hot-rolled steel in the United States and that producers in four countries are receiving counteravailable subsidies.[61] These cases must still go before the ITC for injury determinations.

---

[56] *AMM,* "Steel's National Security Argument Has Gained Resonance," (October 8, 2001).

[57] Francois and Baughman, p. 1.

[58] See table in AISI press release, May 15, 2001. A definitive listing of all U.S. steel AD/CCVD orders in effect as of August 17, 2001, is in the ITC *Prehearing Report,* overview pp. 2-6; a table of all foreign government counteravailable subsidies found by the U.S. Commerce Department is in *ibid.,* overview pp. 27-30.

[59] *AMM,* August 13 and September 25, 2001.

[60] *DER,* U.S. Producers File Trade Case Against Cold-Rolled Steel Exporters," October 1, 2001; *AMM,* October 2, 2001.

[61] *DER,* "Commerce Finds Nine Countries are Dumping Hot-Rolled Steel," September 26, 2001.

Trade Law Reform

The steel industry's problems have helped insure efforts in the 106th Congress to change U.S. trade laws, as they affect import relief. This effort has been renewed in the present Congress. In H.R. 1988, a bipartisan group of House Ways and Means Committee members has renewed an effort to make it easier for import-impacted industries to win safeguard and AD/CVD cases before the ITC, as well as to implement an import monitoring system that would provide quicker reports on sensitive products. This legislation would also require the ITC to exclude in-house "captive production" when calculating the market to determine levels of import penetration. A companion Senate bill (S. 979) has been introduced.[62] On the other hand, Rep. Jim Kolbe and two co-sponsors on August 2, 2001, introduced a measure establishing conditions under which "industrial users" of imported products subject to AD/CVD penalties could appeal to have duties removed on a temporary basis for up to one year (H.R. 2770). The legislation would also establish standing for consumers of products in AD/CVD cases.

The Byrd Amendment (Continued Dumping and Subsidy Offset Act)

Inspired in part by the ongoing financial difficulties of parts of the U.S. steel industry, the Continued Dumping and Subsidy Offset Act (CDSOA), was signed into law in October, 2000. The CDSOA is known as the "Byrd Amendment," because the West Virginia senator, then ranking minority member of the Appropriations Committee, succeeded in adding it as a rider to the FY2001 Agriculture appropriations bill (P.L. 106-387).[63] It requires antidumping and countervailing duties to be deposited in a special account, from which the original domestic industry petitioners who meet eligibility criteria may draw funds to offset expenses incurred as a result of the dumped or subsidized imports.

On June 26, 2001, the Customs Service proposed rules to implement the Byrd Amendment. A preliminary list of eligible "affected domestic producers" has been identified by the ITC based on plaintiffs in 400 active dumping cases. This list of 2,000 potentially eligible producers has been posted on the Customs website.[64] To be eligible for a distribution, producers must still be in operation and making the product for which a dumping or subsidy injury was found. The Customs Service is required to make final distribution to claimants within 60 days of the beginning of the next fiscal year starting October 1, 2001. Funds may be used by claimants for a wide range of purposes, including training, employee health care and pension benefits, as well as improvement of manufacturing technology and equipment, and R&D expenditures.[65] The final rules for CDSOA distribution were promulgated on September 21, 2001, and the final date for submitting certification of eligibility was October 2, 2001.[66]

U.S. trading partners believe that use of penalty tariffs to subsidize a competing domestic industry, as under the Byrd Amendment, contravenes WTO rules. The European Union,

---

[62] For a general view of trade law reform, see the CRS report, *Trade Remedy Law Reform in the 107th Congress.*

[63] P.L. 106-387; see *ibid.,* pp. 7-8.

[64] See http://www.customs.gov/news/fed-reg/notices/dumping.pdf.

[65] *Federal Register,* June 26, 2001, pp. 33920-26 and August 3, 2001, pp. 40782-40800.

[66] *Federal Register,* Sept. 21, 2001, pp. 48546-55 and Sept. 27, 2001, p. 49451.

Japan, Canada, Mexico and eight other U.S. trading partners have initiated WTO consultations. On July 12, 2001, the EU, Japan, and a number of the other countries in this group formally requested a WTO dispute settlement panel.[67] The WTO Dispute Settlement Body has agreed to hear the complaint.

The EU also announced on July 20 that it will file a claim against the U.S. countervailing duties on steel imports from Germany, Italy, France, Spain and Sweden. If the EU wins the case, it could reduce the collected penalty duties available for the CDSOA program and require a decision on how to repay any duties that may have been distributed to eligible U.S. recipients. The basis for this case is a WTO panel decision in 2000 that American countervailing duties against imports from the private-sector successor to the British Steel Corporation were illegal. The U.S. duties were based on the theory that the new company still benefits from the forgiveness by the British government of past loans. The European Commission now holds that similar duties are being applied by the United States in other cases involving European exporters, for whom, in the Commission's view, there are no continuing subsidies being paid by national governments.[68] Hufbauer and Goodrich criticize the WTO decision in the British Steel case as providing cover for high rates of subsidization of allegedly "privatized" foreign steel companies. They suggest that this ruling could be reversed as part of a WTO negotiation aimed at establishing new steel trade rules, as called for by President Bush.[69]

Export-Import Bank Loans

The Senate Banking committee on July 18, 2001, considered an amendment to the U.S. Export-Import Bank reauthorization bill to prevent it from lending to any project associated with a foreign company accused of dumping. This followed a December 2000 loan guarantee of $18 million, over the reported objections of the Clinton Administration, to upgrade the Benxi, China steel mill, which the Commerce Department subsequently found to be dumping in the U.S. market. Sens. Bayh, Shelby, and Stabenow co-sponsored an amendment in committee to ban any financial support by Ex-Im to foreign companies accused of dumping, but the amendment was withdrawn. Meanwhile, Ex-Im itself on July 16, 2001, announced proposed modifications to its procedures for consideration of potentially adverse U.S. domestic economic impact of proposed Ex-Im loans and guarantees.

On the House side, Reps. Peter Visclosky and Alan Mollohan reacted by co-sponsoring an amendment to the Foreign Operations appropriations bill (H.R. 2506) to reduce Ex-Im support by the $18 million amount that the bank guaranteed for the Benxi project. After a sustained floor debate, the Visclosky-Mollohan amendment passed by a vote of 258-162. The subsidy appropriation for loan guarantees was reduced by $15 million and a further $3 million was deducted from Ex-Im's administrative expenses appropriation. The funds were transferred to the child health and survival programs in Title II of the same bill.[70]

On September 20, Ex-Im announced the final changes in its own internal review procedures. The bank will not prohibit outright financing for a company subject to a

---

[67] *Inside US Trade,* "Nine U.S. Trading Partners File WTO Request on Byrd Law," July 13, 2001.
[68] *DER,* EU Will File WTO Challenge to Duties U.S. Imposed on Some Steel Imports," July 23, 2001.
[69] Hufbauer and Goodrich, pp. 13-14.
[70] *Congressional Record,* July 24, 2001, pp. H-4437-47.

preliminary AD or CVD investigation, but has decided that an investigation is a "potential indicator" of commodity oversupply. It would be a "yellow flashing light," though not a "stop sign," for a proposed transaction. But the next day Rep. Patrick Toomey offered an amendment in a Financial Services subcommittee markup of the Ex-Im reauthorization bill (H.R. 2871), which would have banned financing for "any entity" subject to AD, CVD and Section 201 investigations. Toomey's amendment was criticized by supporters of Eximbank and U.S. business interests and lost by a single vote (11-10).[71]

The Iron Ore and Semi-Finished Steel Section 232 Case

Under Section 232 of the Trade Expansion Act, the President may act to "adjust imports," if the Secretary of Commerce has found that they threaten to impair national security. Among the criteria for determining the effect on national security are the effect on "the economic welfare of any domestic industry essential to our national security" and the "displacement of any domestic products causing substantial unemployment..." Administrations have rarely taken positive action under Section 232, although in 1979 and 1982, Section 232 was used as the legal basis to ban oil imports from Iran and Libya.[72]

In January, 2001, Reps. James Oberstar and Bart Stupak wrote outgoing Secretary of Commerce Norman Mineta to request a Section 232 investigation into the upstream iron ore and semi-finished steel industry, which has been under heavy pressure from import competition.[73] On February 1, 2001, the Commerce Department announced that it was initiating an investigation under this provision to "determine the effects on the national security of imports of iron ore and semi-finished steel." Section 232 investigations are conducted by the Bureau of Export Administration. By law the Commerce Department has nine months to complete its report, including public hearings and receipt of any public comments. Public hearings were held in July, 2001, in Minnesota and Michigan, and the agency plans to complete its report by October 29, 2001. The President then has three months to consider the Department's findings and recommendations for action.[74]

The Defense Department is participating in the Section 232 process. Its Office of Industrial Affairs has indicated that use of steel in weapons systems, primarily in shipbuilding, is 250,000 tons annually, or about 0.2% of domestic U.S. output. The Defense Department restricts procurement to U.S. suppliers (or countries covered by defense procurement agreements) in the case of specialty steels used in weapons system applications, but does not apply such restrictions to upstream products used in the manufacture of finished steel.[75]

---

[71] *DER*, "House Panel Narrowly Defeats Amendment Restricting Ex-Im Funding," September 24, 2001.

[72] U.S. Department of Commerce. Bureau of Export Administration, Office of Strategic Industries and Economic Security. *Section 232 Investigations: The Effects of Imports on the National Security* (January, 2001).

[73] Text of letter in *Inside US Trade* (January 26, 2001).

[74] U.S. Department of Commerce. Bureau of Export Administration, Office of Strategic Industries and Economic Security. "National Security Investigation of Imports of Iron Ore and Semi-Finished Steel," www.doc-bxa.bmpcoe.org/dmrii_ironore.html; *Federal Register*, Feb. 6, 2001, p. 9067.

[75] The Department of Defense Office of Industrial Affairs has provided a brief series of Q8As regarding the role of the steel industry in U.S. national security.

The Steel Revitalization Act (H.R. 808/S. 957)

Introduced by Reps. Visclosky and Quinn, this is a comprehensive measure addressing the issues that affect the steel industry. The bill had 222 House co-sponsors by July 2001. A companion bill has been introduced in the Senate (S. 957), by Sen. Wellstone and three co-sponsors.

Title I of H.R. 808 would require the President to establish import quotas on steel products for five years, with monthly imports not to exceed the average of the three-year period leading up to the import surge that started in mid-1997. This title is modeled on H.R. 975, which passed the House in the 106th Congress by a vote of 289-141. The earlier bill, however, mandated quotas for only three years, in line with WTO standards, at least with respect to the length of temporary trade remedies. The five-year relief period in H.R. 808 would exceed WTO rules. Furthermore, when WTO rules allow for such trade remedies, they first require an investigation to be conducted to determine whether relief is warranted. Section 101 of H.R. 808, in contrast, would mandate that the President take action to restrict steel imports within 60 days of enactment. This title also would require Executive Branch action to achieve legislatively specified import quotas, with or without the cooperation of other trading partners. WTO rules generally prohibit members from placing quantitative restrictions on imports and import surcharges (such as those authorized in Section 101 (a) of H.R. 808). A major purpose of the WTO Safeguards Agreement is to eliminate quotas, export restraints, "orderly marketing arrangements," and other "voluntary" agreements that impose barriers to imports. Existing arrangements of this type are being phased out.[76]

Title II of H.R. 808 would establish a 1.5% sales tax on U.S.-made steel products and imports to finance the health care benefits of certain steelworker retirees ("legacy costs"). This provision reflects an assessment that the financially troubled domestic steel industry can no longer support the health care commitments that were made in exchange for labor's acceptance of earlier downsizing agreements. H.R. 808 would establish a Steel Retiree Health Care Board in the Department of Labor, which would include labor and industry representatives. It would administer a Health Care Benefit Costs Assistance Program and a Steelworker Retiree Health Care Trust Fund, both to be established in this bill. The bill further establishes eligibility rules for participation in these programs. The Board would make projections on a yearly basis to determine necessary funds based on the size of the retiree pool. As the pool shrinks, the tax would be automatically reduced until it is phased out.

The USWA is the leading proponent of the legacy-cost-sharing provision of H.R. 808. It states that, "much of the domestic steel industry is heavily burdened by overwhelming retiree health care costs due to the massive layoffs that occurred during the 1970s and 1980s."[77] The same source calculates that the largest companies with unfunded retiree health insurance plans are Bethlehem Steel, USX Corp. (U.S. Steel Group), LTV Steel, and AK Steel. Together, these four companies in 1999 accounted for 63% of $10.6 billion in unfunded post-retirement health insurance obligations.[78] The USWA takes the position that a tax on steel sales is appropriate to support the legacy health care costs of steelworkers who were involuntarily retired during the 1980s or who may have lost their jobs during the late 1990s.

---

[76] Articles 10-11, Agreement on Safeguards, Uruguay Round Final Act of 1994. The provisions on quantitative restrictions and surcharges are in Articles II and XI of the original GATT text.

[77] USWA. *The U.S. Steel Revitalization Act.* [http://www.uswa.org/sra/srasummary.htm]

[78] USWA. *Domestic Steelmakers, Retiree Health Insurance Costs, 1999.* (Table prepared by USWA).

For the major integrated producers, the USWA reports that total retireee health care and pension benefit costs amount to $65 per ton ($50 for pension benefits and $15 for health care benefits), or 14% of the average weighted price of a ton of steel.[79] This amounts to an estimated $965 million in health care benefits to approximately 400,000 retired employees and their families. The USWA argues that these companies are at a competitive disadvantage against domestic companies that do not face legacy costs or foreign manufacturers whose governments are responsible for the provision of health care. Companies (such as Nucor) that operate mini-mills, have a younger work force, few retirees, and no unfunded post-retirement obligations.[80]

Although Title II addresses the legacy issues affecting the integrated steel producers, these companies do not at present support the legacy cost provisions. The steel industry is divided over the question of providing financial assistance to companies that face large legacy costs. The mini-mills, in particular, are actively opposed. The Steel Manufacturers Association, which represents them as a group, has taken the position that "government assistance to troubled steel companies for continued operation or legacy costs is unacceptable. That assistance is unfair to those steel companies who are not troubled."[81]

Title III of H.R. 808 would modify and extend the Emergency Steel Loan Guarantee Act of 1999. This issue will be discussed in detail below in the following subsection. Title IV would create a new environmental compliance grant program for merged steel companies worth up to $100 million per company, but with the proviso that recipient companies cannot downsize production or employment more than marginally for a period of ten years, without being required to repay some or all of the grant. In addition to H.R. 808/S. 957, Sen Rockefeller has also introduced a bill (S. 910), which includes only the health care and environmental compliance titles of H.R. 808.

Alone among industry stakeholders, the USWA supports H.R. 808/S. 957. The American Iron and Steel Institute has adopted a "neutral" position, favoring some corrective trade action, but preferring actions consistent with the WTO under Section 201, instead of legislatively mandated quotas.[82] There is also no consensus in the industry on the bill's legacy costs and other domestic remedy provisions. The Steel Manufacturers Association supports Section 201 action on trade, but, as noted above, opposes "legacy cost" policies that it believes would aid some elements of U.S. industry over others. CITAC, representing steel users, is sharply critical of H.R. 808, as well as of President Bush's action in initiating a Section 201 of investigation.

---

[79] USWA. *The Crisis in American Steel.* May 22, 2001. Major integrated steelmakers are U.S. Steel, Bethlehem Steel, LTV Steel, AK Steel, national Steel, Ispat Inland and WHX Corp.

[80] USWA. *Domestic Steelmakers: Retiree Health Care Legacy Costs.* No date. This document states that since December 1997, 18 steel companies have declared bankruptcy as a result of unfairly traded foreign steel imports. It also asserts that these bankruptcies put at risk the health benefits of 35,000 employees and more than 100,000 retirees. The calculation does not include Bethlehem Steel, which declared bankruptcy on October 15, 2001.

[81] Steel Manufacturers Association. *On Ending the Steel Crisis: Statement on a Program Needed and Principles Underlying Its Implementation* (Feb. 9, 2001).

[82] "Steel Associations Trade Program," reproduced in *Inside US Trade* (March 16, 2001).

The Emergency Steel Loan Guarantee Act of 1999 (P.L. 106-51)

This act established a program to guarantee loans for restructuring and modernizing steel companies that were financially distressed following the 1997-98 import surge and industry financial crisis. The program guarantees loans up to a total of $1 billion (maximum of $250 million per company), with a maturity date through the end of 2005. In practice, the loan guarantee program has not played a major role in alleviating the latest industry problems. It has issued only one guarantee, for a loan of $110 million, that a company has subsequently been able to take up. The fixed deadline of now less than five years for loan maturities means that the guarantees are decreasingly attractive to would-be lenders and investors.[83]

H.R. 808 includes extension of the maturity date on guaranteed loans to the end of 2015. The bill would also increase the total amount of guaranteed loan coverage from $1 billion to $10 billion, increase the individual company limit to $500 million, and increase the portion of a loan eligible for the guarantee from 85 to 95%. H.R. 808 would also expand the definition of eligible companies to include coke-producing companies and eliminate the current $30 million program cap on loans to iron ore companies.

The Senate or July 12, 2001, accepted an amendment to the Interior Department and related agencies appropriations bill to extend and modify the Steel Loan Guarantee Program. It would prolong by 10 years, from the end of 2005 to the end of 2015, the deadline when loans guaranteed under the program must be repaid, as in H.R. 808. In conformity with this change, the amendment would extend the deadline for loan guarantee authorizations from 2001 to Dec. 31, 2003. The amendment also provides that the portion of a loan covered by a guarantee may be increased from the present level of 85% to 90% or 95%, provided that no more than $100 million in total loans may be outstanding at any one time under program guarantees at each of the higher guarantee rates, nor may any single loan at each higher rate be greater than $50 million.[84] On October 9, House conferees accepted the Interior appropriations bill with the Senate-passed steel loan guarantee provision.[85]

Trade Adjustment Assistance

Workers whose positions were eliminated because of the impact of direct trade competition are eligible for additional unemployment compensation and retraining assistance through Trade Adjustment Assistance (TAA), a program administered by the Department of Labor. In addition, firms that have been negatively affected by trade are also eligible for technical assistance in adjusting to the new competitive circumstances, in a small program administered by the Commerce Department, primarily through regional Trade Adjustment Assistance Centers. Both of these programs were set to expire on Sept. 30, 2001. TAA was

---

[83] U.S. Department of Commerce. *Emergency Steel Loan Guarantee Program/Emergency Oil and Gas Guaranteed Loan Program: Annual Report of the Secretary of Commerce to the Congress for Fiscal years 1999 and 2000;* see also the General Accounting Office report, *Financial Management: Emergency Steel Loan Guarantee Program* (GAO-01-714R).

[84] *Congressional Record,* July 12, 2001, pp. S7559-60, S7566; see also *Congress Daily PM,* "Senate GOP Refusing to Agree to Approps Time Limits," July 17, 2001; and, *Inside US Trade, "Senate Approves Steel Program with Better Loan Terms for Companies," July 20, 2001.*

[85] *AMM,* October 12, 2001.

renewed for the short term (through October 16, 2001) by the continuing resolution that became law on September 28.[86]

On October 5, the House Ways and means Committee approved by voice vote a simple renewal of the present TAA statute through the end of FY 2003 (H.R. 3008). The Ways and means committee action avoided a more thoroughgoing re-examination and reform of the TAA program. In response to complaints in the committee regarding the short notice given for the reauthorization bill, Chairman William Thomas stated that the action was "the beginning, not the end" of congressional debate on TAA renewal.[87]

In the other body, Sen. Jeff Bingaman introduced a TAA bill (S. 1209) that would significantly expand the programs on July 19, 2001. The measure would allow the President or either of the congressional trade committees to initiate industry-wide certification for TAA relief, and also require the Labor Department to initiate such a process concomitant with the start of ITC investigations. Maximum income support under TAA would be expanded from 52 to 78 weeks, and the government would pick up 50% of the cost to an individual for continuing employer-provided healthcare coverage after loss of a job (so-called "COBRA" participation) through a refundable tax credit. A new TAA program would also be created for communities where mass job loss (at least 300 or 500 workers, depending on whether the location is rural or urban) has occurred because of a plant closure due to the impact of trade. S. 1209 is not industry-specific, but senators from steel-producing states and union representatives have supported it, because of its relevance to the steel industry legacy cost issue, as well as the prospect of large-scale industry closings and bankruptcies.[88]

Hufbauer and Goodrich in particular are strong supporters of using an enhanced form of TAA to address the trade impact issue affecting distressed U.S. industries such as steel. In their analysis, coverage of "legacy costs" through enhanced TAA and existing Pension Benefit Guarantee Corporation programs over a ten-year period would cost the U.S. economy only one-tenth of the cost to steel consumers of a high level of protectionism through a new program of import quotas. This payment would come in the form of a direct federal outlay of $170-360 million annually, as opposed to trade protection through an import quota system, in which the cost of adjustment would be borne mostly by private sector steel users, at some economic disadvantage to themselves and, it is assumed, the economy as a whole.[89] Moreover, Hufbauer and Goodrich calculate that average steelworker pay and benefits are worth $72,000 per year, a figure substantially higher than in many other industries. And this makes the loss of a steel mill job an economically catastrophic event for most steelworkers; 30% are not re-employed elsewhere, and 50% of those who are report earnings losses greater than 30%.[90]

---

[86]   CRS   electronic   briefing   book   entries,   *Trade   Adjustment   Assistance   for   Workers* [http://www.congress.gov/brbk/html/ebtra85] by Paul Graney and Celinda Franco, and *Trade Adjustment Assistance for Firms,* [http://www.congress.gov/brbk/html/ebtra57], by J.F. Hornbeck.

[87] *DER,* "House-Panel OKs Renewal of TAA Program, Extension Measure for GSP Duty-Free Relief," October 9, 2001.

[88] *AMM,* July 23, 2001.

[89] Hufbauer and Goodrich, pp. 10-13.

[90] *Ibid.,* p. 10.

THE OUTLOOK FOR U.S. POLICY ON STEEL

Congress has given President Bush the lead in resolving steel trade issues, now that the President has decided to take action under Section 201 of U.S. trade law. President Bush's announcement of June 5, 2001, and the USTR request to the ITC have essentially taken the urgency out of congressional proposals to change U.S. trade remedy law for the time being.

It has been suggested that the President, as a self-proclaimed supporter of the WTO-based international trading system, may be seeking through the Section 201 process to show that his Administration can provide relief to the steel industry under WTO rules. If the ITC makes a positive injury determination in November, 2001, then the ITC and the Administration may seek a remedy that conforms to WTO rules, provides real and effective industry relief, and does not seriously impair the competitiveness of steel users. If the ITC determination is negative, then the focus will be on whether Congress should change the terms of reference in injury determinations. Legislation has already been introduced, H.R. 1988/S. 979, which would eliminate the requirement for imports to be "substantial" cause of injury or threat of injury in Section 201 cases. Moreover, a determination of no substantial injury from imports under Section 201 would also most likely stimulate interest in legislation to provide trade and industry relief with little regard for WTO rules, as in, for example, some provisions of H.R. 808.

An ITC finding of injury, followed by proposed U.S. trade remedies, brings into play the reaction of other WTO members. Although U.S. policies on steel have been partly overturned already by WTO rulings on AD.CVD cases and are increasingly under challenge from U.S. trading partners, these actions to date are still in the nature of preliminary skirmishes. Should President Bush decide to take positive steps to implement trade remedies, the issue will be whether such steps can be blended into a new multilateral approach to overcapacity and other steel industry issues, or whether they are viewed as a unilateral and protectionist U.S. response to help its industry. It is almost certain, as indicated by the EU reaction to date, that any resolution of the global overcapacity situation will be internationally controversial and would be challenged, if it does not include some reduction of U.S. steelmaking capacity.

In any case, much of the U.S. steel industry remains financially troubled, and sees little prospect of improvement in the domestic economic outlook. The outcome of the Section 201 trade case and international negotiations may be too far in the future to provide relief that is needed now. As noted earlier, the DRI analysis foresees one form of relief for the industry as a whole in the permanent closure of some domestic capacity through financial distress and trade relief that may be too little or too late to rescue the most seriously affected operations. But contrariwise, higher domestic steel prices, if they result from trade remedy action, could have adverse competitive consequences for industries that use steel and prolong their recovery from the present period of slower economic growth.

Congress is likely to remain engaged with short-term industry relief measures, even while the Section 201 case moves along. Some of these measures may well have international repercussions that will change the overall negotiating environment. One prime example is the implementation of the Byrd Amendment, which has already been challenged in the WTO. Another could be strengthened loan guarantee program, which may be questionable under WTO subsidy rules, but which has not so far been challenged, possibly because it has not guaranteed many loans. If the legacy cost issue is addressed as a domestic welfare problem through TAA, as suggested for example by Hufbauer and Goodrich, then there may be no

WTO issues. On the other hand, assistance to steel companies intended to enable them to stay in business so they can continue to cover retiree and current employee benefits, would not only be controversial domestically, as it already is, but could raise international trade competition issues as well.

Chapter 3

THE U.S.-EUROPEAN BANANA DISPUTE

Charles E. Hanrahan

SUMMARY

The United States and the European Union (EU) reached an agreement in April 2001 that resolved a long-standing dispute over the EU's rules for importing bananas. Objections to the agreement by other banana exporting countries, such as Ecuador and Caribbean banana exporters, have been withdrawn. The U.S.-EU banana agreement provides for a transition to a tariff-only system of imports in 2006. In the meantime, the EU will establish quotas and a licensing system based on historical trade shares that should increase the prospects for Latin American banana imports in the EU market, especially bananas marketed by U.S. firms like Chiquita Brands International. In November 2001, the WTO granted waivers of WTO rules allowing the EU to continue preferential treatment for banana exports of developing countries that are former EU member country colonies. These waivers paved the way for full implementation of the agreement by January 2002. Trade policy officials on both sides of the Atlantic expressed hopes that the banana agreement would contribute to a climate for resolving other thorny trade disputes and for bilateral and multilateral cooperation. Members and committees of the 107th Congress will be monitoring implementation of the agreement and its effects on U.S-EU trade relations.

BACKGROUND AND HISTORY

The Banana Regime and WTO Rulings

In 1993, the EU implemented a single EU-wide regime to regulate banana imports. The regime gave preferential entry to bananas from the overseas territories and former colonies of EU member countries and restricted entry from other countries, including several in Latin America where U.S. companies predominate, and Ecuador.

The banana regime was part of the EU's move toward a single, unified market which was inaugurated in 1992. Before the single market, individual EU member countries imported bananas under an assortment of national practices. For example, France imported bananas from its Overseas Departments of Guadeloupe and Martinique and from former colonies, Cote d'Ivoire and Cameroon; Spain was supplied exclusively by domestic production in the Canary Islands; other EU countries imposed a 20% tariff while Germany allowed tariff-free entry.

The EU regime, which entered into force on July 1, 1993, established a multilayered system of quotas for banana imports. Imports from EU or overseas territories' producers were unrestricted. Imports from traditional suppliers in the African, Caribbean, and Pacific (ACP) countries, former colonies of EU countries, were tariff-free up to 857,000 tons. Imports from nontraditional ACP suppliers were assessed a tariff of 150% ad valorem. Imports from third countries (including Latin American countries) were assigned a tariff-rate quota (IRQ) of 2.2 million tons, with in-quota tariffs of about 20% ad valorem for countries that had signed a framework agreement with the EU (Colombia, Costa Rica, Nicaragua, and Venezuela) and 30% ad valorem for non-framework countries. Above the quotas, there was a 250% ad valorem tariff. In addition to the quotas and tariffs under the regime, the EU issued licenses which allocated the quotas among banana distributors. Import licenses were distributed to traditional importers from third countries (approximately two-thirds of the IRQ) and to European and ACP importers and new importers in the market since 1992 (about one-third of the TRQ).

The banana import regime was challenged in World Trade Organization (WTO) dispute settlement by the United States, Ecuador, Guatemala, Honduras, and Mexico. The WTO found the import regime illegal in 1997 on grounds that its system of allocating licenses discriminated against growers and marketing companies in the complaining countries. A revised import regime was established on January 1, 1999. The revised system consisted of a 2.553 million metric ton TRQ with an additional quantity (850,000 MMT) assigned to ACP countries. The new system was also ruled illegal by a WTO dispute settlement panel because it set aside a quantity of banana imports reserved exclusively for ACP imports and because the licensing system continued to discriminate against suppliers of Lathi American bananas.

Subsequently a WTO arbitration panel ruled that compensation of about $192 million was due the United States for lost banana sales. The EU, foregoing its right to appeal, indicated that it would abide by the decision and bring its banana import regime into compliance with WTO rules. The United States imposed tariffs of 100% on $192 million worth of EU imports into the United States, none of which were agricultural products.[1] The United States and EU continued discussions over what would constitute a WTO-compatible banana import regime during much of 2000.

In October 2000, the EU floated a new proposal for bringing its banana import regime into compliance with WTO rules.[2] The proposal called for three quotas for bananas comparable to the TRQs proposed earlier-850 thousand tons for ACP countries; 2.2 million tons for Lathi American bananas; and an additional 353,000 tons for Latin American bananas. The in-quota duty on Latin American bananas would be 75 Euro (around $66) per ton, while ACP bananas would enjoy a 300 Euro ($255) per ton tariff preference. Effectively, ACP bananas would enter the EU duty free. The quotas would be administered on a "first-come,

---

[1] The retaliation list can be found at http://www.ustr.gov/releases/1999/01/banl-14.pdf

[2] Commission of the European Communities, *Communication from the Commission to the Council on the 'First Come, First Served' Method for the Banana Regime and the Implications of a 'TariffOnly' System,* Brussels COM(2000), October 4, 2000.

first-served (FCFS)" basis that would establish a pre-allocation procedure. Companies would declare their intention to import a specified quantity of bananas when vessels were a sailing distance from Europe to avoid discrimination against countries that are farther away. The pre-allocation procedure would be managed on a fortnightly or weekly basis. This transitional TRQ system would be changed to a tariff only system in 6 years.

The United States also rejected the October 2000 proposal.[3] The basis of the U.S. opposition was that maintaining a separate quota for ACP bananas virtually guarantees that those countries would be able to export their entire production, while Latin American countries would be severely restricted. The proposal, according to the Office of the U.S. Trade Representative (USTR), also would have continued the discrimination between companies that supply the EU with Latin American bananas and companies, primarily European, that supply the EU with ACP bananas. The U.S. statement noted also the opposition of nearly all Latin American countries, with the exception of Ecuador, to the FCFS system and the opposition of Caribbean countries together with the lack of support from the African countries for the EU proposal. Rather than FCFS, the United States insisted on the allocation of banana import licenses based on an historical reference period which would maintain or enhance market share for U.S. companies. Despite lack of agreement, the United States did not re-enter WTO dispute settlement on the banana dispute, but continued discussions with the EU.

RECENT DEVELOPMENTS: THE U.S.-EU AGREEMENT

In April 2001, the United States and the EU reached an agreement on their longstanding dispute over banana imports. Under the Agreement, the EU will establish a tariff-only regime for imports of bananas by January 1, 2006. As of July 1, 2001, the EU will implement an import regime for bananas on the basis of historical licensing, although a quota with tariff preferences would be maintained for developing country exporters of bananas to the EU. Licenses mainly would be allocated to traditional exporters, i.e., those who held licenses during the reference period, 1994-1996, with a smaller proportion of licenses allocated to newcomers, i.e., those not operating in the historical reference period. Once the new regime is in place, the United States will terminate its imposition of increased duties on $192 million of imports from the EU. These duties were suspended as of July 1, 2001 and will be terminated on January 1, 2002.

The Agreement calls for the establishment of a bound tariff-rate quota, (quota A) of 2.2 million metric tons and an additional quota of 350,000 mts (quota B) which will be managed as one, with a tariff of E75 per ton (about $66), A TRQ, designated as quota C, will be set at 850,000 mts. Although within each TRQ, licenses may be used to import bananas from any source, the A and B quotas are essentially for Latin American bananas, while the C quota is for ACP bananas. Within each TRQ, licenses may be used to import bananas from any source. However, licenses to import bananas into TRQ "C" cannot be used to import bananas into TRQs "A" or "B" and vice versa.

---

[3] Office of the U.S. Trade Representative, United States Position on European Commission Proposal for a First Come, First Served Licensing System for Importation of Bananas, October 5, 2000.

Import licenses for 83% of the A and B quotas will be distributed to "traditional" operators based on their 1994-1996 average annual final reference volume of imports. The EU will finalize licensing procedures for C quota bananas. Additionally, a nontraditional or newcomers operator category will be created for 17% of the A and B TRQs. Non-traditional importers cannot become traditional in subsequent periods. In phase II of the agreement (which begins "as soon as possible" and which requires both approval of the EU Council of Ministers and European Parliament), the ACP quota will be reduced by 100,000 mts which will be added to B quota. The 750,00 mts remaining in the C quota will be reserved for bananas of ACP origin.

Compatibility of the agreement with World Trade Organization (WTO) rules was an issue. Ecuador or other banana exporting countries in Central and South America or the Caribbean could have requested a review of compliance of the new regime with WTO requirements. Or these same countries could have challenged the new regime under WTO dispute settlement as discriminatory because the new regime does not treat all WTO members equally. The WTO has ruled in the past against discriminatory licensing systems for bananas, but has not spelled out what would be a non-discriminatory licensing system. Waivers of Articles 1[4] and XIII,[5] which the EU sought, could defuse arguments about the WTO compatibility of the new regime.

As part of the agreement, the United States pledged to support the EU's bid for a waiver of Article 1 of the GATT 1994 that the EU had requested for the preferential access it accords goods originating in former EU member country colonies (the ACP countries) under the ACP-EU Partnership Agreement (which governs trade relations between the EU and former colonies). The United States agreed also to promote the acceptance in the WTO of the EU's request for a waiver of Article XIII of the GATT 1994 needed for managing the quota extended to ACP country banana exports. The approval of both these waivers during the WTO's Fourth Ministerial Conference (in Doha, Qatar, November 9-14), removed the final obstacles to full implementation of the banana agreement.[6]

IMPLICATIONS OF THE AGREEMENT

U.S.-EU Trade Relations

The banana agreement removed a significant dispute from the U.S.-EU bilateral trade agenda. The agreement contributes, some say, to a more favorable climate for resolving other contentious trade disputes and for cooperation both bilaterally and multilaterally in the WTO. Others do not think, however, that it gets at fundamental differences that complicate, for example, the U. S. -EU meat hormone dispute or disagreement on the agenda of a new round of multilateral trade negotiations.[7]

---

[4] Article 1 of GATT 1947 is the general most-favored nation treatment provision which requires that member countries conduct trade on the basis of non-discrimination.

[5] Article XIII Of GATT 1994 requires nondiscriminatory administration of quantitative restrictions.

[6] For the texts of these WTO waivers see http://www-heva.wto-ministerial.org/english/thewto_e/mst_e/min01 _e/mindecl_acp_ec_agre_e.htm   and   http://www-heva.wto-ministerial.org/english/   thewto_e/mst_e/min01_ e/mindecl_ec_bananas_e.htm.

[7] For a discussion of U.S-EU differences over agriculture in the new round of multilateral trade negotiations, see *Agriculture in WTO Negotiations*, CRS Report RS20185, December 7, 2001.

Banana Marketing Companies

According to analysts, the U.S. banana marketing companies, Chiquita Brands International and the Dole Food Company, will be the primary beneficiaries of the banana agreement. Estimates are that these two will share about 44% of the licenses issued under the agreement. That share would be virtually guaranteed until 2006 when the transition to a tariff-only regime would occur. Chiquita and Dole benefit from the definition of "primary operators", i.e., those that either grew or bought green bananas to sell them in Europe during the 1994-96 reference period. According to analysts, two-thirds of the 44% would go to Chiquita and the remaining third to Dole. Although Dole is expected to experience a net loss of licenses under the new regime, the USTR calculates that it and other U.S. firms will obtain a substantial increase in the volume of bananas they are able to import into the EU market. Dole, nevertheless, expressed its opposition to the agreement.

U.S. Businesses and Consumers

Overlooked to some extent are the effects of the agreement on U.S. businesses that import products on the retaliation list and on consumers of those products. Lifting sanctions means that the 100% duties will be eliminated as of July 1, 2001, thus importers and consumers of products like handbags, bed linens, or folding cartons and boxes will be economically better off. Legislation to exempt small businesses from inclusion in such retaliation was introduced in the 106th Congress.

Ecuador and Other Latin American Exporters

The 100,000 addition to the "B" quota is intended to benefit Ecuador and other Latin American exporters. Ecuador, however, initially announced its opposition to the U.S.-EU agreement, but at the same time began negotiations with the EU, according to sources, on ways to get additional market share through the "newcomer category" Rules for administering the newcomer category appear to give Ecuador a substantial share, especially of organic bananas, of that category. Ecuador also withdrew its request for consultation with the EU which could have led to a compliance review or to formation of a panel to hear arguments in a formal dispute. While consultation is the first step in WTO dispute settlement, consultation under Article 21.5 of the Dispute Settlement Understanding to determine compliance with a WTO panel decision, according to some legal analysts, does not necessarily lead to formal dispute settlement.

Developing Country Exporters

Among the major beneficiaries of the EU's 1993 banana import regime have been the Caribbean countries, especially those of the Windward Islands in the eastern Caribbean. While the Windward Islands account for only 3% of world banana trade, they supply 20% of EU imports. They and other ACP producers fear that they would be driven out of business if preferences were eliminated since it would force them to compete with more efficient suppliers. Ecuador, the world's largest producer and exporter of bananas, for example, produces bananas at a cost of about $162 per metric ton, while ACP costs can be as high as $515 per ton.

On balance the ACP countries appear to benefit from the agreement. Although the agreement reduces the size of the quota for bananas initially provided to ACP countries, they nevertheless will benefit from an assured market of 750,000 tons. In addition, the WTO waiver of Article I of GATT 1947 insures that they will continue to receive preferential treatment. While the EU and the ACP countries are enthusiastic about the continuation of trade preferences, some economists maintain that the ACP countries and especially the Caribbean producers need financial and technical assistance to diversify their agriculture away from high-cost banana production instead of, or in addition to, preferences.

ROLE OF CONGRESS

In the 107th Congress, Members and committees that deal with trade issues will be monitoring implementation of the U.S.-EU banana agreement. Partly in response to EU slowness in implementing WTO banana rulings, the 106th Congress enacted legislation (Section 407 of the Africa Growth and Opportunity Act, P.L.106-200) that requires the President periodically to rotate or change the types of products targeted for trade retaliation.[8] This so-called "carousel" provision was aimed partly at maintaining pressure on the EU to come to a speedy resolution of the banana dispute and also the meat hormone dispute[9] by penalizing a wider range of foreign industries and regions. Supporters of the carousel provision urged the USTR to rotate its retaliation lists for bananas and meat hormones. The USTR, on the other hand, appeared reluctant to invoke the carousel provision because of its potential to aggravate another EU-U.S. dispute over the tax treatment of Foreign Sales Corporations (FSC).[10] With a banana agreement, some of the pressure to use the carousel provision has been mitigated.

---

[8] See *Trade Retaliation: the "Carousel" Approach* by Lenore Sek, RS20715, October 27, 2000.

[9] See *The European Union's Ban on Hormone-Treated Meat* by Charles E. Hanrahan, RS20142

[10] The EU successfully challenged U.S. foreign sales corporations (FSC) as an export subsidy in WTO dispute settlement. U.S. and EU negotiators currently are engaged in negotiations over compliance of a U.S. replacement for the FSC and over the level of retaliation that might be imposed by the EU which it estimates at more than $4 billion. See *The Foreign Sales Corporation (FSC) Tax Benefit for Exporting: WTO issues and an economic analysis* by David Lee Brumbaugh, RL30684.

Legislation was also introduced in the 106th Congress to prevent the United States from retaliating altogether against the EU for its banana preference system (H.R. 1361). The support of the ACP countries for the agreement, and especially its continuation of preferential treatment for ACP bananas, makes the introduction of similar legislation in the 107th Congress less likely. Similarly, there may be less pressure in the wake of the agreement on banana imports for legislation like H.R. 4478 introduced in the 106th Congress which would have exempted small businesses from increased tariffs imposed against products of the EU in response to the banana import regime.

Chapter 4

U.S. – EUROPEAN UNION TRADE RELATIONS: ISSUES AND POLICY CHALLENGES

Raymond J. Ahearn

SUMMARY

The United States and European Union (EU) share a huge and mutually beneficial economic partnership. Not only is the U.S.-EU trade and investment relationship the largest in the world, it is arguably the most important. Agreement between the two economic superpowers has been critical to making the world trading system more open and efficient.

Given a huge level of commercial interactions, trade tensions and disputes are not unexpected. While trade tensions in the past have tended to ebb and flow, some observers believe that this year's threat of a trade war is more serious than before. A dispute over steel trade is the proximate cause of rising trade tensions, but other high-profile disputes involving tax breaks for U.S. exporters and the treatment of genetically-engineered (GE) products lurk in the background.

Resolution of U.S.-EU disputes has become increasingly difficult in recent years. Part of the problem may be due to the fact that the U.S. and the EU are of roughly equal economic strength and neither side has the ability to impose concessions on the other. Another factor may be that many bilateral disputes now involve clashes in domestic values, priorities, and regulatory systems where the international rules of the road are inadequate to provide a basis for effective and timely dispute resolution.

In order to build a smoother relationship, Brussels and Washington may have to resolve a number of these disputes and avoid outbreak retaliatory actions this year. The agreement to launch a new round of multilateral trade negotiations at the WTO trade ministerial held last November in Doha, Qatar has facilitated this effort. But the recent passage of U.S. legislation increasing farm spending could complicate efforts to move the Doha Round forward and thwart the new round's potential beneficial impact on resolving other disputes.

The two sides now must deal with the fall-out from the Bush Administration's March 5, 2002 decision to impose temporary tariffs of up to 30% on approximately $8 billion in steel imports. Reacting angrily to this action, the EU on March 27, 2002 announced provisional tariffs of its own on steel. More provocatively, the EU took initial steps under an untested provision of the WTO to impose retaliatory tariffs by June 18, 2002 on U.S. exports without an explicit authorization to act. If Brussels pursues this course, U.S.-EU trade tensions are likely to escalate and potentially more explosive disputes involving the U.S. foreign sales corporation tax benefit for exports ant the EU's policy towards approval of new GE products could become more difficult to manage.

The major U.S.-EU trade and investment policy challenges can be grouped into six categories: (1) avoiding a "big ticket" trade dispute associated with steel or the tax breaks for U.S. exporters; (2) resolving longstanding trade disputes involving Airbus production subsidies and beef hormones; (3) dealing with different public concerns over new technologies and new industries (4) fostering a receptive climate for mergers and acquisitions; (5) strengthening the multilateral trading system; and (6) reaching understandings on foreign policy sanctions that have a trade impact.

MOST RECENT DEVELOPMENTS

The European Union and Japan on May 15, 2002 notified the World Trade Organization of their intent to retaliate against U.S. steel safeguard tariffs if the United States does not provide concessions either in the form of compensation or steel exclusions.

President Bush at the May 2, 2002 U.S.-EU summit stated that he will work with Congress to insure the U.S. will comply with the WTO ruling in the foreign sales corporation tax benefit case.

The European Commission on April 19, 2002 proposed to EU member states a list of U.S. exports, ranging from fruits and rice to steel and apparel products, that would be subject to an additional 100% tariff by mid-June in retaliation for a steel safeguard imposed by the Bush Administration in March.

On March 20, 2002 the European Union indicated that it will notify the WTO of its intent to adopt countermeasures against the U.S. steel tariffs. If the U.S. refuses to negotiate a compensation package by reducing tariffs on over $2 billion in EU exports, the EU could retaliate by raising tariffs on an equivalent amount of U.S. exports.

A senior European Union official stated the Commission intends to begin a process of progressively approving biotechnology products beginning on October 17, 2002.

U.S. Trade representative Robert Zoellick stated on February 7, 2002 that the United States is considering filing a formal complaint against the EU in the WTO over its moratorium on imports of genetically modified organisms (GMOs).

The World Trade Organization's highest appeals body on January 14, 2002 made a final judgment that the U.S. Foreign Sales Corporation Replacement and Extraterritorial Income Exclusion Act is an illegal export subsidy. Barring a negotiated settlement, the EU will be free to impose retaliatory duties on U.S. exports possibly in the range of $4 billion. The amount of the retaliatory duties that can be imposed will be determined by a WTO arbitrator, with a decision due June 17, 2002.

OVERVIEW

The United States and the European Union (EU) share a huge and mutually beneficial economic partnership. Not only is the U.S.-EU trade and investment relationship the largest in the world, but it is also arguably the most important. Agreement between the two partners in the past has been critical to making the world trading system more open and efficient.

Given the high level of U.S.-EU commercial interactions, trade tensions and disputes are not unexpected. While trade tensions in the past have tended to ebb and flow, some observers believe that this year's threat of a trade war is more serious than before. A dispute over steel trade is the proximate cause of rising trade tensions, but other high-profile disputes involving tax breaks for U.S. exporters and the treatment of genetically-engineered (GE) products lurk in the background.

The two sides face a major challenge this year in avoiding an outbreak of tit-for-tat retaliation. While the agreement reached to launch a new round of multilateral trade negotiations at last November's WTO trade ministerial in Doha, Qatar provides a basis for building a smoother relationship, the 2002 U.S. farm bill may complicate continuing U.S.-EU cooperation on this front. Congress in its response to both EU practices and Bush Administration initiatives will play a key role in managing the U.S.-EU economic relationship.

Closer Economic Ties

The United States and the European Union share the largest bilateral trade and investment relationship in the world. Annual two-way flows of goods, services, and foreign investment transactions exceeded $1.1 trillion in 2000. Viewed in terms of goods and services, the United States and EU are each other's largest trading partners. Each purchases about one-fifth of the other's exports of goods and about one-third of the other's exports of services. And much of the trade in goods is increasingly in high-technology and sophisticated product areas where incomes and tastes are the primary determinants of market success.

Based on a population of some 377 million citizens and gross domestic product of about $7.8 trillion (compared to a U.S. population of 284 million and a GDP of $9.9 trillion) in 2000, the fifteen members of the EU provide the single largest market in the world. Given the reforms entailed in the introduction of the European single market in the early 1990s, along with the introduction of a single currency, the euro, for twelve members, the EU market is also increasingly open and standardized. Over the next decade, with a possible enlargement to 27 countries, the EU market could become even more important as a destination for U.S. exports and investments.

The fact that each side has a huge investment position in the other's market may be the most significant aspect of the relationship. By the year-end 2000, the total stock of two-way direct investment reached $1.37 trillion (composed of $802 billion in EU investment in the United States and $573 billion in U.S. investment in the EU), making U.S. and European companies the largest investors in each other's market. This massive amount of ownership of companies in each other's market translates into an estimated 3.5 million Americans who are employed by European companies and an equal number of EU citizens who work for American companies in Europe.

Growing Strains

Given the huge volume of commercial interactions, it is commonly pointed out that trade disputes are quite natural and perhaps inevitable. While the vast majority of two-way trade and investment is unaffected by disputes, a small fraction (often estimated at 1%) of the total often gives rise to controversy and litigation. Historically, with the possible exception of agriculture, the disputes have been handled without excessive political rancor.

Over the past several years, however, trade relations are being strained by the nature and significance of the disputes. The EU Commissioner for Trade, Pascal Lamy, stated on November 20, 2000 that the "problems seem to get worse, not better." Richard Morningstar, then U.S. Ambassador to the EU, said in a January 23, 2001 speech that the inability of our two sides "to resolve our list of disputes, which are growing in both number and severity, is beginning to overshadow the rest of the relationship." Moreover, some of the efforts at dispute resolution have led to escalation and "tit-for-tat" retaliation with the potential to harm the multilateral trading system.

In 1999 the United States imposed punitive tariffs on $308 million of EU exports of mostly higher value-added agricultural products such as Danish ham and Roquefort cheese. This action was a response to a refusal by the EU to change its import regimes for bananas and hormone-treated beef which the World Trade Organization (WTO) determined to be in violation of world trade rules. EU pique over U.S. pressures on bananas and beef, in turn, led the EU to threaten retaliation against $4 billion dollars in U.S. exports that the WTO found in violation of an export subsidy agreement. In addition, the EU has filed numerous WTO dispute resolution petitions alleging that a variety of U.S. trade laws violate international obligations in some technical fashion, contributing to an impression that these challenges are part of a concerted EU strategy to weaken or gut U.S. trade laws.

The underlying causes of the trade disputes are varied. Some conflicts stem primarily from traditional demands from producer or vested interests for protection or state aids. Other conflicts arise when the United States or the EU initiate actions or measures to protect or promote their political and economic interests, often in the absence of significant private sector pressures. Still other conflicts are rooted in an array of regulations that deal mostly with issues that are considered domestic policy.

Resolution of these disputes has proven difficult in recent years. Part of the problem may rest in the fact that the EU and United States are of roughly equal economic strength and neither side has the ability to impose concessions on the other. Another factor may be that numerous new disputes involve clashes in domestic values and priorities where the international rules of the road are inadequate to provide a basis for effective and timely dispute resolution.

Current Trade Agenda

The United States and European Union have full plate of high profile bilateral disputes this year. Several of the disputes may need to be resolved and new potential disputes avoided if the bilateral trade strains are to be contained and a smoother trade relationship is to develop. Moreover, progress on the bilateral front could provide a foundation for the two trading giants to make progress in efforts to begin the process of multilateral trade negotiations as prescribed by the Doha Ministerial Declaration.

Resolution of disputes over steel and the FSC are at the top of the list of bilateral challenges. President Bush's March 5, 2002 decision to provide protective tariffs to the U.S. steel industry for a three year period was widely criticized in Europe, and prompted a quick response. On March 27, 2002, citing a threat of diversion of steel from the U.S. market to Europe, the EU announced provisional tariffs of 15% to 26% on 15 different steel products. More provocatively, the EU took initial steps under an untested provision of the WTO to impose a retaliatory tariffs by June 18, 2002 on U.S. exports without explicit authorization to act.

If Brussels decides on swift retaliation rather than waits for the WTO to rule on whether the U.S. steel tariffs are a violation of world trade rules, U.S. trade officials will be under great pressure to retaliate against the retaliation. In this context, U.S.-EU trade tensions could spillover and affect potentially more explosive disputes involving the FSC tax benefits for U.S. exports and the EU's policy towards approval of new GE products.

MAJOR ISSUES AND POLICY CHALLENGES

Major EU-U.S. trade and investment issues and policy challenges can be grouped into six different categories: (1) avoiding a "big ticket" trade dispute; (2) resolving two longstanding trade disputes; (3) dealing with disputes involving new technologies or industries; (4) fostering a receptive climate for mergers and acquisitions; (5) strengthening the multilateral trading system; and (6) accommodating trade-related foreign policy sanctions. A summary and status update of each challenge follows.

Avoiding A "Big Ticket" Trade Dispute

Perhaps the most serious trade disputes that currently could the bilateral relationship deal with steel and tax breaks for U.S. exporters. If not managed properly, either could lead to a massive disruption of trade and a major increase in political tensions.

Steel Trade[1]

Conflict over steel is again a high priority issue. Although the EU industry has undergone significant consolidation and privatization in recent years, the U.S. government alleges that many EU companies still benefit from earlier state subsidies and/or engage in dumping steel products (selling at "less than fair value") in foreign markets. U.S. steel companies have aggressively used U.S. trade laws to fight against EU steel imports by filing antidumping and countervailing duty petitions that include imports from EU countries. In return, the EU has countered with five recent challenges in the WTO against the alleged U.S. misuse of its countervailing duty and antidumping laws. Moreover, the EU, along with eight other petitioning countries, initiated on July 10, 2001 a WTO dispute resolution complaint against the so-called "Byrd" law, which allows duties collected under the U.S. antidumping and

---

[1] Prepared by Stephen Cooney, Industry Analyst, Resources, Science, and Industry Division.

countervailing duty statutes to be returned to the injured U.S. industry. The law was passed with major backing of the U.S steel industry.

In addition to "unfair" trade disputes, President Bush announced June 5, 2001 that his Administration would call upon the U.S. International Trade Commission (ITC) to begin an investigation on international trade in steel under Section 201 of U.S. trade law. He also announced that he would seek multilateral negotiations with U.S. trading partners on fundamental issues of global overcapacity and government subsidies. The President was reacting to continued problems in the U.S. steel industry, parts of which still have not recovered from a major import surge in 1997-98. The rise in imports to more than a quarter of U.S. finished steel consumption was stimulated by financial crises in Asia, Latin America and Russia, which reduced demand on those markets, and by the dramatically lower dollar-equivalent prices for many foreign producers. After a partial recovery in 1999-2000, the U.S. industry has again been affected by imports rising to more than 20% of finished steel consumption, record-high levels of semi-finished products and falling market demand and prices.

Section 201 relief, often referred to as "safeguard," provides for temporary restrictions on imports that have surged in such quantities as to cause or threaten to cause serious injury to a domestic industry. The procedure is compatible with the rules of the World Trade Organization (WTO). A Section 201 case does not in itself need to demonstrate dumping, subsidization or other unfair practices by U.S. trading partners.

The ITC in October determined that U.S. producers of about 80% of U.S.-made steel are being injured by imports. The decision does not automatically mean that quotas or duties will be imposed on the products found to be causing the injury. The decision is left to the President, following recommendations from ITC on what remedy to impose.

On March 5, 2002, President Bush announced trade remedies for all products on which the ITC had found substantial injury except two specialty categories. All remedies or import restrictions will be for a three-year period beginning on March 20, 2002. The tariffs will be up to 30% on approximately $8 billion in steel imports. Canada, Mexico, and other U.S. free trade partners were exempted from all tariffs.

The U.S. decision raised cries of indignation and protectionism from European leaders, and prompted a quick response. On March 27, 2002, citing a thread of diversion of steel from the U.S. market to Europe, the EU announced provisional tariffs of 15% to 26% on 15 different steel products. More provocatively, the EU took initial steps under an untested provision of the WTO safeguards agreement to impose retaliatory tariffs by as early as June 18, 2002 on U.S. exports without an explicit authorization to act.

If Brussels decides on swift retaliation rather than waits for the WTO to rule on whether the U.S. steel tariffs are a violation of world trade rules, U.S. trade officials will be under great pressure to counter-retaliate. In this context, U.S.-EU trade tensions are likely to escalate and potentially more explosive disputes involving the tax benefit for U.S. exports and the EU's policy towards approval of new GE products could become more difficult to manage.

U.S. Tax Benefits for Exports[2]

The controversy between the European Union (EU) and the United States over U.S. tax benefits for exports has been simmering for years. Since 1984, the U.S. tax code provided an export tax benefit known as the Foreign Sales Corporation (FSC) provisions, which enabled U.S. exporters to exempt between 15% and 30% of their export income from U.S. tax. According to Internal Revenue Service data, FSC was used in connection with almost half of U.S. annual exports of goods. In 1998, however, the EU lodged a complaint with the World Trade Organization (WTO), arguing that the United States' FSC tax benefit was an export subsidy and was, therefore, in violation of the WTO agreements.

An aspect of the controversy concerns why the EU waited almost 14 years to challenge the U.S. tax provision. While EU officials maintain they never formally agreed that the FSC was legal, many of the U.S. side suspect that the challenge had much to do with EU pique over U.S. challenges in the WTO to the EU's import regimes for beef and bananas. Winning a case that involved a large amount of trade may also have been seen by some Europeans as providing significant negotiating leverage that could be used to settle other trade disputes as well. The EU responded that the challenge was prompted by an effort to level the playing field, but there is little indication that European companies, with the possible exception of Airbus, were proponents of the challenge.

In October 1999, a WTO panel issued a report that essentially upheld the EU's position. An appeal by the United States was denied, and, under WTO procedures, the United States had until October 2000, to bring its tax system into WTO-compliance or face possible retaliatory measures by the EU.

In November 2000, the United States repealed the FSC and put in its place the "extraterritorial income (ETI)" regime. The ETI provisions consist of a tax benefit for exports of the same magnitude as FSC, but also extend tax free treatment to a certain amount of income from exporters' foreign operations. The partial tax exemption for extraterritorial income is the design feature of the ETI provisions that is intended to achieve WTO compliance. However the EU maintains that the ETI provisions provide an export subsidy in the same manner as FSC, and has asked the WTO to rule against it. The EU also requested the authority to impose $4 billion in retaliatory duties on U.S. goods, an amount 12 times greater than the $300 million in punitive duties the U.S. imposed in the beef and banana cases.

An interim WTO report, which was delivered to the United States and EU on June 22, 2000, indicated that the new law continues to provide export subsidies and also that it provides less favorable treatment to imported products than that accorded U.S. made products. U.S. Trade Representative Robert Zoellick called the report a "nuclear bomb."

The Bush Administration opted to appeal the WTO ruling. But the appeal was rejected by the WTO on January 14, 2002, thereby leaving both sides with difficult choices. The options for a settlement include U.S. efforts to enact further changes in its tax laws to conform to WTO rules; U.S. offers of compensation to the EU for trade damages; or U.S. acceptance of EU trade retaliation. To date, the Bush Administration and Congress are exploring the legislative option and EU officials have vowed to allow the U.S. time to make the necessary changes as long as there is a clear indication that progress is being made.

---

[2] Prepared by David Brumbaugh, Specialist in Public Finance, and Jane G. Gravelle, Senior Specialist in Economic Policy, Government and Finance Division.

But in the interim, a WTO arbitrator is scheduled to set the level of trade damages by June 17, 2002. The U.S. has argued that the EU may have the right to impose $1.05 billion to $1.11 billion in annual punitive duties but the EU has argued that the trade damages amount to $4.04 billion. The European Commission has prepared a draft list of U.S. exports that could be targeted for retaliation anytime after June 17, 2002 in the event that the tacit agreement between Washington and Brussels on the process for changing the U.S. tax provision in dispute breaks down.

Resolving Longstanding Disputes

Airbus Production Subsidies[3]

On December 19, 2000, Airbus announced that it had formally launched a program to construct the world's largest commercial passenger aircraft, the newly numbered Airbus A380. In the spring of 2001, Boeing dropped its support of a competing new large aircraft, opting instead to focus on the development of a new class of higher speed commercial aircraft. The Airbus action potentially reopens a long-standing trade dispute between the United States and Europe about subsidization of aircraft projects that compete directly with non-subsidized U.S. products, in this case the Boeing 747 series aircraft.

The large commercial aircraft (jet aircraft with 100 or more seats) production industry is essentially a duopoly consisting of an American manufacturer, Boeing, and a European manufacturer, Airbus. Until recently Airbus was a consortium of national aviation firms, some with close government ties, who cooperated to produce commercial aircraft. As a result of recent European aerospace industry consolidation, Airbus is now owned by just two firms, EADS and BAE systems. Airbus itself is reforming as a public firm under the name Airbus Integrated Company. In recent years, after two decades of trying, Airbus has come close to achieving parity in sales with Boeing.

The basic premise of the dispute between the U.S. and EU is whether, as U.S. trade policymakers contend, Airbus is a successful participant in the market for large commercial jet aircraft not because it makes competitive products, which by all standards it does, but because it has received significant amounts of governmental subsidy and other assistance, without which it probably would not have been able to enter and participate in the market. The assistance from the governments of France, Germany, Spain and Great Britain arguably has included equity infusions, debt forgiveness, debt rollovers and marketing assistance, including political and economic pressure on purchasing governments. Airbus, not surprisingly, does not accept the U.S. view of the reasons for its success.

At issue in the A380 development is at least $3.1 billion in already identified direct loans to be provided by seven of the nine EU Member State governments in the A380 development. The total cost is estimated to be $12 billion. The United States is concerned that the level of state-aid needed for this project could violate Member States' adherence to their bilateral and multilateral obligations, including the WTO Agreement on Subsidies and Countervailing Measures (SCM). The United States has urged the Airbus member governments to ensure that the terms and conditions of their support for the A380 are consistent with commercial terms and rates and with their international obligations.

---

[3] Prepared by John W. Fischer, Specialist in Transportation, Resources, Science, and Industry Division.

To date, the Bush Administration has not changed U.S. policy on this issue. At a June 6, 2001 meeting of the WTO Committee on Civil Aircraft, Bush Administration officials pressed the EU for more information on the financing of the A380. The EU responded with the provision of mostly general information about the scope and nature of their member states' support for the A380. The United States is still seeking more detailed information, including information on the critical project appraisal – Airbus' projections on costs and sales of the A380. In response, the EU raised questions concerning alleged subsidies Boeing receives from the U.S. government and its dealings with the Department of Defense.

Beef Hormones

The dispute over the EU ban, implemented in 1989, on the production and importation of meat treated with growth-promoting hormones is one of the most bitter disputes between the United States and Europe. It is also a dispute, that on its surface, involves a relatively small amount of trade. The ban affected an estimated $100-$200 million in lost U.S. exports – less than one-tenth of one percent of U.S. exports to the EU in 1999.

The EU justified the ban to protect the health and safety of consumers, but several WTO dispute settlements panels subsequently ruled that the ban was inconsistent with the Uruguay Round Sanitary and Phytosanitary (SPS) Agreement. The SPS Agreement provides criteria that have to be met when a country imposes food safety import regulations more stringent than those agreed upon in international standards. These include a scientific assessment that the hormones pose a health risk, along with a risk assessment. Although the WTO panels concluded that the EU ban lacked a scientific justification, the EU refused to remove the ban primarily out of concern that European consumers were opposed to having this kind of meat in the marketplace.

In lieu of lifting the ban, the EU in 1999 offered the United States compensation in the form of an expanded quota for hormone-free beef. The U.S. government, backed by most of the U.S. beef industry, opposed compensation on the grounds that exports of hormone-free meat would not be large enough to compensate for losses of hormone-treated exports. This led the way for the United States to impose 100% retaliatory tariffs on $116 million of EU agricultural products from mostly France, Germany, Italy, and Denmark, countries deeded the biggest supporters of the ban.

The U.S. hard line is buttressed by concerns that other countries might adopt similar measures based on health concerns that lack a legitimate scientific basis according to U.S. standards. Other U.S. interest groups are concerned that non-compliance by the EU undermines the future ability of the WTO to resolve disputes involving the use of SPS measures.

Recent occurrences of "mad cow disease" in several EU countries and the outbreak of foot-and-mouth disease (FMD) in the United Kingdom and three other EU countries have contributed to an environment that is not conducive to resolving the meat hormone dispute. The EU has recently indicated its intention to make the ban on hormone-treated meat permanent, while at the same time expressing some openness to renewing discussions about a compensation arrangement which would increase the EU's market access for non-hormone treated beef from the United States. In discussions held June 11, 2001, a U.S. industry proposal for expanded access to the EU market for hormone-free beef for a period of 12 years was rejected by the EU. In response, the EU countered with a 4-5 year period for compensation. The compensation talks have since languished. But a February 20, 2002 EU

Standing Veterinary Committee proposal to repeal the requirement that 20% of beef imported from the U.S. be tested for the presence of hormones could remove an important obstacle in the compensation talks by making it easier for U.S. non-hormone beef producers to take advantage of any improved market access conditions.

In pursuing compensation talks, the Bush Administration is faced with a divided industry position. Then American Meat Institute and the American Farm Bureau prefer carousel retaliation to settle the dispute while the American Cattlemen's Beef Association supports efforts to gain increased access for non-hormone treated beef in exchange for dropping the retaliatory tariff on EU exports. Thus far, EU offers of compensation for lost U.S. meat exports in lieu of lifting the ban have been rejected by the United States.

The Bush Administration has maintained that it would not use so-called "carousel" retaliation (rotating the products subject to retaliation) while the negotiations for compensation are on-going. Some observers speculate that both the EU and the U.S. have made a political decision to handle the dispute by insisting that they are making progress toward a resolution. This arguably could shield USTR from congressional and private sector pressures to apply the carousel provision against the EU.

Resolution of the dispute could remove a critical irritant to the overall U.S.-EU trade relationship. How it is resolved could also have important implications for future WTO disputes involving the use of SPS measures to restrict trade.

Dealing with Different Public Concerns Over
New Technologies and New Industries

The emergence of new technologies and new industries is at the heart of a growing number of disputes. Biotechnology as a new technology and e-commerce (and related data privacy concerns) as a new industry are emerging issues that have great potential for generating increases in transatlantic welfare, as well as conflict. These issues tend to be quite politically sensitive because they affect consumer attitudes, as well as regulatory regimes.

Bio-technology[4]

Differences between the United States and the EU over genetically engineered (GE) crops and food products that contain them pose a potential threat to, and in some cases have already disrupted, U.S. agricultural trade. Underlying the conflicts are pronounced differences between the United States and EU about GE products and their potential health and environmental effects.

Widespread farmer adoption of bio-engineered crops in the United States makes consumer acceptance of GE crops and foods at home and abroad critical to producers, processors, and exporters. U.S. farmers use GE crops because they can reduce input costs or make field work more flexible. Supporters of GE crops maintain that the technology also holds promise for enhancing agricultural productivity and improving nutrition in developing countries. U.S. consumers, with some exceptions, have been generally accepting of the health and safety of GE foods and willing to put their trust in a credible regulatory process.

---

[4] Prepared by Charles E. Hanrahan, Senior Specialist in Agricultural Policy, Resources, Science, and Industry Division.

In contrast, EU consumers, environmentalists, and some scientists maintain that the long-term effects of GE foods on health and the environment are unknown and not scientifically established. By and large, Europeans are more risk averse to the human health and safety issues associated with bio-engineered food products than U.S. citizens.

In 1999 the EU instituted a *de facto* moratorium on any new approval of GE products. The moratorium has halted come $300 million in U.S. corn shipments. EU policymakers also moved toward establishing mandatory labeling requirements for products containing GE ingredients. Subsequently, the EU has put in place legislation to restart the process of approving GE crop varieties, but has yet to complete regulations on labeling GE foods. On July 25, 2001, the European Commission proposed stringent rules on labeling and traceability of GM food and animal feed. U.S. biotechnology, food, and agriculture interests are concerned that these regulations, if adopted by the EU governments and EU Parliament, will deny U.S. products entry into the EU market and may seek to challenge them in the WTO.

The Bush Administration in late August 2001 reiterated its view that regulatory approaches toward products of biotechnology should be transparent, predictable, and based on sound science. Moreover, the administration made clear that it would mount an aggressive campaign against proposed EU labeling and traceability regulations by pressing the EU not to adopt regulations that would violate WTO rules or hurt U.S. exports. On February 7, 2002, USTR Zoellick stated that the United States is "very strongly" considering filing a formal dispute settlement complaint in the WTO over the EU's failure to lift its moratorium on imports of GMOs. EU Trade Commissioner Pascal Lamy countered that U.S. action along these lines would be immensely counterproductive" because it would be seen as a challenge to "consumer fears and perceptions."

The April 2002 National Trade Estimates report, released by the Office of the U.S. Trade Representative, warned the U.S. is evaluating its next steps for altering the EU moratorium. A U.S. trade official defined that as including both continued consultations with the Commission, which is trying to unblock the approval process, as well as bringing a WTO case. Few observers predict a change in the EU approval process will occur this year.

E-Commerce and Data Privacy

The EU Council of Ministers in December 2001 reached agreement on a proposed directive on the taxation of e-commerce. The agreement was to adapt and apply existing taxes on e-commerce, not to levy any new or additional taxes as had been actively considered. The proposed directive considers that e-commerce transactions that do not involve the delivery of physical goods still constitute the provision of a service subject to each Member State's value-added-tax (VAT). The VAT is a consumption tax payable on deliveries of goods and services. The proposed directive requires that non-EU suppliers register with a VAT authority in a single Member State. The VAT on digital products supplied from outside the EU would be levied at the rate applicable in the customer's country of residence, and VAT revenue then reallocated from the supplier's country of registration to that of the customer.

U.S.-based companies have questioned whether the proposed Directive treats U.S. suppliers of digital products less favorably than EU suppliers. One problem cited is that U.S. suppliers would be required to collect and remit the VAT at 15 different rates in accord with the consumer's Member State of residence. By contrast, EU suppliers would only be obliged to collect and remit VAT at the rate of the single Member State in which that supplier is registered. If the Directive is formally adopted by Member States this year, it would likely be implemented by 2003.

The related issue of data privacy rights is also a source of friction. While the EU supports strict legal regulations on gathering consumer's personal data, the United States has advocated a self-regulated approach. Controversy emerged when the EU adopted a directive forbidding the commercial exchange of private information with countries that lack adequate privacy protections. The issue appeared resolved by the "Safe Harbor" agreement of 2000, whereby U.S. companies that agree to abide by privacy principles can enter a safe harbor protecting them from the EU directive barring data transfers to countries that do not adequately protect citizens' privacy. But U.S. companies have been slow to participate in the Safe Harbor by self-certifying to the Department of Commerce (only 35 had signed on as of May 2002). Currently, only entities whose activities fall under the regulatory authority of the Federal Trade Commission or the Department of Transportation are eligible to participate in the Safe Harbor. Whether or how other sectors, particularly financial services, will be considered in relation to Safe Harbor has not yet been determined.

The U.S. financial services industry argues that existing U.S. laws (Gramm-Leach-Bliley Act and the Fair Credit Reporting Act) adequately protect data privacy. In a May 11, 2001 letter to Treasury Secretary Paul O'Neill, some Members of Congress expressed concern with the "EU's unwillingness to grant an adequacy determination to U.S. financial services firms."

FOSTERING A RECEPTIVE CLIMATE
FOR MERGERS AND ACQUISITIONS

Consistent with the trend of increased globalization, U.S. and European companies have engaged in hundreds of mergers and acquisitions (M&A) in recent years. In 1999 European companies reportedly spent over $200 billion on acquisitions of U.S. companies compared to U.S. company expenditures of $90 billion for European companies. Although concerns regarding foreign control and ownership of companies in particular sectors, such as telecommunications or mass media, have been raised from time to time, M&A activity has been pretty much noncontroversial. That was until July 3, 2001, the day the European Commission blocked the merger of General Electric and Honeywell, opening a debate on the need for better U.S.-EU antitrust cooperation.

Enhanced Antitrust Cooperation

As M&A activity has accelerated in recent years among U.S. and European companies, the U.S. Justice Department and the European Union's competition directorate have worked closely in passing judgment on proposed deals. Pursuant to a 1991 bilateral agreement on antitrust cooperation between the European Commission and the United States, the handling of these cases has been viewed generally as a successful example of transatlantic cooperation. In reviews of several hundred mergers over the past 10 years, there has been substantial agreement between regulators in Brussels and Washington on antitrust decisions. However, the EU's recent rejection of General Electric's $43 billion merger with Honeywell International has highlighted major differences in antitrust standards and processes employed by the EU and the United States. In the process, some observers have argued that the GE-Honeywell case points to a need for closer consultations or convergence in antitrust standards.

The GE-Honeywell merger would have combined producers of complementary aircraft components. GE produces aircraft engines and Honeywell makes advanced avionics such as airborne collision warning devices and navigation equipment. GE and Honeywell do not compete over any large range of products. The combined company arguably would have been able to offer customers (mostly Boeing and Airbus) lower prices for a package that no other engine or avionics company could match. In its review, the U.S. Justice Department concluded that the merger would offer better products and services at more attractive prices than either firm could offer individually, and that competition would be enhanced.

With regard to the European Commission's merger review (which occurs over any merger between firms whose combined global sales are more than $4.3 billion and that do at least $215 million of business in the European Union), the legal standard employed for evaluating mergers is whether the acquisition creates or strengthens a company's dominant position as a result of which effective competition would be significantly impeded. The commission's Task Force on Mergers concluded that, together, GE-Honeywell's "dominance" would be increased because of the strong positions held by GE in jet engines and by Honeywell in avionics products.

EU antitrust regulators relied, in part, on the economic concept of "bundling" to reach its decision. Bundling is the practice of selling complementary products in a single, discounted package. The combined company makes more profits than the pre-merger companies and prices are lower, making consumers better off. But the EU concluded that the lower prices and packages of products that could be offered by the merged entity would make competition a lot more difficult for other producers of airplane equipment such as Rolls Royce, Pratt & Whitney, and United Technologies. In the long run, European regulators had concerns that the merger could force weaker competitors out of the market, thereby leaving GE-Honeywell free over time to raise prices.

GE officials countered that the commission relied on a theory that is not supported by evidence, particularly in the aerospace industry. Boeing and Airbus, for example, tend not to be weak or passive price takers, but are strong and sophisticated customers that negotiate all prices. And even if the new company offered discounted "bundled" packages, the winners would be the airlines, and ultimately, their customers.

In short, the GE-Honeywell case crystallized differences in standards and processes employed by antitrust regulators in Washington and Brussels. One of the most striking differences is that the European process clearly affords competitors more leeway to oppose mergers by allowing for testimony behind closed doors and places more weight on economic models that predict competition will be reduced and competitors eliminated in the long-run. U.S. antitrust regulators tend to presume that any post-merger anti-competitive problems can be taken care of later by corrective antitrust enforcement action.

Since the GE-Honeywell dispute, there have been few cases that have tested whether an emerging rift on antitrust policy may be developing. One reason is that M&A activity has been slow in 2001 and again this year to date. The next test, however, could be the EU's handling of the Microsoft case. The EU is expected to take action on Microsoft by year-end 2002. U.S. antitrust officials reportedly have been urging the EU to adopt sanctions modeled on the U.S. settlement.

Strengthening the Multilateral Trading System

After three years of efforts, including the ill-fated ministerial held in Seattle in 1999, trade ministers from the 142 member countries of the WTO agreed to launch a new round of trade negotiations last November in Doha, Qatar. At Doha the WTO members agreed to launch a new round of trade negotiations and agreed to give priority attention to a number of developing country concerns.

By most accounts, U.S.-EU cooperation played a major role in producing agreement at Doha. USTR Zoellick and EU Trade Commissioner Lamy reportedly worked closely together, agreeing that making concessions to developing countries on issues of priority concern was necessary to move the trading system forward. Their Cooperation began early in 2001 with the settlement of the long-running banana dispute and tacit agreement to settle other disputes without resort to retaliation. Each also recognized that both trading superpowers would have to make concessions at Doha to achieve their overall objectives.

At Doha, both the U.S. and EU shared the goal of liberalizing markets in which each enjoyed competitive advantages and to preserve as many protected and less advanced sectors as possible. To gain support from other WTO members, the United States agreed to allow negotiations on its trade remedy laws and on patent protection while the EU agreed to greater liberalization of the agricultural sector than some Member States wanted. Both also agreed to support a number of capacity building initiatives designed to help developing countries better take advantage of world trade opportunities.

The agenda agreed to at Doha calls for a comprehensive three-year negotiation to be completed by 2005. The negotiations will cover trade in services, industrial tariffs, and agriculture. The broad agenda provides scope for negotiators to derive balanced packages of concessions from all participating countries.

Agriculture is an issue that could prove divisive once the negotiations pick up momentum. Transatlantic trade tensions over agriculture delayed the conclusion of the Uruguay Round by several years in the early 1990s. The U.S. has been a longstanding demander for the liberalization of agricultural trade barriers and domestic support programs, while the EU has been reluctant to put agriculture on the negotiating agenda. However, passage of the 2002 farm bill could offset this standard calculation. As the bill increased subsidies for a number of major crops, U.S. farm support levels could well approach limits on farm support set by the Uruguay Round. Whether higher levels of U.S. farm spending will serve as a prod for further negotiations or provide the EU with an excuse to put agriculture on the negotiating table, with the politically difficult reform of the Common Agricultural Policy that would require, remains to be seen.

Accommodating Foreign Policy Sanctions
That Have An Impact on Trade

U.S. legislation that requires the imposition of economic sanctions for foreign policy reasons has been a major concern of the EU. While the EU often shares many of the foreign policy goals of the United States that are addressed legislatively, it has opposed the extraterritorial provisions of certain pieces of U.S. legislation that seek to unilaterally regulate or control trade and investment activities conducted by foreign companies outside the United States. Most persistent EU complaints have been directed at the Cuban Liberty and Democratic Solidarity Act of 1996 (so-called Helms-Burton Act) and the Iran and Libya Sanctions Act (ILSA), which threatens the extraterritorial imposition of U.S. sanctions against European firms doing business in Cuba, Iran, and Libya.

In May 1998 the EU reached an understanding with the Clinton Administration concerning Helms-Burton and ILSA. Regarding Helms-Burton, the Clinton Administration agreed to continue to waive title III (at six month intervals, as allowed by law), which allows lawsuits for damages in U.S. courts over investment in expropriated U.S. property in Cuba, in order to avoid a major dispute with the EU. The Clinton Administration also pledged to work with Congress to amend the law's provision (Title IV) barring entry into the United States of executives working for companies that have invested in property confiscated by the Cuban government. This permanent waiver of Title IV would be undertaken in exchange for the EU's efforts to promote democracy and human rights in Cuba. The understanding also tried to insulate the EU from sanctions under ILSA, which threatened sanctions on foreign oil companies that invest more than $20 million in one year in Iran's energy sector, or $40 million in one year in Libya's energy sector.

EU Commissioner for External Affairs Christopher Patten called on the Bush Administration to endorse the 1998 understanding at a March 6, 2001 press conference. President Bush, in turn, has continued to suspend implementation of Title III. On July 16, 2001, President Bush made the decision to continue to suspend the implementation and cited efforts by European countries and other U.S. allies to push for democratic change in Cuba. On January 16, 2002, President Bush once again suspended implementation of Title III for a six-month period. Concerning ILSA, the House and Senate both passed bills (H.R. 1954, S. 1218) extending ILSA for an additional five years. H.R. 1954, also provides for termination of the bill with the passage of a joint resolution of the Congress.

Chapter 5

U.S.-EU TRADE TENSIONS: CAUSES, CONSEQUENCES, AND POSSIBLE CURES

Raymond J. Ahearn

SUMMARY

The United States and the European Union (EU) share a large and mutually beneficial trade and investment relationship. Given a huge volume of commercial interactions, trade tensions and disputes are not unexpected. While trade tensions in the past have tended to ebb and flow, some observers believe that this year's threat of a trade war is more serious than before. A dispute over steel trade is the proximate casue of rising trade tensions, but other high-profile disputes involving tax breaks for U.S. exporters and the treatment of genetically-engineered (GE) products lurk in the background. The steel dispute is characterized by feelings on both sides of the Atlantic that the other side has taken actions that are unreasonable and inconsistent with the rules of the World Trade Organization (WTO). Moreover, both Washington and Brussels have palyed hardball in crafting retaliation lists aimed at influencing each other's domestic political process. While fears of an all-out trade war are likely exaggerated, the trade disputes may impede U.S.-EU cooperation in other areas. A number of ways have been suggested to diffuse current trade tensions including greater reliance on compensation as opposed to retaliation and greater emphasis on diplomatic as opposed to legalistic solutions to disputes. While potentially helpful, the fact that some of these high-profile disputes have been unresolved for decades suggests the difficulty of finding permanent solutions. Congress has a strong interest in these disputes and plays a significant legislative role, particularly on the export subsidy issue.

INTRODUCTION

The United States and European Union (EU) are parties to the largest two-way trade and investment relationship in the world. Annual two-way flows of goods, services, and investments now exceed $1 trillion. While only a tiny fraction of these interactions lead to disputes, the dominant role that both economic powers play in the world economy makes settlement of the disputes particularly important.[1]

U.S.-EU trade tensions have ebbed and flowed in recent years. During the summer of 2000, the two sides bickered over the EU's discriminatory policies affecting imports of bananas and beef treated with hormones. The United States imposed 100% tariffs on about $300 million of mainly luxury items such as Danish ham, truffles, Roquefort cheese, and Italian handbags. The EU countered by challenging a U.S. tax benefit for export sales known as the Foreign Sales Corporation (FSC). This case eventually provided the EU with a huge bargaining chip - authorization from the WTO to impose trade sanctions on a value of U.S. exports that could range from $1 billion - $4 billion. A WTO arbitration panel is scheduled to decide the exact amount by June 17, 2002.[2]

With the onset of the Bush Administration in 2001, cooperation began to supercede confrontation. Pascal Lamy, the EU Commissioner for Trade, and Robert Zoellick, the U.S. Trade Representative, reached agreement on the banana dispute and U.S. retaliatory tariffs associated with bananas were lifted in April. The two sides agreed to disagree on the hormone dispute, and the EU consented to provide the United States more time to bring its tax law in conformity with its WTO obligations. Moreover, Lamy and Zoellick collaborated to launch a new round of WTO negotiations last November in Doha, Qatar.

Last year's lull in trade threats was broken on March 5, 2002 when President Bush announced his decision to impose fairly steep, albeit temporary, tariffs of up to 30% on approximately $8 billion in steel imports. Canada, Mexico, Israel, and Jordan - countries that have a free trade agreement with the U.S. - were exempted from all tariffs.[3]

The President's decision to rely on a trade remedy and to impose the tariffs in a selective fashion raised cries of indignation and protectionism from European leaders, and prompted a quick response. On March 27. 2002, citing a threat of diversion of foreign steel from the U.S. market to Europe, the EU announced provisional tariffs of 15% to 26% on 15 different steel products. More provocatively, the EU took initial steps under an untested provision of the WTO to impose retaliatory tariffs by June 18, 2002 on U.S. exports without an explicit authorization to act.

If Brussels decides on swift retaliation rather than waiting for the WTO to rule on whether the U.S. steel tariffs are a violation of world trade rules, U.S. trade officials will be under great pressure to retaliate against the retaliation. In this context, U.S.-EU trade tensions are likely to escalate and potentially more explosive disputes involving the U.S. tax benefit for exports and the EU's policy towards approval of new GE products could become more difficult to manage.[4]

---

[1] For background, see CRS Report RL30608, EU-U.S. Economic Ties: Framework, Scope, and Magnitude, by William H. Cooper, and CRS Issue Brief IB 10087, U.S.-European Union Trade Relations: Issues and Policy Challenges, by Raymond J. Ahearn.

[2] For background, see CRS Report RS20746, Export Tax Benefit and the WTO: Foreign Sales Corporation (FSCs) and the Extraterritorial (ETI) Replacement Provision, by David L. Brumbaugh.

[3] For background, see CRS Report RL31107, Steel Industry and Trade Issues, by Stephen Cooney.

[4] For background on the GE products dispute, see CRS Report RL31107, Agricultural Trade Issues in the 107th Congress, by Charles Hanrahan, Geoffrey Becker, and Remy Jurenas.

CAUSES

Escalation of U.S.-EU trade tensions in 2002 has been spurred by three factors. First, each side views actions the other has taken as unreasonable and motivated by narrow political considerations. Second, each side believes that the other is skirting WTO rules and shirking WTO obligations. Third, each side sees the other playing political hardball in crafting retaliation lists that clearly attempt to influence internal political deliberations.

Narrow Political Actions

Balancing divergent domestic and foreign goals - a strong domestic economy, responsiveness to domestic political interests, promotion of an open world trading system, and fostering strong relationships with key allies - is part of trade policy decision-making. When decisions are skewed toward achieving one of these objectives, controversy often ensues. In this context, the Bush Administration's steel decision was viewed as unreasonable by many Europeans who saw it as driven primarily by narrow domestic political calculations, not broader domestic economic or foreign policy interests. Whether valid or not, many Europeans believed that the decision was motivated by electoral considerations. Moreover, many Europeans were incensed by the discriminatory manner in which the tariffs were implemented, targeting the EU hardest and excluding countries that have a free trade agreement with the United States.

On the contrary, Washington has been irked by EU actions that appear to have narrow political motivations of another kind. The EU's decision to challenge a provision of the FSC export tax benefit is a case in point. While the FSC was enacted in 1984, the EU did not challenge the provision until November 1997. Many on the U.S. side suspect that the challenge had much to do with an attempt by the European Commission to gain negotiating leverage over the United States, as well as with getting even for U.S. pressures over beef and bananas. The fact that few European companies were complaining about the FSC as disadvantaging them commercially further suggests a calculated political motive for launching the case.

Skirting WTO Rules

The EU aggressive reaction is related, in part, to its belief that the conduct of the U.S. steel decision violates numerous WTO rules. An essential element of the EU's complaint is that its steel exports to the United States declined by 33 percent between 1998 and 2001, and that the WTO Agreement on Safeguards permits temporary restrictions on imports only when imports are increasing. EU officials also question whether the U.S. decision adequately links the remedy to the actual level of injury caused by imports as opposed to other causes. In addition, they are skeptical that the U.S. decision to exclude its free trade partners from the tariffs is permitted under the most-favored nation principle of the WTO.

U.S. officials say that EU concerns about whether its steel action complies with its WTO obligations should be determined by a formal WTO dispute settlement panel- a process that normally takes up to two years. But the EU maintains that the WTO safeguards agreement allows it to adopt countermeasures immediately because the United States did not show an absolute increase in imports over the most recent three year period. Accordingly, the EU has argued that it is entitled to retaliate as of June 19, 2002 on about $320 million worth of U.S. exports. U.S. trade officials have responded that any immediate unilateral retaliation against the United States would be unprecedented in the history of the WTO and would "strike at the heart of the multilateral trading system."

Retaliation and **Domestic Politics**

The WTO permits retaliation (imposition of very high tariffs on a trading partner's exports) when recalcitrant governments fail to comply with dispute panel rulings against them. While it is used sparingly, both the United States and EU have imposed or threatened retaliation in ways that have sparked a raw nerve on both sides of the Atlantic.

When the Clinton Administration levied retaliatory tariffs on European exports over the banana and beef hormone disputes in 2000, the hope was that the Danish, German, Italian, and French exporters affected by higher prices would lobby their respective governments to change the EU policies that were in violation of WTO rules. While some of the "targeted producers" did lobby to change the policies, the retaliation may have stiffened the resolve of other Europeans not to give in to U.S. pressures. This is because many Europeans view retaliation as a frontal assault on European unity — an effort to set one Member State off against another in an attempt to influence EU decision-making.[5]

Despite its condemnation of retaliation as a trade weapon, the EU in the aftermath of the Bush steel decision emulated previous U.S. efforts to devise a retaliation list with domestic political considerations in mind. The EU list includes products from regions such as citrus from Florida, steel from the mid-west, and textiles from North Carolina that are considered politically important to President Bush. Leaving no mistake about intent when he released the list, EU Trade Commissioner Pascal Lamy expressed hope that the threatened countermeasures would help persuade the U.S. Administration to lower its steel barriers.

CONSEQUENCES

On the one hand, the good news is that the U.S.-EU steel trade spat and associated disputes are unlikely to get out of hand. Some trade disputes may even facilitate greater trade liberalization and industrial restructuring over time if they serve as a prelude to international negotiations. On the other hand, the bad news is that the current tensions and mutual recriminations may make U.S.-EU cooperation in other areas more difficult, and they clearly threaten the viability of the WTO trading system.

Good News

An all-out trade war between the two sides appears remote due to domestic political opposition and the high level of economic integration that now exists. As retaliation hurts

---

[5] For background, see CRS Report RS21185, *Trade Policy making in the European Union,* by Raymond J. Ahearn.

consumers, retailers, and companies dependent on "targeted" products for inputs into their production processes, these groups lobby Brussels and Washington intensively to keep specific products off any retaliation list that may be drawn up.

Moreover, given the huge stake each side has in the other's market through direct investments and merger and acquisition activity, both European and American multinational companies (MNCs) serve as powerful lobbies that caution restraint. Any imposition of across-the-board and high trade barriers could create massive disruptions in the worldwide production arrangement of MNCs and also deflate economic activity on both sides of the Atlantic. These factors, in turn, limit the scope and flexibility that U.S. and EU trade officials have in devising a politically acceptable retaliation list or in imposing across-the-board and high trade barriers.

Selective trade disputes may have consequences that some view as positive. For example, President Bush's decision to raise steel tariffs reportedly was motivated in part to enlist the support of legislators from steel producing states for passage of Trade Promotion Authority (TPA) legislation, USTR Zoellick argued that the President's willingness to raise tariffs was a short term necessary step for obtaining the leverage TPA may provide for negotiating new sweeping trade liberalization agreements later on. In addition, the Bush Administration argued that higher U.S. tariffs would help spur international negotiations to facilitate the restructuring of the steel industry worldwide.

Bad News

Escalating trade tensions, however, are not cost-free. Polls indicate that trade disputes likely have some effect on public attitudes, contributing to a perception of each other as inward-looking, egotistical, and hypocritical free traders. Trade tensions and mutual recriminations may also make cooperation in other areas more difficult. This includes efforts to settle other trade disputes if media and public pressures intensify for linking disputes. Most assuredly it also includes efforts to make quick progress in the recently launched Doha Round of multilateral trade negotiations. Transatlantic trade tensions over agriculture, for example, stalled progress on the Uruguay Round of trade negotiations for several years in the early 1990s.[6]

What impact trade tensions may have on cooperation on broader foreign policy issues, such as the war on terrorism, remains uncertain. But high profile trade disputes are likely to raise sharper and more critical questions concerning the benefits of such cooperation. If trade tensions work to undermine the notion that the United States and Europe share common values or lead to a view that a weaker America or a weaker Europe is in the other's interest, then the consequences could be more significant.

The most serious consequence of escalating trade tensions may be the strain placed on the WTO system itself. As the EU and U.S. are the WTO's two biggest parties and most important leaders, their relationship and example are critical to the smooth functioning of the multilateral trading system. When either party does not comply with WTO obligations, acts

---

[6] Recent passage of U.S. farm legislation could serve as an additional complication in efforts to move the Doha Round forward. The increased spending for U.S. farmers could serve as an excuse for the EU to avoid further agricultural liberalization or as a prod to serious negotiations.

unilaterally, or uses the dispute resolution system to score political points, the WTO-centered world trading system arguably suffers.

POSSIBLE CURES

Several cures or recommendations to ameliorate current trade tensions have been put forth. These include greater reliance on compensation (as opposed to retaliation), and greater emphasis on diplomatic as opposed to legal solutions to disputes. While helpful, the fact that some of these high-profile trade disputes have been on-going in one form or another for several decades suggests how difficult dispute resolution can be.

Compensation Instead of Retaliation

When a country refuses to comply with a final dispute resolution ruling, the primary enforcement mechanism is WTO authorized retaliation. Many observers maintain that the system should place more stress on trade compensation in order to limit the negative consequences of retaliation. Trade compensation would require the defending country to open other markets in compensation for the markets it restricts. Instead of restricting trade, compensation would bias dispute resolution towards lowering trade barriers - the essential goal of the WTO.

The hurdles to greater reliance on compensation are both political and legal. In the steel safeguards case, for example, if the United States were to reduce tariffs on textile imports as compensation for raising tariffs on steel, one industry would be asked to "pay" for another industry's protection. Moreover, payment of compensation before the WTO rules whether the U.S. steel safeguard action was imposed consistent with WTO rules could be viewed as admission of wrongdoing.

Greater Emphasis on Diplomatic Solutions

The U.S. and EU are the heaviest users of the WTO dispute resolution system. Some of the disputes between the two sides have been submitted to a WTO panel for resolution without strenuous efforts at resolving the dispute beforehand. Some disputes arguably have been initiated out of a desire to score political points by winning cases that show the other side in technical violation of WTO provisions. Once the dispute panel is formed, neither side is inclined to seek a negotiated solution out of fear of compromising important principles and obtaining a ruling on who is "right" or "wrong." In the process, numerous disputes have become acrimonious and have hurt the credibility of the WTO as an institution.

To deal with problems accompanying a confrontational approach, many observers have emphasized the desirability of greater reliance on a diplomatic approach that stresses conciliation and problem-solving over legal precision. In a sense, this is the route U.S. trade policymakers may be taking in the steel dispute by offering selective EU member states favorable consideration of their exporters' requests that specific products be exempted from U.S. steel tariffs. Exemption from U.S. tariffs, in turn, may help shore up opposition in member states such as Germany, Sweden, and Great Britain to precipitous EU retaliation.

Another form of diplomacy may be helping resolve the FSC dispute - a dispute where the EU has repeatedly emphasized that it does not want to retaliate against the United States, but rather wants the United States to comply with the WTO panel ruling. To show good faith that it is moving in that direction, congressional leaders are reportedly discussing a process for changing the U.S. tax provision in dispute.[7]

[7] *Inside U.S. Trade,* "Thomas Sees Procedural Arrangement for FSC If Legislation Fails," May

Chapter 6

Trade Retaliation: The "Carousel" Approach

Lenore Sek

Summary

Section 407 of the Trade and Development Act of 2000 (P.L. 106-200) requires the U.S. Trade Representative (USTR) to periodically revise the list of products subject to retaliation when another country fails to implement a World Trade Organization (WTO) dispute decision. This periodic revision of the product list has become known as "carousel retaliation." The intent of switching products is to exert more pressure on a trading partner to comply with a WTO ruling. The impetus for more pressure came principally from U.S. banana and livestock exporters, who had become frustrated with the European Union (EU) and its repeated postponement of compliance with WTO dispute rulings. To date, the USTR has not revised a product list under Section 407, but credits the threat of action under carousel authority with helping to resolve the banana case, and says that carousel authority might be used as leverage in the future. An EU challenge of U.S. carousel retaliation still stands in the WTO dispute process.

Setting the Stage: The WTO Banana and Beef Disputes

Many U.S. policymakers have expressed concern over the effectiveness of the WTO dispute resolution process to convince other countries to remove various trade barriers. Two WTO dispute cases were especially exasperating to U.S. exporters because of the length of time to decide the cases and the improbability that the losing party would change its practices. These involved banana and beef trade disputes with the European Union (EU).[1] They were

---

[1] For more information on these cases, see CRS Report RL30789, *Agricultural Trade Issues in the 106th Congress: A Review of Issues,* by Geoffrey S. Becker, Charles E. Hanrahan, and Remy Jurenas; CRS Report RS20130, *The*

the main reason that Congress considered alternative ways to pressure a trading partner to implement a WTO dispute decision.

All WTO disputes follow a procedure that normally takes about 2-3 years from start to finish. Disputes are administered by WTO members, who act as the Dispute Settlement Body (DSB). Parties to the dispute first engage in consultations. If a satisfactory solution is not reached, the complainant may request a panel to hear the dispute. Once a panel report is issued, it will be adopted by the DSB, unless a party to the dispute appeals it or all DSB members vote not to adopt it. If the report is appealed, the Appellate body submits its findings, along with the panel's report as modified by the appeal, to the DSB, which will adopt the reports unless all DSB members vote not to do so. If the complaining party prevails, the losing party is given a "reasonable period of time" for implementation; an arbitrator might decide that time. The original panel can be called on to decide whether or not the losing party has implemented the decision. If a country does not implement the decision within the agreed upon time period, there are two possible alternatives for the complaining party. One is compensation, which is negotiated between the disputing parties. The other is suspension of concessions, or stated simply, retaliation. The complainant estimates its loss, the losing party can request arbitration on the level of the loss, and the DSB approves the final level.[2]

Banana Case

The WTO banana dispute began in 1995, the WTO's first year, but challenges of the EU banana regime had begun earlier.[3] The EU had a complicated import regime that gave preferences to banana imports from its former colonies and preferential licenses to European banana importers. In September 1995, the United States, Guatemala, Mexico, and Honduras requested consultations with the EU. Ecuador later joined the request. A panel was established and issued a report finding that the EU banana import regime violated certain WTO rules. The EU appealed the report. The Appellate Body upheld the panel's principal findings, and the DSU adopted the Appellate report. An arbitrator set a "reasonable time" for EU implementation at 15 months, or by January 1999. The EU argued that it came into compliance during the 15 months, but special panels to examine the question did not agree. The United States asked to suspend %520 million in trade concessions. The EU requested arbitration. The arbitrators decided the amount should be $191.4 million, and the DSB authorized the United States to suspend concessions in that amount.[4] On April 19, 1999, the United States imposed 100% tariffs on a list of eight items representing $191.4 million in imports from the EU. [This case was resolved in April 2001. See **Recent Developments** below.]

In selecting items for the retaliation list, U.S. officials wanted to increase tariffs on items from EU countries that supported the banana regime. The higher tariffs would increase the

---

U.S.-European Union Banana Dispute, by Charles E. Hanrahan; and CRS Report RS20142, *The European Union's Ban on Hormone-Treated Meat,* by Charles Hanrahan.

[2] For further information on the WTO dispute process, see CRS Report RS20088, *Dispute Settlement in the World Trade Organization: An Overview,* by Jeanne J. Grimmett.

[3] Several countries in Central and South America requested action on the EU banana regime in the early 1990s under the General Agreement on Tariffs and Trade (GATT), which was predecessor to the WTO. Those panel reports were not adopted.

[4] The DSB also authorized Ecuador to suspend concessions in the amount of $201.6 million.

total cost of the items and hurt EU exporters. To illustrate, U.S. officials selected "bath preparations, other than bath salts" as one of the items on the U.S. list. Before the increase in tariffs, the U.S. duty on imports of these items from the EU was 4.9% ad valorem. That rate rose to 100% in April 1999. The two leading EU exporters of bath preparations in 1998 were the United Kingdom and France. These countries not coincidentally were also the leading supporters of the EU banana regime. In the four quarters before the 100% tariffs were imposed, the United States imported $7.6 billion in bath preparations from the United Kingdom and $7.5 billion from France. In the four quarters after the imposition of 100% tariffs, U.S. imports fell to $1.3 billion (83% decline) and $4.1 billion (45% decline) respectively.

Hormone Case

In January 1996, the United States requested consultations with the EU on its directive on the use of hormones in livestock. The directive restricted imports of meat produced with hormones. The United States requested a dispute panel. (Canada also challenged the EU practice.) The panels reported that the EU ban was inconsistent with the WTO Sanitary and Phytosanitary Agreement. The EU appealed, and the Appellate Body upheld some of the panels' findings but reversed others. The DSB adopted the Appellate Body report and the panels' reports as modified. An arbitrator set a reasonable time for implementation at 15 months, or by May 1999. A month before the time expired, the EU said it may not be able to comply with the DSB ruling and would consider offering compensation by the deadline. The United States requested authorization for suspension of concessions of $202 million. The EU requested arbitration, and arbitrators set the level at $116.8 million. The DSB authorized suspension of concessions in that amount. On July 27, 1999, the USTR announced duties in the amount authorized by the DSB. The time for consultation to retaliation in both the banana and hormone cases was about three and a half years.

THE CONGRESSIONAL RESPONSE TO NON-COMPLIANCE

On September 22, 1999, two months after the USTR increased tariffs in the hormone dispute, Senator Mike DeWine, on behalf of nine other Senators, introduced s. 1619, the Carousel Retaliation Act of 1999.[5] The bill proposed an amendment to the "section 301" trade program to require the USTR to "carousel," or rotate, a retaliation list when a country does not implement a WTO dispute settlement. It would have required the USTR to rotate items 120 days after the first list of items and every 180 days thereafter. The USTR would not be required to rotate the list if compliance was imminent, or if both the USTR and the petitioners agreed that rotating was not necessary in that particular case.

The legislation attempted to more effectively place pressure on foreign governments, through their domestic exporters, to change their position on the disputed practice. In his statement introducing S. 1619, Senator DeWine said that "...some [WTO] member nations are simply undermining this entire [dispute] process by refusing to comply with the final dispute

---

[5] On October 1, 1999, Representative Larry Combest introduced identical bill H.R. 2991 with 12 original cosponsors.

settlement decision, even after losing their cases on appeal."[6] He said that the EU had ignored WTO rulings, ignored the U.S. retaliation, and now was preparing to subsidize the products that had been identified for U.S. retaliation. Farm and cattle groups and the Hawaii Banana Industry Association supported the bill.

The Senate approved the language of S. 1619 as an amendment to H.R. 434, a broader bill that also dealt with trade with the Caribbean and with Africa, on November 3, 1999. The House-approved version of H.R. 434 had not included a carousel provision. Section 407 of the conference report included the carousel provisions of the Senate bill and added a section on including reciprocal goods on the retaliation list. The conference report was released on May 3, 2000. The same day, a European spokesperson was quoted as saying that the carousel approach was a "very dangerous game" and that "the United States has to realize that one day this can be used against them."[7] The House and Senate approved the conference report, and the President signed the measure on May 18, 2000 (The Trade and Development Act of 2000; P.L. 106-200).

Summary of Section 407 of P.L. 106-200

In the event that the United States initiates a retaliation list or takes other action under section 301 of the Trade Act of 1974 because a country fails to implement the recommendations of a WTO dispute settlement proceeding, the USTR shall periodically revise the list or action to affect other goods of the foreign country. The USTR is not to revise the list or action if the USTR determines that the country is about to implement the recommendation or if the USTR and the petitioning party agree that it is unnecessary. The USTR must review and revise the list 120 days after the date of the retaliation list and every 180 days thereafter. The USTR is to revise the list in a way that is mostly likely to result in the country's implementing the recommendation or in achieving a satisfactory solution. The USTR is to include on retaliation lists the reciprocal goods of the industries affected by the failure of the foreign country(ies) to implement the recommendation made in the dispute.

Although U.S. banana and meat producers clearly supported the carousel provision, other U.S. businesses did not. Many businesses claimed that the carousel approach would create confusion and cause hardship for retailers by continually raising and lowering tariffs. On May 17, 2000, the day before the President signed H.R. 434 into law, Representative Robert Menendez introduced H.R. 4478, the small Business Trade Protection Act, for himself and six others. The purpose of H.R. 4478 was to exempt certain small businesses from the increased tariffs and other retaliatory measures imposed against EU products in response to the EU banana and beef hormone regimes. The bill would have exempted small importers (defined generally as those with fewer than 100 employees) from the higher tariffs. It capped the exemption at 125% of the amount of the product imported the prior year from the countries concerned. It also provided that small importers who lost 50% or more of their revenues as a result of higher tariffs in the disputes would be eligible for full rebates of those tariffs. In related legislation, Representative Maxine Waters introduced H.R. 1362, a bill to bar the

---

[6] Congressional Record, Sept. 22, 1999, p. S11260.
[7] Pruzin, Daniel. EU Warns US Against Africa-CBI Provision Adopting 'Carousel' Approach to Retaliation. Bureau of National Affairs, Inc. *Daily Report for Executives,* may 4, 2000.

imposition of increased tariffs or other retaliatory measures against EU products in response to the banana regime of the European Union.

RECENT DEVELOPMENTS

On May 26, 2000, just eight days after the President signed the Trade and Development Act of 2000, the USTR issued a press release calling for comments on modification of the retaliation lists in the banana and beef hormone cases.[8] The press release said that the USTR was particularly interested in comments from small- and medium-sized businesses.

On the same day that the USTR issued its press release, EU members authorized the EU Commission to seek consultations with the United States on the carousel measure under WTO dispute procedures. On June 5, 2000, the EU made a formal request for consultations. In its submission requesting consultations, the EU argued that the carousel approach violated the WTO dispute Settlement Understanding because the carousel approach was a unilateral means to impose trade retaliation and had not been agreed to multilaterally. The EU also argued that continual switching on the retaliation list caused more harm than that allowed under WTO dispute procedures. Other countries wanted to join the EU complaint. According to one report, 10 other countries, including Japan and Australia, sided with the EU at the July 27, 2000 meeting of the Dispute Settlement Body.[9]

In its press release calling for comments, the USTR said that the Administration's goal was to announce modifications to the retaliation lists by June 19, 2000, which was the first business day that was 30 days after Section 407 entered into force.[10] That date passed without modifications. An early reason for delay might have been many U.S. companies used possibly targeted products as inputs or sold such products, and did not want these products on the list. According to one report at the time, "Over 500 requests were received from US businesses and members of Congress looking to protect US firms that rely in EU imports from being unduly hurt by the 100 percent duties."[11]

To date, the USTR has not revised the lists of products for retaliation. A principal reason has been a link between carousel retaliation and the U.S.-EU dispute over U.S. tax benefits for foreign sales corporations (FSC). In that dispute, the EU brought and won a case against the U.S. practice, and the United States subsequently amended its law. A decision is pending in the WTO on whether or not the amended U.S. law is now in compliance with WTO rules. The EU and the United States informally agreed that the EU would not seek sanctions in the FSC case while the decision is pending. However, the EU has since announced that if the United States revises its product lists under the carousel provisions, it will ignore the informal agreement and pursue sanctions in the FSC case. The FSC sanctions are much greater than those in the banana and beef hormone cases.

---

[8] USTR. USTR Announces Procedures for Modifying Measures in EC Beef and Bananas Cases. Press Release 00-41. May 26, 2000.

[9] U.S. Faces EU on 'Carousel' and Bananas. Trade Reports International Group. *Washington Trade Daily.* July 28, 2000.

[10] The conference report to accompany H.R. 434 (H.Rept. 106-606) stated that for cases in which the USTR had already taken a retaliatory measure and the initial statutory deadline had already passed, conferees expected the USTR to take initial action no later than 30 days after enactment.

[11] 'Carousel' List Still held Up. Trade Reports International Group. *Washington Trade Daily.* August 2, 2000.

In April 2001, the United States and the EU reached an agreement in the banana dispute. As part of the agreement, the United States agreed to suspend its retaliatory tariffs from July 1, 2001. Revision of the retaliation list in this case then will no longer be an issue. In the hormone case, however, retaliatory tariffs remain in place. European officials have mentioned possible compensation in the form of increased market access for U.S. hormone-free beef, but nothing has been decided. In a hearing before the House Agriculture Committee on May 23, 2001, U.S. Trade Representative Zoellick reportedly said that the carousel authority had been used successfully as a tool in the banana case, and that it might be used in other disputes in the future.[12]

POLICY CONSIDERATIONS

There are at least three policies to consider in relation to the question of non-compliance with a WTO dispute decision. One policy is acceptance of non-compliance under the current WTO dispute procedures. The General Accounting Office (GAO) has found that a majority of WTO disputes involving the United States have resulted in greater market access or more protection of intellectual property rights.[13] So, the WTO dispute process generally benefits U.S. interests. However, in a few cases, the outcome is not greater market access. As the banana and hormone cases showed, a WTO dispute decision against a country does not necessarily result in the timely removal of its trade restrictive practice. In those instances, the losing country may face higher tariffs or pay compensation, neither of which is a goal of dispute settlement.

A second policy is to seek further reform of multilateral dispute settlement procedures to increase the likelihood of compliance. If WTO Members find that retaliatory measures do not always effectively induce compliance and that this situation poses significant challenges to the overall effectiveness of the WTO dispute settlement system, Members may seek to revisit existing dispute remedies. The United States has already proposed in the current WTO dispute settlement review that the dispute procedures provide for the carouselling of retaliation lists. Some commentators have also suggested more aggressive monitoring of a defending party's compliance activities during the implementation period, especially where the period is long; automatic authorization of compensation for prevailing parties; and remedies for past damage resulting from violations of WTO obligations.

A third policy for consideration is unilateral action in an attempt to increase the chance of compliance. Unilateral action such as carousel retaliation might or might not improve compliance with WTO dispute decisions. If unilateral action is successful, the domestic industry is better off because it faces a less restrictive foreign market. If not successful, the domestic industry still faces the restrictive foreign market, U.S. consumers of imported goods on the retaliation list have to pay higher prices, and foreign exporters lose sales. In any case, continuous changes in retaliation lists could hurt some U.S. companies, especially small and medium-sized businesses and importers of items on the lists. The EU challenge in the WTO also could have international consequences. For example, if the U.S. practice is upheld, will

---

[12] Yerkey, Gary G. U.S. Will use 'Carousel' law as 'Leverage' to Open Foreign Markets, USTR Zoellick Says. Bureau of National Affairs, Inc. *International Trade Reporter*. May 31, 2001.

[13] U.S. General Accounting Office. World Trade Organization: Issues in Dispute Settlement. Report to the Chairman, Committee on Ways and means, House of Representatives. August 2000. GAO/NSIAD-00-210. p.8.

other countries impose similar measures? Depending upon the point of view, carousel retaliation promotes the WTO by strengthening the dispute process, or undermines the multilateral system through unilateral action.

Chapter 7

CHINA'S TRADE WITH THE UNITED STATES AND THE WORLD

Thomas Lum and Dick K. Nanto

SUMMARY

International trade of the People's Republic of China (PRC) has become an issues as the United States has granted permanent normal trade relations (PNTR) status to China and the PRC has entered the World Trade Organization (WTO). As the Chinese market has opened to world trade, it has become both a source of imports into the United States and a destination for U.S. exports and investments. In 2001, China was the fourth largest trading partner of the United States while the United States was the PRC's second largest trading partner, largest export market, and largest source of foreign investment.

With the exception of 1993, when the PRC government temporarily loosened state controls on imports, China ran merchandise trade surpluses with the world throughout the 1990s, although its current account surpluses have been smaller because it runs deficits in trade in services. In 2000, China ran its largest trade surplus with the United States ($83.8 billion), followed by the European Union ($44.9 billion), and Japan ($24.9 billion). In 2000, China surpassed Japan as the country with which the United States runs its largest trade deficit. In 2001, the United States incurred its highest merchandise trade deficits with China ($83.0 billion), Japan ($68.9 billion), and Canada ($53.2 billion). Among other Asian nations, the United States also incurred large trade deficits with Taiwan ($15.2 billion), Malaysia ($12.9 billion), and South Korea ($12.9 billion). In 2000, the United States was the second largest supplier of utilized foreign direct investment to China ($4.4 billion), after Hong Kong ($15.5 billion).

In 2000, the United States was the third largest exporter to China ($16.2 billion), after Japan ($30.4 billion) and the EU ($24.5 billion), excluding Hong Kong and Taiwan. However, China still represents a smaller market for U.S. goods than Taiwan ($24 billion), with a population of 21 million, and Singapore ($17 billion), with a population of 3.5 million.

The United States was China's largest overseas market ($100 billion), followed by the EU ($69.5 billion) and Japan ($55.3 billion).

In the 1990s, the most dramatic increases in the value Chinese imports to the United States have not been in sectors such as footwear and apparel – traditional labor-intensive industries in which China is already quite competitive – but in high technology sectors, such as office and data processing machines, telecommunications and sound equipment, and electrical machinery and appliances as well as in miscellaneous manufactured items. China has also become a major supplier of furniture, building fixtures, and travel goods and handbags to the United States.

Over the medium term, China is expected to continue to run trade surpluses with the world, although likely at lower levels than those reached during 1997-98. If China opens its economy as required under the WTO, its current account surplus is projected to turn into a deficit in 2004 and continue in deficit through the end of the decade as its deficit in its services trade grows.

INTRODUCTION

International trade of the People's Republic of China (PRC) has become an issue as the United States has granted permanent normal trade relations (PNTR) status to China and the PRC has entered the World Trade Organization (WTO).[1] As the Chinese market has opened to world trade, it has become both a source of imports into the United States and a destination for U.S. exports and investments. In 2001, China was the fourth largest trading partner of the United States while the United States was the PRC's second largest trading partner, largest export market, and largest source of foreign investment. In 2000, China surpassed Japan as the country with the biggest trade deficit with the United States.

This report provides basic data and analysis of China's international trade with the United States and with the world. The purpose of this report is both to provide actual data and charts of China's merchandise trade, to highlight certain trends in the trade flows, and to briefly discuss policy options. Both Chinese and trading partner data are presented for China's trade with the United States, Japan, and the European Union. Charts showing import trends by sector for the United States highlight China's growing market shares in many industries and also show import shares for Japan, Canada, Mexico, the European Union, and ASEAN (Association for Southeast Asian Nations). Data on foreign direct investment in China also are included.

China not only runs a surplus in its trade with the world, but it runs a surplus most of the time with the world's three industrial centers: the United States, the European Union, and Japan. The U.S. trade deficit with China at $83.8 billion in 2000 ($83.0 in 2001) was the largest, while that of the EU with China at $44.9 billion was over half as large, and that of Japan at $24.9 billion nearly a third as large.

How does the U.S. trade deficit with China compare with the U.S. trade deficit with other nations? In 2001, the largest U.S. merchandise trade deficits were with China ($83 billion), Japan ($69 billion), Canada ($53 billion), Mexico ($30 billion), and Germany ($29 billion).

---

[1] P.L. 106-286 granted permanent normal trade relations treatment to the People's Republic of China, effective upon the PRC's accession to the WTO (an event that occurred on December 11, 2001).

Among major Asian nations, the United States incurred large trade deficits with Taiwan ($15 billion), Malaysia ($13 billion), South Korea ($13 billion), Thailand ($8 billion), Indonesia ($7 billion), and the Philippines ($3.6 billion).

The U.S. trade deficit with China has two unusual characteristics. First is its size - $83 billion. Second is the large gap between imports from and exports to China. Japan in 2001, for example, exported 2.2 times more to the U.S. than it imported, while Canada exported 1.3 times more than it imported. China, by comparison, exported 5.3 times more to the U.S. market in 2001 than it imported. This suggests that the Chinese market is vastly underdeveloped as a destination for U.S. exports.

Between 1996 and 2001, however, China's imports from the United States have grown faster (up 10%) than those by Canada (4.2%) or by Japan (-3.6%), although China's have been increasing from a low base. By joining the World Trade Organization China is required to lower import barriers on many products in which the United States is competitive. This is expected to increase U.S. export opportunities there.

According to Japanese, European, and U.S. data, in 2002, Japan was the largest overseas supplier of products to China with $30.4 billion in exports. The EU was the second largest supplier with $24.5 billion, while the United States exported only $16.2 billion worth of merchandise to the PRC in 2000 and $19.2 billion in 2001. Considering that the United States is the world's largest trading nation and exported $57 billion to Japan in 2001, its exports to China seem rather low. In 2001, the United States exported more to South Korea ($22 billion), France ($22 billion), and almost as much to Taiwan ($18 billion) as it did to China.

The United States is China's largest overseas market with $100 billion in U.S. imports from China in 2000, followed by the EU with $69.5 billion in imports from China, and Japan with $55.3 billion. China was the fourth largest source of imports for the United States in 2000. Canada ($229 billion), Japan ($146 billion), and Mexico ($135 billion) exported more to the United States in 2000 than did China, but China sold more to the American market than did Germany ($58 billion), the United Kingdom ($43 billion), Taiwan ($40 billion), or South Korea ($40 billion). In short, China (with the help of foreign investors) is a major supplier of products to the U.S. market. According to Chinese data, the United States was the PRC's second largest trading partner in 2000 after Japan. Bilateral trade between China and the United States totaled $74 billion compared with $83 billion between China and Japan.

In terms of the balance of trade with China by major sector, the sectors in which the United States runs the largest trade deficits are those that depend on abundant and low-cost labor. These include toys, sports equipment, footwear, apparel, leather bags, and textiles. Among the large deficit sectors, however, are electrical machinery, machinery, and motor vehicles (mostly motorcycles and auto parts). Some of China's competitiveness in these sectors may be based on its underlying economic advantages combined with foreign technology and manufacturing processes, but in certain areas, such as moto5r vehicles, the Chinese surplus appears to be based primarily on import restrictions. Under China's WTO accession agreement, tariffs on automobiles are to drop from 100% to 25%. Moreover, in plastic, optical and medical instruments, books and magazines, soaps and waxes, cosmetics, and cotton yarn, the United States runs a surplus in its balance of trade with the world but a deficit with China. These deficits run counter to market expectations.

The sectors in which the United States runs a trade surplus with China mirror U.S. competitive advantages and include aircraft and agricultural products. In two sectors, a deficit in U.S. trade with China has turned into a surplus. Edible fruit and nuts went from a $30 billion deficit in 1999 to a surplus of $7 billion in 2001. Likewise, miscellaneous food went from a deficit of $17 billion to a surplus of $23 billion. This indicates that China's market for agricultural products may becoming more open to U.S. exports.

U.S. imports from China are moving up the technology ladder. While imports in sectors such as footwear and apparel continue to grow, imports in many high technology sectors are growing faster. These include office and data processing machines (up 1,055% between 1993 and 2001), electrical machinery and appliances (up 428%), and telecommunications and sound equipment (up 343%). In sectors such as footwear, building and light fixtures, furniture, and handbags, imports from China have been displacing those from South Korea, Singapore, Thailand, and other newly industrializing Asian nations. More than half of U.S. imports of footwear and travel goods/handbags now come from China.

Current U.S. policy toward trade with China has been aimed primarily at integrating China into the global trading system through China's accession to the WTO, the granting of permanent normal trade relations status, assisting the country in establishing a modern commercial, legal, regulatory, and financial infrastructure, promoting American businesses interests there, and in ensuring that China complies with its commitments to liberalize its markets.[2] The task is large because even though for the past two decades China has been in transition from a closed communist economy to an open, market-based socialist economy, many trade and investment barriers still remain. In the 2002 report by the U.S. Trade Representative on foreign trade barriers, the section on China takes up 27 pages and includes high import duties, problems with tariff classification, non-tariff barriers, import quotas, import licenses, lack of transparency, trading rights, standards, government procurement, and lack of intellectual property rights enforcement.[3] Many of these barriers, however, are expected to be reduced as China implements the conditions of its WTO accession agreement. Most countries now appear to be taking a wait-and-see attitude while continuing to monitor the problem areas as China attempts to make the changes in its economy required to bring it into compliance with its WTO commitments.

Since China is now a member of the WTO, any change in existing U.S. trade policy toward that country would be subject to WTO rules and dispute settlement procedures. On the other hand, if China does not live up to its WTO commitments, the United States can bring a complaint before the WTO as it has done with other trading partners.

CHINA'S TRADE WITH THE UNITED STATES, EUROPE, AND JAPAN

The data for U.S. trade with China differ from Chinese trade with the U.S. primarily because of the treatment of products that China exports through Hong Kong. China counts Hong Kong as the destination of exports sent there even if those products are transshipped to other markets. The United States and many of China's other trading partners count Chinese exports that are transshipped through Hong Kong as exports from China, not from Hong Kong. This changes the totals for Chinese exports and the size of a country's trade balance with China.

---

[2] For details, see: CRS Issue Brief IB91121, *China-U.S. Trade Issues,* by Wayne M. Morrison.
[3] U.S. Trade Representative. *2002 national Trade Estimate Report on Foreign Trade Barriers.* Washington, U.S. Government Printing Office, 2002. Pp. 44-71.

As shown in **Figure 1** and **Appendix Table A1**, with the exception of 1993 (according to Chinese data), China has run a trade surplus in goods (merchandise) each year over the past decade. That surplus emerged at the beginning of the 1990s, changed to a $11 billion deficit in 1993 (when the government temporarily loosened controls on imports), and then rose to a $46.5 billion surplus in 1998 before dropping to $24.1 billion in 2000. In the 1980s, the U.S. ran trade deficits with China in all but the first years of the decade.

Figure 1. China's Exports, Imports, and Balance of Merchandise Trade, 1980-2000

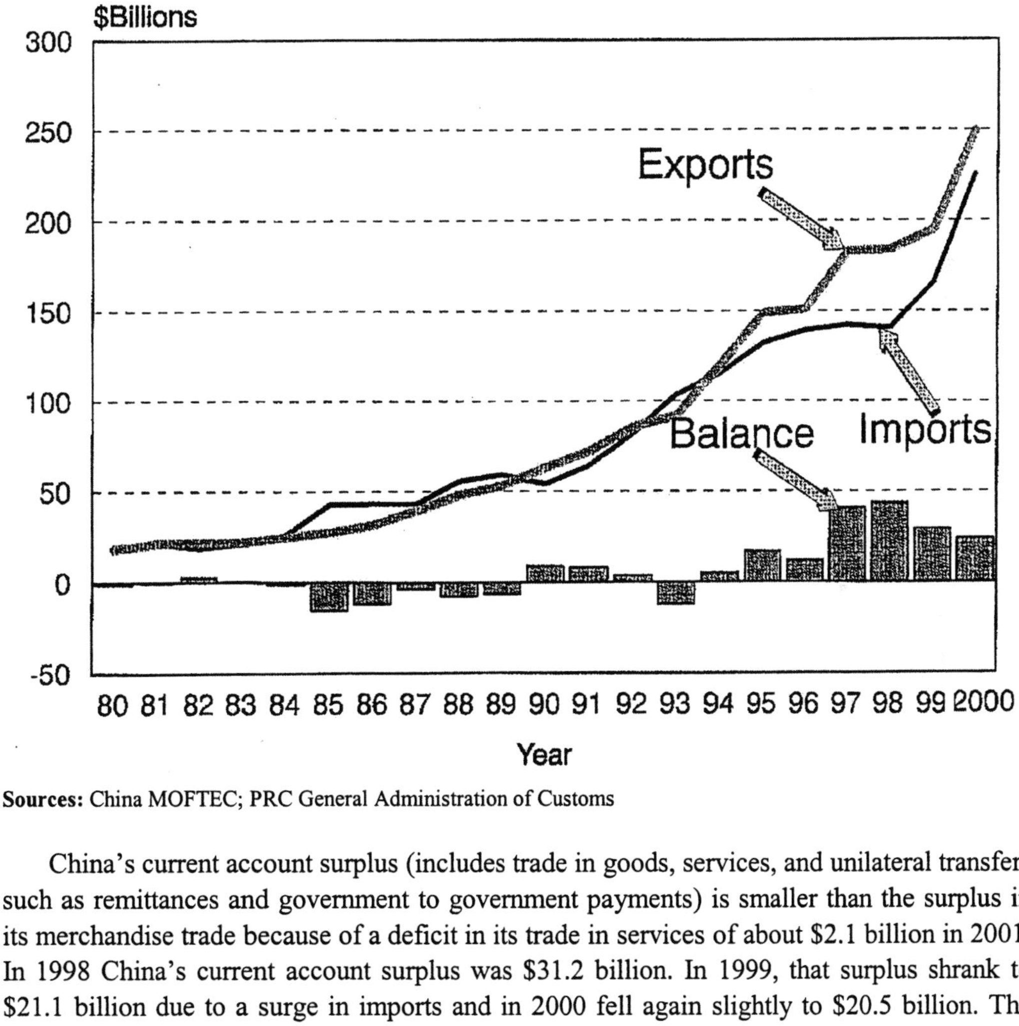

Sources: China MOFTEC; PRC General Administration of Customs

China's current account surplus (includes trade in goods, services, and unilateral transfers such as remittances and government to government payments) is smaller than the surplus in its merchandise trade because of a deficit in its trade in services of about $2.1 billion in 2001. In 1998 China's current account surplus was $31.2 billion. In 1999, that surplus shrank to $21.1 billion due to a surge in imports and in 2000 fell again slightly to $20.5 billion. The continued growth in imports, deficit in its services balance, and stalled U.S. economy reduced China's current account surplus to $16.5 billion in 2001. If China opens its economy as required under the WTO, its current account surplus is expected to turn into a deficit in 2004 and to remain in deficit throughout the decade.[4]

---

[4] DRI-WEFA. *International Analysis – China.* March 2002.

**Figure 2. U.S. Exports, Imports, and Balance
of Merchandise Trade with China, 1980-2000**

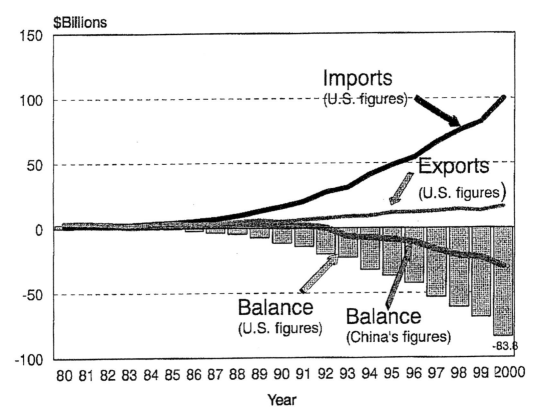

Sources: U.S. Department of Commerce; China MOFTEC; PRC General Administration of Customs.

As shown in **Figure 2** and **Appendix Table A1**, by either Chinese or U.S. data, China runs a trade surplus with the United States. Although the Chinese figures show it at only $28.1 billion in 2001, the United States reported it to be $83 billion.

As shown in **Figure 3** and **Appendix Table A2**, the European Union also runs a similar trade deficit with China. At a merchandise trade deficit of $31.8 billion in 1999, the deficit rose to 44.9 billion in 2000. This trade deficit also began in the latter 1980s and has continued through the 1990s. According to Chinese figures, however, the EU deficit with China began in the late 1990s and was only $7.3 billion in 2000.

Figure 3. European Union/European Economic Community Exports, Imports, and Balance of Merchandise Trade with China, 1980-2000

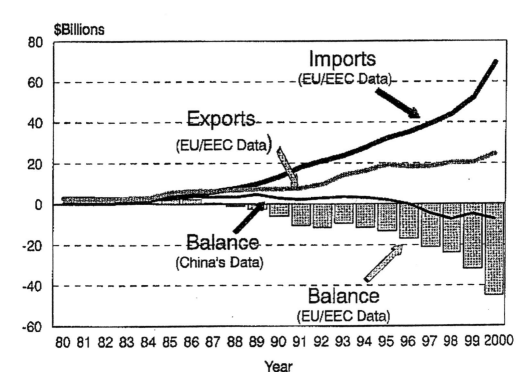

Note: For 1980-88, data are for the EEC12 nations. After 1988, for the EU 15.

Sources: IMF, *Direction of Trade Statistics yearbook (1999); Eurostat;* China MOFTEC; PRC General Administration of Customs.

Japan likewise since 1988 has been running a trade deficit with China. As shown in **Figure 4** and in **Appendix Table A3**, Japan's balance of trade with China (according to Japanese data) dropped from a surplus of $6 billion in 1985 to a deficit of $5.9 billion in 1990 and $24.9 billion in 2000. Considering Japan's reputation for protecting its own markets, its widening trade gap with China seems remarkable. According to Chinese data, however, China has run more annual trade deficits with Japan than surpluses. In 1993, China reported a $7.5 billion deficit with Japan. In 2000, the PRC reported a $142 million surplus.

Figure 4. Japan's Merchandise Imports, Exports, and Balance of Trade with China, 1980-2000

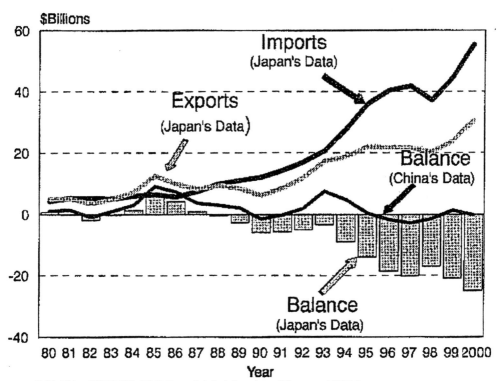

Sources: IMF; China MOFTEC; PRC General Administration of Customs; JETRO.

In summary, China not only runs a surplus in its trade with the world, but it runs a surplus most of the time with the world's three industrial centers: the United States, the European Union, and Japan. (See **Figure 5.**) The U.S. trade deficit with China at $83.8 billion in 2000 was the largest, while that of the EU at $44.9 billion was about half as large, and that with Japan at $24.9 billion nearly a third as large.

Within the EU, in 2000, Germany's trade deficit with China was $8.3 billion, the U.K.'s was $4.4 billion, and France's was $4.4 billion. South Korea, by contrast, ran a $6.6 billion surplus with China in 2000. As shown in **Appendix Table A4**, however, China's trade statistics indicate smaller European trade deficits and a larger South Korean surplus.

Figure 5. U.S., European Union, and Japan's Merchandise Trade Balances with China, 1980-2000

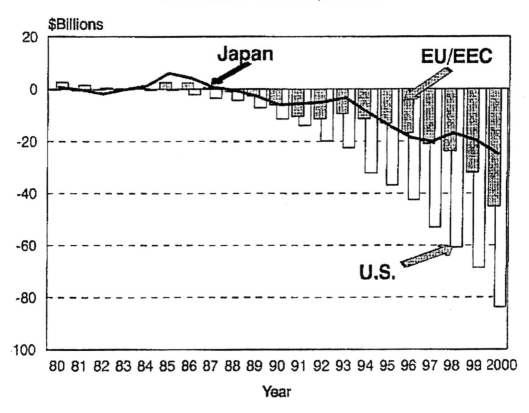

U.S. Department of Commerce; IMF. Direction of Trade Statistics; Eurostat; JETRO.

How does the U.S. trade deficit with China compare with the U.S. trade deficit with other nations? In 2001, the largest U.S. merchandise trade deficits were with China ($83 billion), Japan ($69 billion), Canada ($53 billion), Mexico ($30 billion), and Germany ($29 billion). Among major Asian nations, the United States incurred large trade deficits with Taiwan ($15 billion), Malaysia ($13 billion), South Korea ($13 billion), Thailand ($8 billion), Indonesia ($7 billion), and the Philippines ($3.6 billion). (See **Figure 6** and **Appendix Table A5.**)

The U.S. trade deficit with China has two unusual characteristics. First is its size. Second is the large imbalance between imports from and exports to China. Japan in 2001, for example, exported 2.2 times more to the U.S. than it imported, while Canada exported 1.3 times more than it imported. China, by comparison, exported 5.3 times more to the U.S. market in 2001 than it imported. This indicates that the Chinese market has been vastly underdeveloped as a destination for U.S. exports. China's imports from the United States (up 10% between 1996 to 2001) recently have grown faster than those by Canada (4.2% over the same time period) or by Japan (-3.6%), although China's have been growing from a low base.[5] By joining the World Trade Organization China is required to lower import barriers on many products in which the United States is competitive. This is expected to increase U.S. export opportunities there.

---

[5] U.S. International Trade Commission.

Figure 6. U.S. Merchandise Trade Balances with Selected Countries in 2001

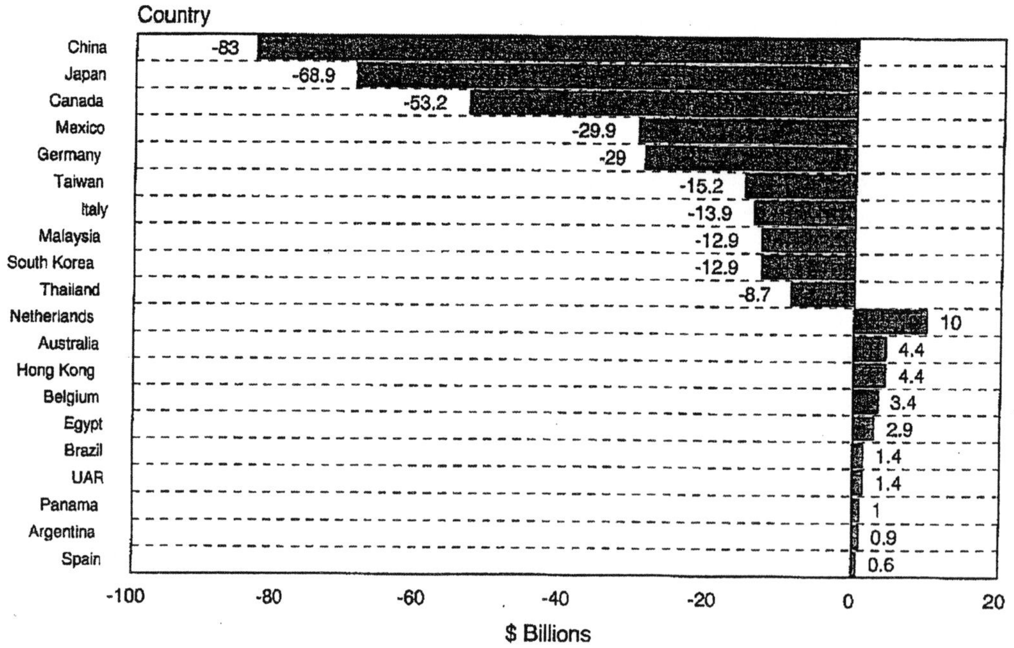

Country

Country	$ Billions
China	-83
Japan	-68.9
Canada	-53.2
Mexico	-29.9
Germany	-29
Taiwan	-15.2
Italy	-13.9
Malaysia	-12.9
South Korea	-12.9
Thailand	-8.7
Netherlands	10
Australia	4.4
Hong Kong	4.4
Belgium	3.4
Egypt	2.9
Brazil	1.4
UAR	1.4
Panama	1
Argentina	0.9
Spain	0.6

$ Billions

Source: Department of Commerce

According to Japanese, European, and U.S. data, in 2000, Japan was the largest overseas supplier of products to China with $30.4 billion in exports. The EU was the second largest supplier with $24.5 billion, while the United States exported only $16.2 billion worth of merchandise to the PRC in 2000 and $19.2 billion in 2001. Considering that the United States is the world's largest trading nation and exported $57 billion to Japan in 2001, its exports to China seem rather low. In 2001, the United States exported more to South Korea ($22 billion), France ($22 billion), and almost as much to Taiwan ($18 billion) as it did to China.

As shown in **Table 1**, among the top twenty U.S. exports to China in 2001, the top five by dollar value were transport equipment, electrical machinery, office machines and automatic data processing machines, telecommunications and sound equipment, and general industrial machinery and equipment.

Table 1. Top Twenty U.S. exports to China, 1993-2001 (Million dollars)

Category	1993	1994	1995	1996	1997	1998	1999	2000	2001
Transport Equip.	2,252	1,929	1,187	1,718	2,127	3,604	2,325	1,695	2,452
Electrical Mach	247	285	408	553	684	931	1,252	1,502	1,842
Office Machines	213	233	306	254	324	830	697	1,154	1,207
Telecom, Sound Recording Equip.	596	561	712	643	621	626	540	777	1,107
Gen. Indust. Equip.	427	515	712	764	756	663	675	812	1,050
Oil Seeds and Fruits	23	9	52	422	419	288	354	1,020	1,014
Metalliferous Ores	136	147	247	198	180	195	281	604	879
Special Machinery	669	670	675	685	765	519	478	744	772
Prof. & Scien. Instr.	336	276	323	327	388	451	465	563	755
Plastics	168	140	280	314	340	320	392	539	623
Power Gen. Equip.	321	282	394	462	590	512	493	301	464
Fertilizers	293	944	1,204	891	1,050	1,064	930	658	415
Hides, Furskins	13	46	100	107	112	126	96	230	402
Organic Chemicals	204	233	260	238	208	210	302	467	369
Misc. Manufactures	90	93	169	335	235	237	223	337	362
Pulp and Waste Paper	46	105	183	187	148	156	189	259	329
Paper Products	111	126	141	248	258	332	339	374	305
Chemical Materials	51	53	110	94	125	143	177	242	281
Metalworking Mach.	270	296	228	240	173	189	159	204	260
Road Vehicles	721	281	126	146	346	132	143	177	217

Note: Ranked by data for 2001.
Source: Data from U.S. Department of Commerce.

Figure 7. Top Six U.S. Imports from China by Industry, 1992-2002

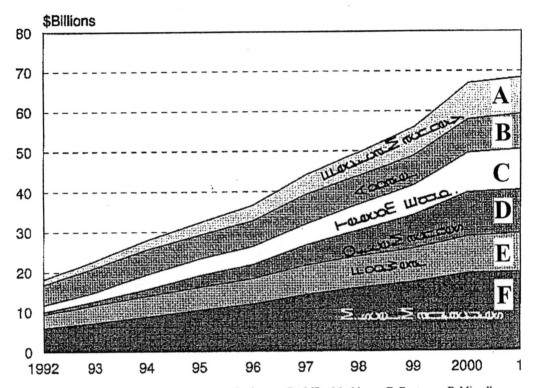

A. Electrical Machinery, B. Apparel, C. Telecom. Equipment, D. Office Machinery, E. Footwear, F. Miscellaneous
Source: U.S. Department of Commerce.

The United States is China's largest overseas market with $100 billion in imports from China in 2000, followed by the EU with $69.5 billion, and Japan with $55.3 billion. China was the fourth largest source of imports for the United States in 2000. Canada ($229 billion), Japan ($146 billion), and Mexico ($135 billion) exported more to the United States in 2000 than did China, but China sold more to the American market than did Germany ($58 billion), the United Kingdom ($43 billion), Taiwan ($40 billion), or South Korea ($40 billion). In short, China (with the help of foreign investors) is a major supplier of products to the U.S. market. According to Chinese data, the United States was the PRC's second largest trading partner in 2000 after Japan. Bilateral trade between China and the United States totaled $74 billion compared with $83 billion between China and Japan.

As shown in **Figure 7** and **Table 2**, among the top twenty U.S. imports from China in 2001 by dollar amount, the top six were miscellaneous manufactured articles, office machines and automatic data processing machines, telecommunications and sound equipment, footwear, electrical machinery, and footwear. The value for miscellaneous manufactured articles alone ($19.7 billion) exceeded the value for all 20 of the top U.S. exports to China ($15 billion). **Figure 7** shows how the top six imports from China have increased over 1992-2001. While U.S. imports in all these categories have increased, the most dramatic percentage changes have not been in sectors such as footwear and apparel – traditional labor-intensive industries in which China is quite competitive – but in high technology sectors, such as office and data processing machines (up 1,055% between 1993 and 2001), electrical machinery and appliances (up 428%), and telecommunications and sound equipment (up 343%).

Table 2. Top Twenty U.S. Imports from China, 1993-2001 (Million dollars)

Category	1993	1994	1995	1996	1997	1998	1999	2000	2001
Misc. Manufactured Articles	7,151	8,690	10,319	11,867	14,155	15,872	17,291	19,445	19,763
Office Machines, Data Processing	932	1,583	2,879	3,562	5,019	6,329	8,239	10,980	10,763
Telecom and Sound Equip.	2,279	3,715	4,215	4,438	5,126	6,405	7,382	9,812	10,118
Footwear	4,505	5,254	5,817	6,367	7,354	8,016	8,438	9,206	9,758
Electrical Machinery, parts, and Appliances	1,723	2,252	3,094	3,874	4,877	5,707	7,022	9,037	9,110
Apparel and Accessories	6,148	6,294	5,850	6,298	7,406	7,133	7,351	8,473	8,866
Furniture and Bedding	497	747	877	1,109	1,545	2,183	3,261	4,476	5,018
Manufactures of Metals	784	976	1,227	1,414	1,816	2,238	2,878	3,651	4,119
General Industrial Machinery	510	659	811	982	1,180	1,449	1,833	2,087	2,414
Building Fixtures/Fittings	440	617	813	1,013	1,194	1,444	2,073	2,555	2,377
Travel goods, Handbags	1,309	1,552	1,607	1,665	1,917	1,942	1,974	2,214	2,171
Nonmetallic Mineral Manufactures	444	614	824	963	1,216	1,441	1,681	2,059	2,165
Photographic Optical Equip, Watches and Clocks	504	682	913	976	1,211	1,400	1,600	2,016	1,935
Textile Yarn, Fabrics	989	1,022	1,155	1,042	1,369	1,432	1,583	1,816	1,854
Road Vehicles	249	321	412	417	574	731	923	1,800	1,406
Professional & Scientific Instruments	204	295	390	524	634	715	837	1,025	1,177
Cork and Wood (Non-Furniture)	150	193	224	255	335	445	568	710	792
Misc. Low-Valued Items	160	167	202	232	282	425	586	759	784
Fish and Related Products	299	259	306	285	321	323	431	579	657
Paper products	128	178	240	267	310	401	471	611	627
Iron and Steel	66	105	242	292	315	398	350	623	443

Note: Ranked by data for 2001.
Source: U.S. Department of Commerce

BALANCE OF TRADE BY SECTOR

In modern economies, trade by sector generally follows two patterns. The first is based on traditional comparative advantage in which one country trades with another in those products in which it has abundant resources. The United States economy is characterized by high technology, extensive farmland and with high agricultural yields, expensive labor, and deep capital. As such, the United States would be expected to be strong in exports of high-technology goods, food and grains, and capital intensive products. The Chinese economy, on the other hand, is characterized by abundant and cheap labor, low capital intensity, and a mix of low, medium and high technology both in manufacturing and agriculture. As such, China would be expected to be strong in exports of labor-intensive manufactures, such as textiles and apparel, shoes, toys, or light manufactures, but also in production of items made under the tutelage of foreign, competitive companies that have invested in Chinese factories. These could include household appliances, furniture, tools, automobile parts, or electronic machinery. One would expect trade that is conducted on the basis of comparative advantage to be unbalanced on a sector-by-sector basis. The United States, for example, would run a surplus with China in aircraft but a deficit in apparel.

The second trade pattern occurs among industrialized countries and is called intra-industry or trade within industrial sectors. This is typical of trade among North America, the European Union, and industrialized nations of Asia (e.g., Japan, South Korea, and Taiwan). The products traded usually carry brand names, are differentiated, and may be protected by intellectual property rights. For example, the United States both imports and exports items such as automobiles, machinery, electronic devices, prepared food, and pharmaceuticals. A considerable share of U.S. intra-industry trade is carried out within a multinational corporation (e.g., between Ford Motors and one of its related companies, such as Mazda in Japan, Jaguar in the United Kingdom, or with other subsidiaries abroad). A large deficit in an intra-industry trading sector in which the United States is competitive indicates that the trading partner country may be using import barriers to tip the trade balance in its favor.

Table 3 shows the U.S. balance of trade with China by major sector. Most of the sectors in which the United States runs the largest trade deficits with China are, as expected, those that depend on abundant and low-cost labor. These include toys, sports equipment, footwear, apparel, leather bags, and textiles. Among the large deficit sectors, however, are electrical machinery, machinery, and vehicles (indicated by shading in the table). Some of China's competitiveness in these sectors may be based on its underlying economic advantages combined with foreign technology and manufacturing processes, but in certain areas the advantage also may be based on trade barriers. In automobiles, for example, a 2.3 liter Honda Accord sold from a plant in the United States that retails for roughly $20,000, sells for the equivalent of about $36,000 in China even though it is assembled at a plant there.[6] Prior to China's accession to the WTO, tariffs on imports of automobiles exceeded 100%. They are to be reduced to 25% by 2005. The tariff on large motorcycles also is slated to fall from 60% to 45% - still relatively high.[7] Moreover, in plastic, optical and medical instruments, books and magazines, soaps and waxes, cosmetics, and cotton yarn, the United States runs a surplus in

---

[6] Zaun, Todd. Foreign Auto Makers Expand production in Chinese Market. *Wall Street Journal,* April 18, 2002, p. D6.

its balance of trade with the world but a deficit with China. These deficits run counter to market expectations.

Table 3 U.S. Balance of Trade with China by Sector, 1999-2001 (Million Dollars)

	1999	2000	2001
Total China	-68,677	-83,833	-83,046
Major U.S. Deficit Sectors			
Electrical Machinery	-13,081	-16,831	-16,295
Toys and Sports Equipment	-11,041	-12,354	-12,186
Footwear	-8,393	-9,142	-9,711
Machinery	-7,617	-9,911	-9,649
Furniture and Bedding	-5,485	-7,117	-7,404
Woven Apparel	-3,746	-4,164	-4,126
Leather Art; saddler; bags	-3,003	-3,827	-3,897
Plastic	-1,947	-2,194	-2,381
Knit Apparel	-2,023	-2,032	-2,273
Iron/steel Products	-1,302	-1,800	-2,020
Optical, Medical Instruments	-1,499	-1,994	-1,511
Vehicles, Not Railway	-856	-1,759	-1,299
Misc. Textile Articles	-963	-1,097	-1,200
Misc. Art of Base Metal	-715	-836	-963
Artificial Flowers, Feathers	-869	-927	-958
Tools, cutlery, of Base Metals	-738	-878	-939
Ceramic Products	-762	-869	-864
Miscellaneous Manufactures	-751	-740	-841
Precious Stones, Metals	-491	-669	-803
Books, Newspapers, Manuscripts	-203	-325	-377
Soap, Wax, Polish, Dental Preps, etc.	-122	-140	-133
Perfumery, Cosmetics, etc.	-74	-86	-132
Cotton & Yarn Fabric	-174	-132	-101
	1999	**2000**	**2001**
Major U.S. Surplus Sectors			
Aircraft, Spacecraft	2,290	1,658	2,389
Misc. Grain, Seed, Fruit	299	968	964
Hides and Skins	127	270	434
Fertilizers	931	607	398
Wood pulp, Etc.	195	274	330
Iron and Steel	-83	-122	265
Copper and Articles Thereof	-31	140	142

Note: Shaded categories are those in which the United States runs a trade surplus with the world but a trade deficit with China. Classification is by Harmonized System tariff codes at the 2-digit level.

Source: Data from U.S. Department of Commerce

[7] U.S. Trade Representative. *2002 National Trade Estimate Report on Foreign Trade Barriers.* Washington, U.S. Government Printing Office. P. 46.

The sectors in which the United States runs a trade surplus with China mirror U.S. competitive advantages and include aircraft and agricultural products. In two sectors, a deficit in U.S. trade with China has turned into a surplus. Edible fruit and nuts went from a $30 billion deficit in 1999 to surplus of $7 billion in 2001. Likewise, Miscellaneous food went from a deficit of $17 billion to a surplus of $23 billion.

U.S. IMPORTS FROM CHINA BY SELECTED SECTORS

This section presents charts and data on U.S. imports from China by selected industrial sectors. The charts show imports from China as compared with imports from other major exporting countries or groups of countries. These include the European Union, the Association of Southeast Asian Nations (ASEAN, which includes, Indonesia, Malaysia, Singapore, Thailand, the Philippines, Brunei, Vietnam, Laos, and Myanmar [Burma]), Taiwan, Mexico, south Korea, Japan, Hong Kong, and Canada. Even though granting permanent normal trade relations status to China and China's accession to the WTO will not change materially the accessibility of Chinese exports to the U.S. market, U.S. industries competing with imports from China (such as apparel and textiles) have opposed increasing trade with the PRC partly for fear of losing U.S. jobs to imports. This has been a particular concern of labor organizations.

The data in this section are presented according to two-digit standard international trade classification (SITC) codes as reported by the U.S. Department of Commerce. The industries selected are those in which the share of imports from China has risen to a significant level or industries in which trade policy has played a significant role (e.g. iron and steel or automobiles), even though U.S. imports from China in those industries might be small.

Figure 8. U.S. Imports of Iron and Steel products (SITC 67) by Country and Group, 1990-2001

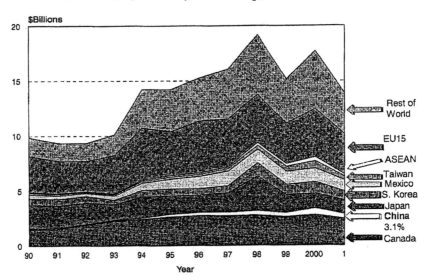

Source: U.S. Department of Commerce

Iron and Steel

In iron and steel products, China is not a major exporter – either to the United States or to the world. In 2001, China accounted for only 3.1% of U.S. imports of iron and steel.

Table 4. U.S. Imports of Iron and steel Products (SITC 67) from Selected Countries and Country Groups, 1990, 1997-2001 (Million dollars)

	1990	1997	1998	1999	2000	2001
Canada	1,504	2,708	2,761	2,607	2,803	2,437
China	71	315	398	350	623	439
Hong Kong	2	1	1	3	2	2
Japan	2,097	1,694	3,063	1,563	1,320	1,213
Korea	574	650	1,206	944	1,019	815
Mexico	357	1,301	1,244	1,202	1,267	1,021
Taiwan	154	249	329	449	649	346
ASEAN	65	130	273	262	389	193
EU15	3,303	4,376	4,372	3,714	4,379	3,672
Rest of World	1,691	4,571	5,403	4,005	5,293	3,720
World	9,818	15,995	19,050	15,100	17,744	13,858

Note: Shaded categories are those in which the United States runs a trade surplus with the world but a trade deficit with China. Classification is by Harmonized System tariff codes at the 2-digit level.
Source: Data from U.S. Department of Commerce

Office Machines and Computers

In U.S. imports of office machines and automatic data processing machines (computers), China is becoming a major supplier – accounting for 14% of U.S. imports of such products in 2001. These imports rose from $117 million in 1990 to $10.7 billion in 2001. China appears to be gaining market share partly at the expense of Japan. The other supplier whose market share is becoming dominant is ASEAN. Imports from ASEAN rose from $5.1 billion in 1990 to $20.6 billion in 2001.

Figure 9. U.S. Imports of Office Machines and Automatic Data Processing Machines (SITC 75) by Country and Group, 1990-2001

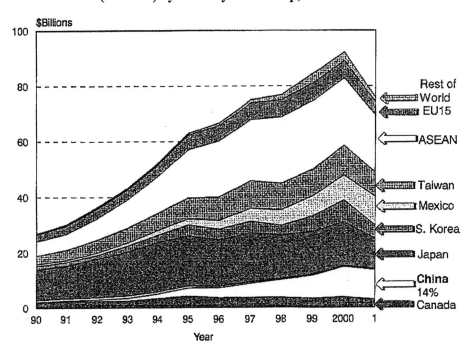

Telecommunications and Sound Equipment

In U.S. imports of telecommunications and sound equipment, China's share has risen to 16%. Such imports from China rose from $1.1 billion in 1990 to $10 billion in 2001. Imports of these products from Canada, Mexico, South Korea, and ASEAN have also been rising. Those from Japan, however, have risen relatively little.

Table 5. U.S. Imports of Office Machines and Automatic Data Processing Machines (SITC 75) from Selected Countries and Country Groups, 1990. 1997-2001 (Million dollars)

	1990	1997	1998	1999	2000	2001
Canada	1,893	3,649	3,701	3,269	3,778	2,942
China	117	5,019	6,329	8,239	10,980	10,761
Hong Kong	809	541	404	303	345	276
Japan	11,001	17,803	15,640	15,648	15,878	11,055
Korea	1,347	4,186	3,449	5,527	7,831	4,657
Mexico	706	4,637	5,483	7,169	9,058	10,377
Taiwan	3,084	9,875	9,560	9,641	10,592	8,751
ASEAN	5,150	21,967	23,956	24,723	24,475	20,674
EU15	2,461	6,127	6,231	6,373	6,156	4,673
Rest of World	297	1,181	1,824	3,451	3,041	1,695
World	26,871	74,985	76,577	84,343	92,134	75,861

Source: U.S. Department of Commerce

Figure 10. U.S. Imports of Telecommunications and Sound Equipment (SITC 76) by Country and Group, 1990-2001

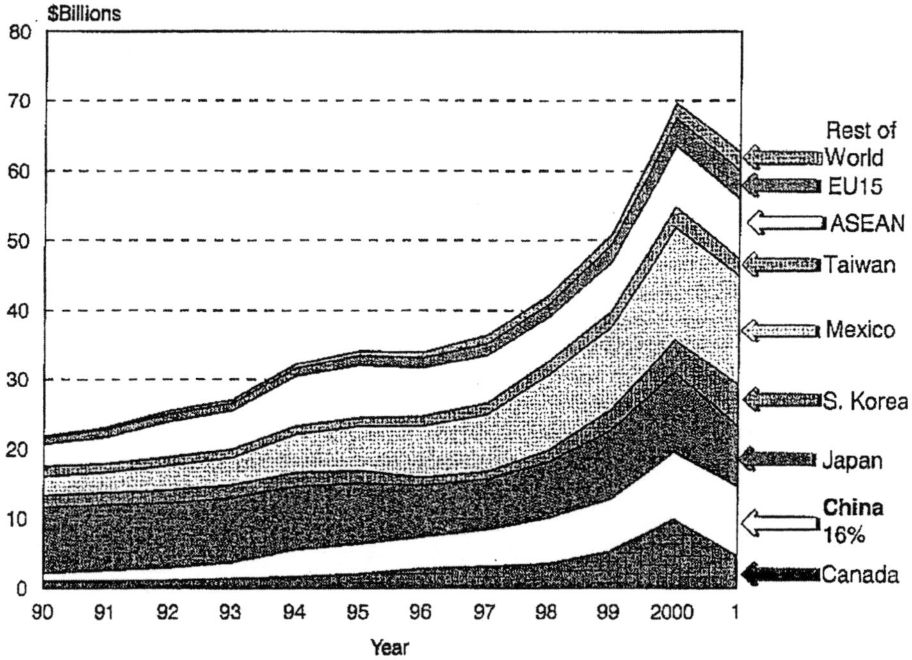

Source: U.S. Department of Commerce

Table 5. U.S. Imports of Telecommunications and Sound Equipment (SITC 76) from Selected Countries and Country Groups, 1990, 1997-2001 (Million dollars)

	1990	1997	1998	1999	2000	2001
Canada	972	3,066	3,434	5,164	9,846	4,533
China	1,142	5,126	6,405	7,382	9,812	10,062
Hong Kong	478	221	249	171	262	224
Japan	9,061	7,127	7,991	9,789	11,429	8,577
Korea	1,632	1,037	1,569	2,896	4,729	6,001
Mexico	2,302	7,722	9,526	11,886	16,073	15,765
Taiwan	1,426	1,590	1,926	2,238	2,986	2,361
ASEAN	3,122	6,876	6,364	6,972	8,779	8,619
EU15	890	1,620	1,759	2,536	3,860	3,990
Rest of World	322	1,224	1,257	1,363	2,118	2,689
World	21,347	35,609	40,480	50,397	69,894	62,821

Source: U.S. Department of Commerce

Figure 11. U.S. Imports of Electrical Machinery/Parts (SITC 77) by Country and Group, 1990-2001

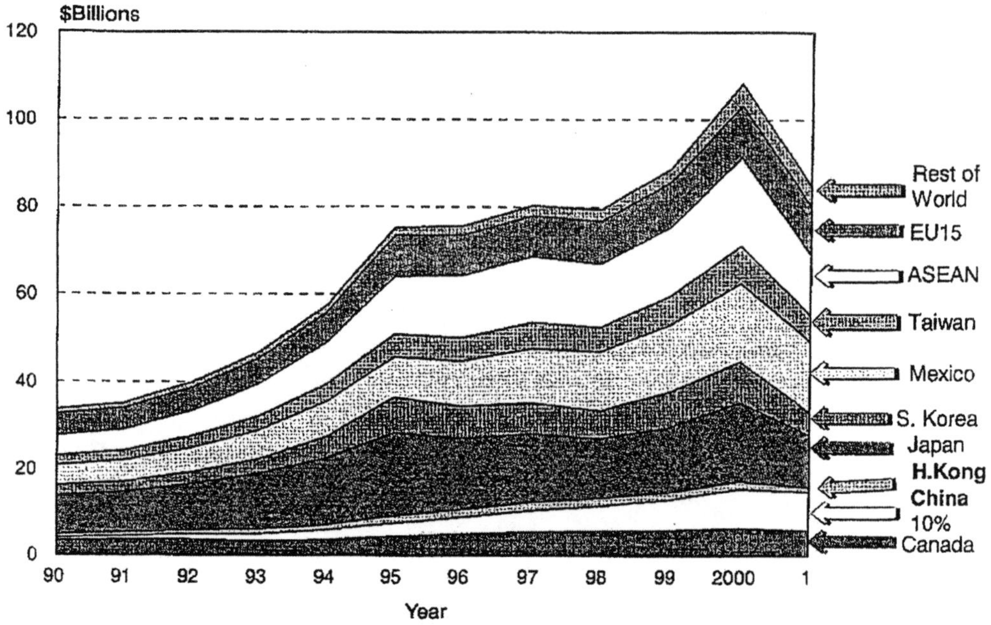

Source: U.S. Department of Commerce

Electrical Machinery and Parts

U.S. imports of electrical machinery and parts have been growing dramatically from nearly all major supplier countries. At 10% of such imports in 2001, China is becoming a significant supplier – surpassing Canada, Taiwan, and South Korea. Other major suppliers are the European Union, Japan, ASEAN, and Mexico.

Table 6. U.S. Imports of Electrical Machinery and parts (SITC 77) from Selected Countries and Country Groups, 1990, 1997-2001 (Million dollars)

	1990	1997	1998	1999	2000	2001
Canada	3,323	5,503	5,768	5,833	6,499	5,871
China	652	4,877	5,707	7,022	9,037	9,047
Hong Kong	792	1,920	1,770	1,747	1,782	1,050
Japan	8,658	15,452	13,650	14,665	18,096	11,941
Korea	2,504	7,092	6,422	8,087	9,327	5,194
Mexico	4,406	12,474	13,506	15,290	17,828	16,290
Taiwan	2,180	5,750	5,438	6,370	8,492	5,878
ASEAN	4,644	14,998	13,249	15,783	20,295	13,755
EU15	4,898	9,223	9,640	10,162	11,922	11,139
Rest of World	1,080	2,395	2,707	3,056	4,988	4,545
World	33,137	79,684	78,857	88,015	108,266	84,710

Source: U.S. Department of Commerce

Road Motor Vehicles

In U.S. imports of road motor vehicles, China is an insignificant player. Most of the imports come from Canada, Japan, the European Union, and Mexico. Imports from China in this sector have primarily been motorcycles and motor vehicle parts.

Figure 12. U.S. Imports of Road Vehicles (SITC 78) by Country and Group, 1990-2001

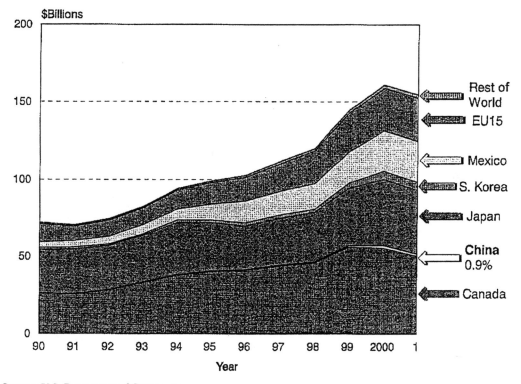

Source: U.S. Department of Commerce

Table 7. U.S. Imports of Road Motor Vehicles (SITC 78) from Selected Countries and Country Groups, 1990, 1992-2001 (Million dollars)

	1990	1997	1998	1999	2000	2001
Canada	26,094	43,849	45,823	56,266	55,703	50,477
China	59	574	731	923	1,800	1,404
Hong Kong	7	11	10	12	30	14
Japan	29,839	32,930	34,102	38,825	42,917	41,429
Korea	1,275	2,102	1,912	3,287	5,222	6,778
Mexico	4,084	15,566	16,750	19,963	25,991	26,246
Taiwan	871	987	1,083	1,168	1,335	1,124
ASEAN	88	184	207	262	249	247
EU15	12,270	17,914	21,824	26,092	27,176	27,680
Rest of World	930	1,392	1,429	1,711	2,205	2,009
World	75,517	115,509	123,871	148,509	162,628	157,408

Source: U.S. Department of Commerce

Building Fixtures/Lighting

In U.S. imports of prefabricated buildings, sanitary, plumbing, heating and lighting fixtures and fittings, China has surged to become a major player. It accounted for nearly half such imports in 2001, although total imports of such products amounted to only $4.9 billion, of which $2.4 billion came from China.

Figure 13. U.S. Imports of Prefab Buildings, Sanitary, Plumbing, Heating, and Lighting Fixtures/Fittings (SITC 81) by Country and Group, 1990-2001

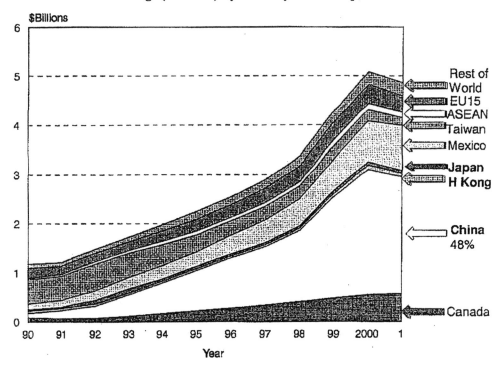

Source: U.S. Department of Commerce

Table 8. U.S. Imports of Prefabricated Buildings; Sanitary, Plumbing, Heating and Lighting Fixtures and Fittings (SITC 81) from Selected Countries and Country Groups, 1990, 1997-2001 (Million dollars)

	1990	1997	1998	1999	2000	2001
Canada	80	337	406	481	544	572
China	94	1,194	1,444	2,073	2,555	2,383
Hong Kong	47	41	48	65	94	70
Japan	28	43	48	62	63	59
Korea	61	44	23	29	26	32
Mexico	117	463	558	642	819	903
Taiwan	495	274	262	261	235	156
ASEAN	27	82	88	126	132	116
EU15	205	296	317	360	384	333
Rest of World	78	173	194	228	255	271
World	1,232	2,946	3,388	4,327	5,107	4,895

Source: U.S. Department of Commerce

Furniture

In U.S. imports of furniture and parts, China is becoming a major supplier. It accounted for 27% of such imports amounting to $5 billion in 2001. This exceeded the $3.2 billion of such imports from Mexico and the $4.4 billion from Canada.

Table 9. U.S. Imports of Furniture and Parts (SITC 82) from Selected Countries and Country Groups, 1990, 1997-2001 (Million dollars)

	1990	1997	1998	1999	2000	2001
Canada	1,209	3,449	4,014	4,337	4,859	4,411
China	145	1,545	2,183	3,261	4,476	5,017
Hong Kong	29	52	69	75	84	98
Japan	162	94	122	145	141	141
Korea	67	48	65	76	85	75
Mexico	578	1,915	2,317	2,885	3,201	3,212
Taiwan	1,009	924	967	1,009	1,031	765
ASEAN	331	1,098	1,204	1,436	1,593	1,492
EU15	1,174	1,491	1,798	2,209	2,473	2,314
Rest of World	299	522	586	742	982	1,086
World	5,003	11,137	13,325	16,175	18,923	18,611

Source: U.S. Department of Commerce

**Figure 14. U.S. Imports of Furniture and Parts (SITC 82) by
Country and Group, 1990-2001**

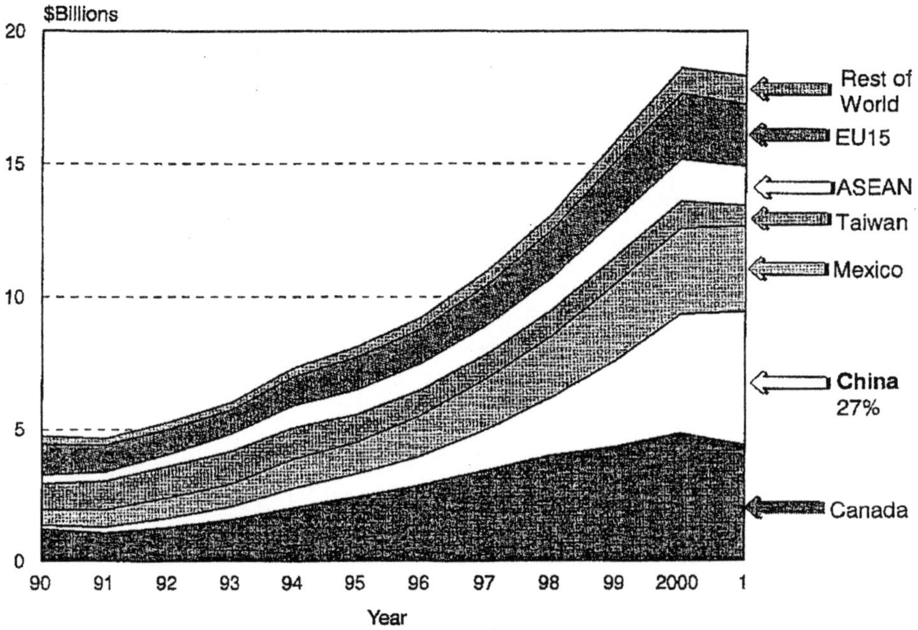

Source: U.S. Department of Commerce

Travel Goods, Handbags

In travel goods, handbags, and similar items, China again has become a major supplier, although total U.S. imports of such products amounted to only $4.3 billion in 2001. Of this, China accounted for 51% or $2.2 billion. ASEAN also is becoming a major source of such products.

**Table 10. U.S. Imports of Travel Goods, Handbags, (SITC 83) from
Selected Countries and Country Groups, 1990, 1997-2001 (Million dollars)**

	1990	1997	1998	1999	2000	2001
Canada	17	34	34	38	42	39
China	692	1,917	1,942	1,974	2,214	2,211
Hong Kong	50	53	48	47	59	46
Japan	3	5	5	7	7	7
Korea	446	177	160	168	143	106
Mexico	46	131	154	161	145	104
Taiwan	406	184	176	149	138	129
ASEAN	114	495	633	726	811	836
EU15	270	439	387	406	430	492
Rest of World	121	344	383	417	412	330
World	2,171	3,779	3,922	4,093	4,401	4,300

Source: U.S. Department of Commerce

Figure 15. U.S. Imports of Travel Goods, Handbags, and Similar Products (SITC 83) by Country and Group, 1990-2001

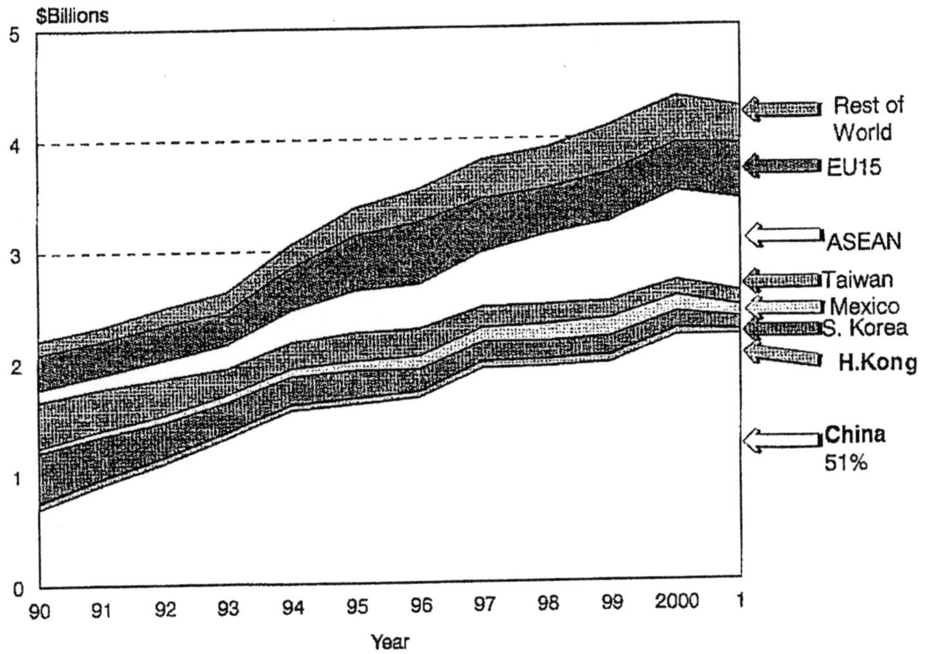

Source: U.S. Department of Commerce

Apparel and Clothing

In U.S. imports of articles of apparel and clothing accessories, the market share from China is rising, but in 2001, it accounted for only 13% of all such U.S. imports or $8.8 billion. Mexico and ASEAN export a similar amount to the United States. The largest increase in import share has come from the "rest of the world."

Table 11. U.S. Imports of Apparel and Clothing Accessories (SITC 84) from Selected Countries and Country Groups, 1990, 1997-2001 (Million dollars)

	1990	1997	1998	1999	2000	2001
Canada	247	1,343	1,555	1,735	1,911	1,764
China	3,422	7,406	7,133	7,351	8,473	8,852
Hong Kong	3,974	4,027	4,493	4,341	4,571	4,282
Japan	158	93	86	93	109	170
Korea	3,244	1,654	2,037	2,256	2,461	2,354
Mexico	709	5,349	6,811	7,845	8,730	8,127
Taiwan	2,475	2,164	2,223	2,076	2,160	1,907
ASEAN	3,404	6,593	7,544	7,949	9,354	9,595
EU15	1,790	2,234	2,437	2,379	2,540	2,599
Rest of World	5,891	17,424	19,345	20,351	23,872	24,211
World	25,314	48,287	53,664	56,376	64,181	63,861

Source: U.S. Department of Commerce

Figure 16. U.S. Imports of Apparel and Clothing Accessories (SITC 84) by Country and Group, 1990-2001

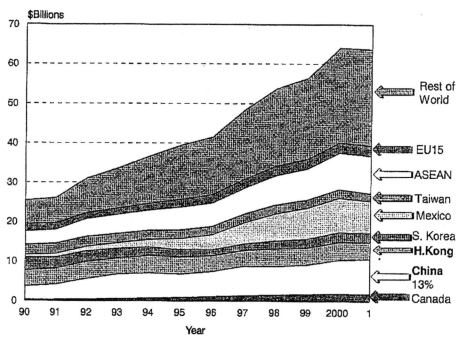

Source: U.S. Department of Commerce

Footwear

Imports of footwear into the United States from China leaped upward during the 1990s. From $1.5 billion in 1990, they rose to $9.7 billion in 2001 or 64% of all such imports. China has largely replaced South Korea and Taiwan as a major source of footwear imports, and imports of such products continue to grow.

Table 12. U.S. Imports of Footwear (SITC 85) from Selected Countries and Country Groups, 1990, 1997-2001 (Million dollars)

	1990	1997	1998	1999	2000	2001
Canada	53	117	100	89	76	78
China	1,475	7,354	8,016	8,438	9,206	9,766
Hong Kong	109	99	62	58	67	81
Japan	5	3	2	2	2	2
Korea	2,558	235	181	162	140	103
Mexico	165	384	349	354	351	311
Taiwan	1,528	183	144	111	92	75
ASEAN	579	1,675	1,291	1,246	1,207	1,185
EU15	1,523	2,087	2,047	2,038	2,044	1,950
Rest of World	1,543	2,087	1,687	1,576	1,671	1,684
World	9,538	13,951	13,879	14,074	14,856	15,235

Source: U.S. Department of Commerce

Figure 17. U.S. Imports of Footwear (SITC 85) by Country and Group, 1990-2001

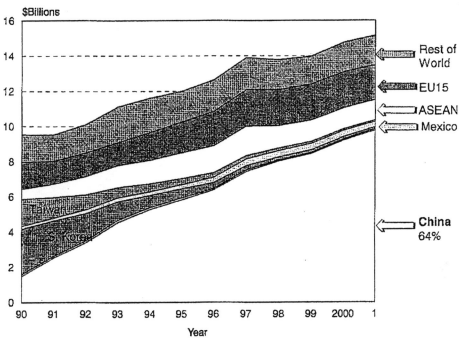

Source: U.S. Department of Commerce

Figure 18. U.S. Imports of Professional, Scientific, and Controlling Instruments (SITC 87) by Country and Group, 1990-2001

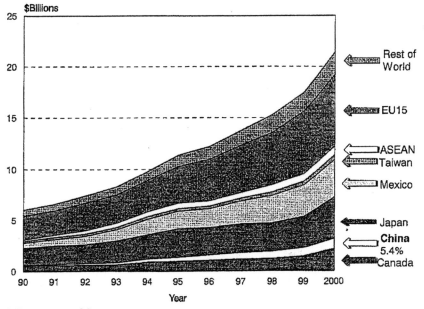

Source: U.S. Department of Commerce

Professional, Scientific, and Controlling Instruments

In U.S. imports of professional, scientific and controlling instruments and apparatus, China is only a minor supplier with 5.4% and $1.1 billion of such imports in 2001. Most originate in the European Union, Mexico, and Japan.

Table 13. U.S. Imports of Professional, Scientific and Controlling Instruments and Apparatus (SITC 87) from Selected Countries and Country Groups, 1990, 1997-2001 (Million dollars)

	1990	1997	1998	1999	2000	2001
Canada	527	1,173	1,222	1,443	2,167	1,793
China	74	634	715	837	1,025	1,172
Hong Kong	82	79	88	73	87	55
Japan	1,494	2,613	2,684	3,085	4,075	3,561
Korea	89	98	113	116	152	152
Mexico	513	2,253	2,716	3,082	3,665	3,895
Taiwan	176	283	341	344	434	372
ASEAN	152	558	715	769	860	1,029
EU15	2,310	4,569	5,030	5,870	6,980	7,050
Rest of World	604	1,408	1,709	1,857	2,177	2,320
World	6,021	13,668	15,333	17,476	21,622	21,399

Source: U.S. Department of Commerce

Photographic/Optical Equipment, Watches/Clocks

In U.S. imports of photographic apparatus, equipment and supplies and optical goods as well as watches and clocks, China is a significantly rising supplier. In 2001, China accounted for 15% of U.S. imports of such products or $1.9 billion. Japan ($3.8 billion) and the European Union ($2.4 billion) still dominate imports.

Figure 19. U.S. Imports of Photographic Equipment/Supplies, Optical Goods, and Watches/Clocks (SITC 88) by Country and Group, 1990-2001

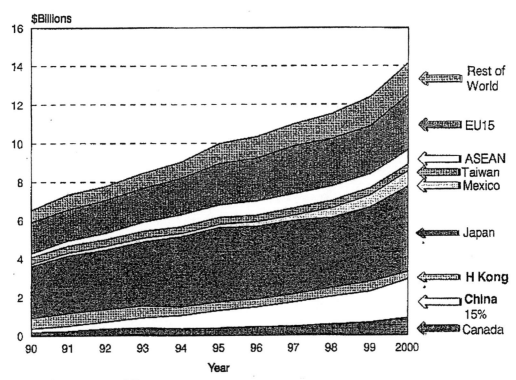

Source: U.S. Department of Commerce

Table 14. U.S. Imports of Photographic Apparatus, Equipment and Supplies and Optical Goods; Watches and Clocks (SITC 88) from Selected Countries and Country Groups, 1990, 1997-2001 (Million dollars)

	1990	1997	1998	1999	2000	2001
Canada	180	467	572	663	904	545
China	191	1,211	1,400	1,600	2,016	1,908
Hong Kong	526	418	389	408	378	236
Japan	2,668	3,776	3,648	3,919	4,450	3,848
Korea	127	191	203	190	179	168
Mexico	128	260	467	620	802	648
Taiwan	334	360	375	361	342	282
ASEAN	199	738	763	737	745	650
EU15	1,619	2,437	2,355	2,363	2,868	2,453
Rest of World	574	1,064	1,295	1,509	1,626	1,506
World	6,546	10,922	11,467	12,370	14,310	12,244

Source: U.S. Department of Commerce

FOREIGN DIRECT INVESTMENT IN CHINA

Foreign direct investment (FDI) is directed toward investments in companies in which the foreign investor has a controlling interest. It is primarily for physical plant and equipment and for the costs of establishing enterprises in China. It is not for portfolio investment on China's stock exchanges. As shown in **Table 15**, China relies heavily upon FDI from Hong Kong and Taiwan. Some of the FDI registered as originating in Hong Kong actually comes from Taiwan. Also, a significant amount of investment from Hong Kong and Macao is actually investment by Mainland Chinese companies via subsidiaries in Hong Kong and Macao. Mainland subsidiaries in Hong Kong and Macao can take advantage of investment incentives for foreign companies on the PRC mainland. In addition, many foreign firms, including U.S. companies, are registered in the Virgin Islands for tax purposes. The industrial sectors in China that have received the most FDI have been manufacturing and real estate. In 2000, U.S. utilized (spent) FDI in China totaled $4.4 billion.

China's accession to the WTO would likely result in higher levels of investment from other countries. China's concessions in order to bring its economy into line with WTO requirements include allowing more foreign investment in industries, such as telecommunications, financial services, and transportation.

Table 15. China's Utilized Foreign Direct Investment Inflows, Top Ten Foreign Investors, 1998-2000 (Billion dollars)

Country or Region	Foreign Direct Investment		
	1998	1999	2000
Hong Kong	18.51	16.36	15.50
United States	3.90	4.22	4.38
Virgin Islands	4.03	2.66	3.84
Japan	3.40	2.97	2.91
Taiwan	2.92	2.60	2.29
Singapore	3.40	2.64	2.17
South Korea	1.80	1.27	1.49
United Kingdom	1.18	1.04	1.16
Germany	0.74	1.37	1.04
France	.90	.88	.85
All Sources	45.46	40.40	40.71

Note: These figures refer to yearly rather than cumulative amounts.
Sources: U.S. Department of State. *FY2000 Country Commercial Guide – China;* U.S. Department of State. *FY2001 Country Commercial Guide – China;* State China [http://www.statchina.com]; China. Ministry of Foreign Trade and Economic Cooperation; Japan External Trade Organization. *JETRO White Paper on Foreign Direct Investment, 1999.* See [http://www.jetro.go.jp].

APPENDIX

Table A1. China's Merchandise Trade with the World and with the United States, 1980-2001 (Million dollars)

Year	China's Trade with the World (Chinese data)			U.S. Trade with China (U.S. data)			China's Trade with U.S. (Chinese data)		
	China Exports	China Imports	China Balance	U.S. Exports	U.S. Imports	U.S. Balance	China Exports	China Imports	China Balance
1980	18,139	19,505	-1,366	3,755	1,164	2,591	983	3,830	-2,847
1981	21,476	21,631	-155	3,603	2,062	1,541	1,505	4,682	-3,177
1982	21,865	18,920	2,945	2,912	2,502	410	1,765	4,305	-2,540
1983	22,096	21,313	783	2,173	2,477	-304	1,713	2,753	-1,040
1984	24,824	25,953	-1,129	3,004	3,381	-377	2,313	3,837	-1,524
1985	27,329	42,534	-15,205	3,856	4,224	-368	2,336	5,199	-2,863
1986	31,367	43,247	-11,880	3,106	5,241	-2,135	2,633	4,718	-2,085
1987	39,464	43,222	-3,758	3,497	6,910	-3,413	3,030	4,836	-1,806
1988	47,663	55,352	-7,689	5,017	9,261	-4,244	3,399	6,633	-3,234
1989	52,916	59,131	-6,215	5,807	12,901	-7,094	4,414	7,864	-3,450
1990	62,876	53,915	8,961	4,807	16,296	-11,489	5,314	6,591	-1,277
1991	71,940	63,855	8,085	6,287	20,305	-14,018	6,198	8,010	-1,812
1992	85,492	81,843	3,649	7,470	27,413	-19,943	8,599	8,903	-304
1993	91,611	103,552	-11,941	8,767	31,183	-22,416	16,976	10,633	6,343
1994	120,822	115,629	5,193	9,287	41,362	-32,075	21,421	13,977	7,444
1995	148,892	132,063	16,829	11,749	48,521	-36,772	24,744	16,123	8,621
1996	151,093	138,949	12,144	11,978	54,409	-42,431	26,731	16,179	10,552
1997	182,917	142,163	40,754	12,805	65,832	-53,027	32,744	16,290	16,454
1998	183,744	140,385	43,359	14,258	75,109	-60,851	38,001	16,997	21,004
1999	194,932	165,717	29,215	13,118	81,786	-68,668	41,946	19,480	22,466
2000	249,212	225,097	24,115	16,253	100,063	-83,810	52,104	22,363	29,741
2001	N/A	N/A	N/A	19,234	102,280	-83,046	26,200	54,300	28,100

Sources: U.S. Department of Commerce; China. Ministry of Foreign Trade and Economic Cooperation; PRC General Administration of Customs.

Table A2. China's Merchandise Trade with the
European Union, 1980-2000 (Million dollars)

Year	EU Trade with China (EU data)			China's Trade with the EU (Chinese data)		
	EU Exports	EU Imports	EU Balance	China Exports	China Imports	China Balance
1980	2,478	2,753	-275	2,363	2,814	-451
1981	2,216	2,682	-466	2,502	2,714	-212
1982	2,105	2,437	-332	2,168	2,178	-10
1983	2,573	2,485	88	2,508	3,390	-882
1984	2,929	2,639	290	2,232	3,323	-1,091
1985	5,484	2,971	2,513	2,283	6,157	-3,874
1986	6,403	4,106	2,297	4,017	7,757	-3,740
1987	6,430	5,945	485	3,916	7,274	-3,358
1988	6,772	7,719	-947	4,746	8,176	-3,430
1989	7,360	9,877	-2,517	5,114	9,785	-4,671
1990	7,373	13,289	-5,916	6,275	9,147	-2,872
1991	7,719	18,160	-10,441	7,127	9,297	-2,170
1992	9,604	20,995	-11,391	8,004	10,863	-2,859
1993	14,301	23,730	-9,429	12,258	15,739	-3,481
1994	16,246	27,644	-11,398	15,418	18,604	-3,186
1995	19,327	32,333	-13,006	19,258	21,313	-2,055
1996	18,387	35,197	-16,810	19,868	19,883	-15
1997	18,445	39,364	-20,919	23,865	19,205	4,660
1998	20,270	44,010	-23,740	28,148	20,715	7,433
1999	20,448	52,252	-31,806	30,207	25,463	4,744
2000	24,545	69,490	-44,945	38,193	30,845	7,348

Note: From 1980-88, data are for the 12 nations of the European Economic Community and after 1988 for the 15 nations of the EU (addition of Austria, Finland, and Sweden). EU data for 2000 are estimates based upon data for 11 months.

Sources: (1980-1998) International Monetary Fund. *Direction of Trade Statistics Yearbook, 1999;* (1999) European Union Delegation of the European Commission, *Eurostat;* China. Ministry of Foreign Trade and Economic Cooperation: PRC General Administration of Customs.

Table A3. China's Merchandise Trade with Japan, 1980-2000 (Million dollars)

Year	Japan's Trade with China (Japanese Data)			China's Trade with Japan (Chinese Data)		
	Japan Exports	Japan Imports	Japan Balance	China Exports	China Imports	China Balance
1980	5,109	4,346	763	4,032	5,169	-1,137
1981	5,076	5,283	-207	4,747	6,183	-1,436
1982	3,500	5,338	-1,838	4,806	3,902	904
1983	4,918	5,089	-171	4,517	5,495	-978
1984	7,199	5,943	1,256	5,155	8,057	-2,902
1985	12,590	6,534	6,056	6,091	15,178	-9,087
1986	9,936	5,727	4,209	5,079	12,463	-7,384
1987	8,337	7,478	859	6,392	10,087	-3,695
1988	9,486	9,861	-375	8,046	11,062	-3,016
1989	8,477	11,083	-2,606	8,395	10,534	-2,139
1990	6,145	12,057	-5,912	9,210	7,656	1,554
1991	8,605	14,248	-5,643	10,252	10,032	220
1992	11,967	16,972	-5,005	11,699	13,686	-1,987
1993	17,353	20,651	-3,298	15,782	23,303	-7,521
1994	18,687	27,569	-8,882	21,490	26,319	-4,829
1995	21,934	35,922	-13,988	28,466	29,007	-541
1996	21,827	40,405	-18,578	30,888	29,190	1,698
1997	21,692	41,827	-20,135	31,820	28,990	2,830
1998	20,182	37,079	-16,897	29,718	28,307	1,411
1999	23,450	43,070	-19,620	32,400	33,768	-1,368
2000	30,440	55,340	-24,900	41,654	41,512	142

Sources: International Monetary Fund. *Direction of Trade Statistics Yearbook, 1999;* International Monetary Fund. *Direction of Trade Statistics Quarterly,* June 2000; Japan External Trade Organization (JETRO); China. Ministry of Foreign Trade and Economic Cooperation; PRC General Administration of Customs.

Table A4. Major Country Merchandise Exports to China, Imports from China, and Trade Balances with China, 1999, 2000 (Billion dollars)

Partner	Trading Partner Data						Chinese Data					
	1999			2000			1999			2000		
	Exp	Imp	Bal	Exp	Imp	Bal	Exp	Imp	Bal	Exp	Imp	Bal
U.S.	13.1	81.8	-68.7	16.3	100.1	-83.8	19.5	41.9	-22.4	22.4	52.1	-29.7
Japan	23.4	43.0	-19.6	30.4	55.3	-24.9	31.5	34.0	-2.5	41.5	41.6	-0.1
EU	20.4	52.3	-31.8	24.5	69.5	-45.0	22.4	30.2	-7.8	30.8	38.1	-7.3
Hong Kong	57.6	77.9	-20.3	69.9	92.4	-22.5	6.9	36.9	-30.0	9.4	44.5	-35.1
Taiwan	21.3	4.5	16.8	26.1	6.2	19.9	19.5	3.9	15.6	25.5	5.0	20.5
Germany	7.4	14.5	-7.1	8.5	16.8	-8.3	8.3	7.8	0.5	10.4	9.3	1.1
S. Korea	15.0	8.2	6.8	17.7	11.1	6.6	17.2	7.8	9.4	23.2	11.3	11.9
Singapore	3.9	5.7	-1.8	5.2	7.0	-1.8	4.1	4.5	-0.4	5.0	5.8	-0.8
U.K.	1.9	5.7	-3.8	2.3	6.7	-4.4	3.0	4.9	-1.9	3.6	6.3	-2.7
France	3.4	6.8	-3.4	3.1	7.5	-4.4	1.0	5.4	-4.4	3.9	3.7	0.2

Sources: International Monetary Fund. *Direction of Trade Statistics Quarterly,* June 2000 and June 2001; U.S. Department of Commerce: China. Ministry of Foreign Trade and Economic Cooperation; PRC General Administration of Customs; Taiwan. Board of Foreign Trade; EU. European Union Delegation of the European Commission, *Eurostat;* Japan. Ministry of International Trade and Industry.

Table A5. U.S. Merchandise Trade Balances with Selected Asian Developing Nations, 1980-2001 (Million dollars)

Year	China	Indonesia	S. Korea	Malaysia	Philippines	Taiwan	Thailand
1980	2,593	-4,114	-17	-1,400	64	-3,146	221
1981	1,540	-5,149	-465	-807	-404	-4,453	3
1982	410	-2,565	-677	-248	-121	-5,434	-95
1983	-305	-4,212	-1,953	-529	-370	-7,714	-131
1984	-377	-4,674	-4,188	-9983	-913	-11,266	-381
1985	-373	-4,152	-4,992	-936	-959	-13,295	-804
1986	-2,135	-2,757	-7,588	-807	-805	-16,069	-1,018
1987	-3,422	-2,955	-10,326	-1,159	-898	-19,221	-904
1988	-4,237	-2,438	-10,578	-1,715	-1,069	-14,314	-1,739
1989	-7,094	-2,618	-7,115	-2,052	-1,102	-14,305	-2,343
1990	-11,488	-1,785	-4,888	-2,071	-1,151	-12,347	-2,597
1991	-14,018	-1,675	-2,224	-2,446	-1,439	-11,038	-2,693
1992	-19,943	-1,927	-2,732	-4,144	-1,870	-10,601	-3,944
1993	-24,927	-3,117	-3,003	-4,858	-1,646	-10,050	-5,214
1994	-32,076	-4,209	-2,346	-7,454	-2,137	-10,864	-5,938
1995	-36,772	-4,599	523	-9,162	-2,070	-10,863	-5,452
1996	-42,431	-4,778	3,286	-9,809	-2,372	-12,610	-4,587
1997	-53,026	-5,222	1,269	-7,695	-3,370	-13,331	-5,699
1998	-56,927	-7,042	-7,456	-10,043	-5,211	-14,960	-8,198
1999	-68,668	-7,575	-8,308	-12,349	-5,153	-16,077	-9,340
2000	-83,810	-7,839	-12,398	-14,573	-5,147	-16,134	-9,747
2001	-83,045	-7,605	-12,988	-12,956	-3,666	-15,239	-8,733

Source: U.S. Department of Commerce

Chapter 8

THE ANDEAN TRADE PREFERENCE ACT: BACKGROUND AND ISSUES FOR REAUTHORIZATION

J.F. Hornbeck

SUMMARY

Following passage by the 102nd Congress, President Bush signed into law the Andean Trade Preference Act (ATPA) on December 4, 1991 (P.L. 102-182, title II), making it part of a multifaceted strategy to counter illicit drug production and trade in Latin America. For ten years, it has provided preferential, mostly duty-free, treatment of selected U.S. imports from Bolivia, Columbia, Ecuador, and Peru. ATPA's goal has been to encourage growth of a more diversified Andean export base, thereby promoting development and providing an incentive for Andean farmers and other workers to pursue economic alternatives to the drug trade. ATPA expired on December 4, 2001 and U.S. tariffs were reimposed, but on February 15, 2002, President Bush acted to defer collection of these tariffs for 90 days. In the meantime, reauthorizing legislation (H.R. 3009) has been passed by the full House and by the Senate Finance Committee and is part of the broader 2002 trade agenda.

In considering the merits of ATPA, it is important to understand that its benefits have been shown to be quantitatively small. Because many imports are not eligible by law for preferential treatment or enter the United States under other preferential trade arrangements, only 10% of imports from ATPA countries enter the United States exclusively under the ATPA provisions. This has not changed in recent years, suggesting that ATPA's trade effects are unlikely to increase, unless the program's parameters are modified. Because the trade response is small, so too are ATPA's likely effects on the Andean economies.

Although the trade effects of ATPA have been relatively small, there is some indication that the composition of trade has changed and that, with a few products, a case can be made that ATPA has supported this change. It is possible that the slightly altered composition of U.S. imports from ATPA countries reflects broader change in what Andean countries are producing and that this in turn points to some indirect evidence that resources once used for drug-related activity are being redirected toward ATPA-eligible products. Isolating ATPA's role from other counternarcotics and economic diversification programs, however, has been a difficult challenge, producing imprecise estimates. Supporters of ATPA argue that its effects are evident and have proposed that it be reauthorized to reinforce the U.S. commitment to the alternative development counternarcotics strategy and that preferential treatment be extended to other Andean exports to broaden the program effects. Both the House and Senate versions of H.R. 3009 express the findings of Congress that extending and expanding trade preferences to ATPA countries is part of an effective U.S. foreign policy to counter illicit drug trafficking from the Andean region. To enhance the effects of ATPA, both bills provide for an extension of trade preferences into 2006 and cover exports previously excluded, including certain textile and apparel articles, canned tuna, watches and parts, petroleum, footwear, and selected leather bags and goods. Although ATPA may be only a small part of a large and long-term counternarcotics effort, expanding duty-free provisions of ATPA to include more exports in growth industries may have a marginal effect on the program's effectiveness.

INTRODUCTION

Following passage by the 102nd Congress, President George Bush signed into law the Andean Trade Preference Act (ATPA) on December 4, 1991 (P.L. 102-182, title II), making it part of a multifaceted strategy to counter illicit drug production and trade in Latin America. For ten years, it has provided preferential, mostly duty-free, treatment of selected U.S. imports from Bolivia, Colombia, Ecuador, and Peru. ATPA's goal has been to encourage growth of a more diversified Andean export base, thereby promoting development and providing an incentive for Andean farmers and other workers to pursue economic alternatives to the drug trade.

ATPA expired on December 4, 2001 and U.S. tariffs were reimposed on affected Andean exports. On February 15, 2002, the Bush Administration acted to defer collection of these tariffs for 90 days, in expectation that Congress would either reauthorize ATPA or temporarily extend the tariff provisions, presumably retroactively. In the meantime, reauthorizing legislation has been passed in the House and by the Senate Finance Committee and is part of a broader trade legislative agenda, including Trade Promotion Authority (TPA), under consideration in 2002.

AN OVERVIEW OF ATPA'S SCOPE AND IMPACT

ATPA was created as part of a broader Andean initiative to address the growing drug trade from Latin America. It provides zero or reduced tariffs on certain U.S. imports from Bolivia, Colombia, Ecuador, and Peru (see **Appendix 1** for program details) to complement crop eradication, interdiction, military training, and other counternarcotics efforts. In 1992, when the program was implemented, supporters expected that ATPA-induced export diversification and growth would encourage economic alternatives to coca production and other drug-related activity, with one estimate projecting as much as a three-fold increase in the U.S. imports from ATPA countries over a decade.[1]

Trade data alone, however, do not provide adequate measures of success, which should link a decline in drug activity with the expansion of ATPA supported industries. Indeed, there has been some movement on the drug front. For example, total coca cultivation has fallen by 13% from 1992 to 2000. This represents significant declines in Bolivia (68%) and Peru (74%), but an offsetting large increase in Colombia (267%). Little coca is grown in Ecuador.[2] Determining the role of ATPA tariff preferences in this trend, however, presents a difficult challenge because their effects must be isolated from other counternarcotics and economic development efforts.

Studies by the U.S. International Trade Commission (USITC) of ATPA's trade effects suggest that overall, the program has had a positive, but small influence on the volume and composition of U.S. imports from ATPA countries. For example, although total U.S. imports from ATPA countries on a dollar-value basis have grown 85% through the decade 1990-99, this is much less than some had hoped for and represents no growth of ATPA imports relative to U.S. import growth worldwide. Further, the composition of U.S. imports from Andean countries has changed only slightly in favor of products that are ATPA eligible. This suggests that there has been no major change in the production structure of ATPA economies, particularly in the biggest ATPA beneficiary, Colombia, which has actually experienced a large increase in coca production in the 1990s.

One of the most telling indicators of ATPA's limited influence is that *U.S. imports given preferential treatment exclusively under ATPA represent only 10% of total imports from the four eligible countries*.[3] This represents a small percentage of trade and has not grown thus far in the life of the program. Without legislative change to the ATPA program, a larger response may be limited in the short run by the Andean export sector's dependence on a limited number of natural-resource based products and simple manufactures, ATPA's program exclusion of many major Andean products (e.g. petroleum products, textiles, certain leather goods), and the fact that many products are already eligible for duty-free or preferential treatment under other trade arrangements.

In short, as discussed below, although there may have been a positive response to the ATPA preferential tariff provisions, the overall impact has been small and operates at the margin of Andean trade. Similarly, the tariff preferences have little effect on the United States economy, suggesting the cost of these preferences is low.

U.S.-ATPA COUNTRY TRADE

Colombia and Bolivia qualified as ATPA beneficiaries in mid-1992, with Ecuador and Peru following one year later. Since then, aggregate U.S. trade with ATPA countries has remained small and has grown in line, more or less, with the average for U.S. trade

---

[1] For more on early expectations, see: CRS Report 92-172 F, *The Andean Drug Initiative: Background and Issues for Congress*, by Raphael F. Perl. February 13, 1992, p. 3.

[2] United States Department of State. Bureau for International Narcotics and Law Enforcement Affairs. *International Narcotics Control Strategy Report (INCSR)*. March 2001. pp. II-11 and II-21.

[3] U.S. International Trade commission. *Andean Trade Preference Act: Impact on U.S. Industries and Consumers and on Drug Crop Eradication and Crop Substitution*. Seventh Report 1999. Publication No. 3358, September 2000. p. 34.

worldwide. For the decade 1990 to 2000, U.S. exports to ATPA countries rose 84%, less than total export growth (see **Appendix 2** for aggregate trade data.) Relative to the rest of the world, U.S. exports to ATPA countries have declined slightly to less than 1% of total exports, although there was an upward trend in the mid-1990s. U.S. imports from ATOA countries, although rising by 105% in dollar terms from 1990 to 2000, also declined slightly on a relative basis to less than 1% of total U.S. world imports.

In addition to trade volume, another indicator of ATPA's possible effects is change in the composition of ATPA imports. **Figure 1** contrasts the composition of U.S. imports from ATPA countries between 1994 and 2000. Because 1994 is the first full year all four countries participated, it provides a base for comparison since it is unlikely to reflect large changes in the trade composition due to ATPA given that insufficient time had passed for industries to have responded fully.[4]

Figure 1. U.S. Imports from ATPA Countries by Product Category

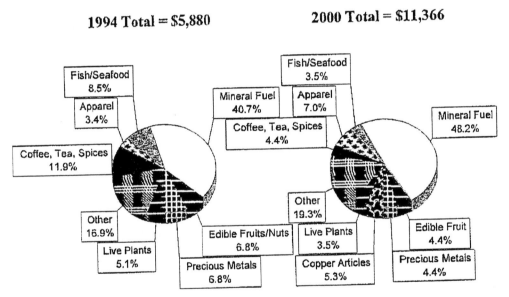

1994 Total = $5,880   **2000 Total = $11,366**

Source: CRS graph based on U.S. International Trade Commission and Department of Commerce data.

For 2000, the major U.S. imports (approximately 80% of the ATPA countries total), by harmonized tariff schedule (HTS) chapter were: HTS 27, mineral fuels (81% of which is crude oil); HTS 71, precious stones and metals (43% gold); HTS 09, spices, coffee, and tea (99% coffee); HTS 08, edible fruit and nuts (91% bananas); HTS 03, fish and seafood (69% crustaceans or shrimp); HTS 61 and 62, knit and woven apparel (73% sweaters, shirts, and

---

[4] 1994 data from the U.S. International Trade Commission. *Andean Trade Preference Act: Impact on U.S. Industries and Consumers and on Drug Crop Eradication and Crop Substitution.* Seventh Report 1999, Publication 2995. September 1996, p. 8. Data for 2000 originated from the U.S. Department of Commerce as reported in World Trade Atlas.

suits); HTS 06, live plants and trees (99% cut flowers); and HTS 74, copper articles (94% unwrought refined and alloy.)

A comparison of the two years suggests that on a broad product category basis, the composition of U.S. imports from eligible countries has changed only marginally since the ATPA program began. Most notable has been the addition of Peru's refined copper cathode imports, which began in 1995 and are ATPA eligible. Petroleum products, which are not eligible for ATPA tariff preferences, remain a large portion of imports, but come predominantly from Colombia. There has been a contrasting relative decline in seafood and coffee imports.

In general, the minimal change in the U.S. import composition reflects three factors. First, most U.S. imports from ATPA countries are natural-resource based products (petroleum, gold, fish, coffee, bananas, cut flowers) or simple manufactures (knit apparel, sweaters, shirts, suits, copper cathodes), many of which are not ATPA eligible. This trend is likely to continue regardless of ATPA reauthorization. Second, the continuing large portion of oil imports on a dollar-value basis in 2000 continues to skew import figures, reflecting in part the worldwide surge in oil prices. Third, Colombia stands out as the dominant ATPA trade pattern, accounting for 62% of total U.S. imports from the group in 2000, followed by Peru and Ecuador, both with 18%, and Bolivia trailing with only 2%.[5]

Given that the relative size and composition of ATPA imports, variables expected to reflect the program's effects, have not changed much during the course of the program, little trade effect seems attributable to the ATPA provisions. A closer look at the trade data at the sectoral level supports this conclusion until the data are further disaggregated by duty treatment and product type. These trends are in keeping with economic reasoning that would suggest a program such as ATPA would not affect the overall structure of trade, but might alter the composition of ATPA imports at the margin and within very specific product categories.

Imports from ATPA Countries by Duty Status[6]

To determine which products are benefiting from ATPA, it is necessary to ascertain what portion would have entered duty-free *exclusively* because of their ATPA eligibility. Many imports qualify unconditionally as duty-free under general tariff rates (e.g. coffee) or through other favorable tariff arrangements such as the Generalized System of Preferences (GSP) or production sharing provisions and can enter under more than one of these arrangements. For example, some products eligible to enter under GSP come in under ATPA. As shown in **table 1**, when these products are subtracted, it turns out that imports eligible exclusively for ATPA preferences represented only 10% of total imports from the ATPA countries.[7] The table contrasts selected Andean country import data in 1995 and 1999 to reflect changes that may have occurred during a time when the ATPA program was in full force. Duty-free imports rose from 59% of total imports in 1995 to 66% in 1999, but because the ATPA-only category

---

[5] U.S. International Trade Commission, *Andean Trade Preference Act,* September 2000, p. 14.
[6] For this section, it was necessary to rely on specialized data produced by the International Trade Commission, which has not been updated for 2000.
[7] Estimates by USITC, ibid, p. 34. It should be noted that the 10% figure was higher during the mid-1990s when the GSP program lapsed on a few occasions, causing greater reliance on the ATPA provisions.

is unchanged, the increase appears due entirely to non-ATPA trade arrangements (general rates, GSP, production-sharing arrangements, or other smaller programs).

Table 1. Duty Status of U.S. Imports from ATPA Countries
(1995 and 1999 in $ millions)

Duty Status	Bolivia	Colombia	Ecuador	Peru	Total	% of Total
1995 Total Imports:	256.8	3,807.4	1,929.2	965.4	6,958.7	100%
Dutiable	19.0	1,717.0	756.6	360.5	2,853.1	41%
Duty-Free	237.8	2,090.4	1,172.7	604.7	4,105.6	59%
(ATPA only)*	Na	Na	Na	Na	699.0	10%
(Other Duty-Free)**	Na	Na	Na	Na	3,406.6	49%
1999 Total Imports:	216.8	5,475.2	1,798.6	1,781.8	9,273.6	100%
Dutiable	40.1	2,059.3	587.8	450.6	3,137.8	34%
Duty-Free	176.7	3,417.1	1,210.8	1,331.2	6,135.8	66%
(ATPA only)*	Na	Na	Na	Na	939.0	10%
(Other Duty-Free)**	Na	Na	Na	Na	5,196.8	56%

Na = not available, per discussion with USITC.
Includes value of both duty-free and reduced-duty ATPA imports. Reduced-duty imports amounted to only 0.3% of total imports from ATPA countries in both years and so are not shown separately.
** Includes all other imports that entered the United States duty-free: 1) under general rates; 2) under non-ATPA programs (e.g. Generalized System of Preferences (GSP) or production sharing provision) and/or; 3) under ATPA, but eligible to enter duty free under another program.
Data source: U.S. International Trade Commission. *Andean Trade Preference Act: Impact on U.S. Industries and Consumers and on Drug Crop Eradication and Crop Substitution.* Publication No. 3358, September 2000. Pp. 17 and 34.

The 10% figure is important because it shows first that the amount of imports entering duty-free exclusively under ATPA is a small portion of trade and second that, over the life of the program, ATPA-eligible imports as a group have not grown any faster than U.S. imports from the four Andean countries as a whole. This is unlikely to change in the short run without legislative action given that many imports already enter the United States duty free, other big items, such as petroleum and textile products, are not eligible for duty-free treatment, and economic diversification into new (ATPA-eligible) areas is a slow process.

Imports from ATPA Countries by Product Level

The major products entering the United States under ATPA appear in **table 2** in descending order of importance. Between 1995 and 1999, cut flowers, most of which come from Colombia, were the largest import item. Copper cathodes from Peru grew to become the second largest ATPA import, rising in 1999 to nearly 19% of the total on a dollar-value basis. Precious metals, mostly jewelry and gold products from Peru, are the third largest import group, comprising some 11% of the total. Colombian pigments (9%), Ecuadorian non-canned tuna (5%), and Peruvian zinc (5%) round out the major ATPA imports.

Table 2. Major U.S. Imports Entering Under ATPA (1995 and 1999, in percent)

HTS*	Article	% 1995	% 1999	Beneficiary Country
06	Live Plants (cut flowers)	39.6	25.0	Colombia – 80% Ecuador – 20%
74	Copper articles (cathodes)	2.9	18.9	Peru – 100%
71	Precious metals (jewelry/gold products)	18.9	10.7	Peru – 70% Bolivia – 30%
32	Pigments	0.3	9.3	Colombia – 100%
16	Tuna (non-canned)	4.2	5.0	Ecuador – 99% Colombia – 1%
79	Zinc	0.8	4.8	Peru – 100%
	Other	33.3	26.3	
	Total	100.0	100.0	

*HTS = harmonized tariff schedule chapter.
Data source: USITC, *Andean Trade Preference Act,* September 2000, pp. 16-24, D-3.

The composition of ATPA imports has changed some over the life of the program, but not in clearly predictable ways. Cut flowers, for example, which remain the largest U.S. import item on a dollar basis, have actually fallen from nearly 40% to 24% of total ATPA imports, reflecting falling demand in the United States for cut flowers and growth in other ATPA imports such as copper cathodes and pigments, which represent new U.S. imports since the ATPA program began. Although there has been a large increase in zinc products coming in under ATPA, this growth is partially due to a shift in duty treatment of zinc products, which previously entered the United States duty-free under the GSP provisions.[8]

The benefits of ATPA fall in line with the overall trade importance of the countries. In 1999, Colombia and Peru benefited most and had 45% and 36% of the dollar value of ATPA imports, respectively. Colombia's percentage has fallen slightly since 1995, reflecting a decline in cut flower imports, offset some by an increase in U.S. pigment imports. Peru is the fastest growing exporter under ATPA, reflecting its new copper cathode manufacturing industry. Ecuador accounted for 15% of ATPA imports in 1999, followed by Bolivia with only 4%. Ecuador accounts for most of the tuna imports and a small portion of cut flowers. Bolivia exports mostly gold jewelry items, which is the only major ATPA item it produces.[9]

Overall, the ATPA trade effects a-pear to be relatively small. Nonetheless, at the product level there has been some indication of a change in trade composition with new products coming on line, at least in part to take advantage of ATPA's duty-free provisions. This reflects some level of Andean economic diversification, but not a net growth in the amount of Andean exports eligible under ATPA on a relative basis. Given that total imports eligible exclusively under ATPA have remained at 10% of total U.S. imports from these countries, it appears that gains in some industries or products have been offset by declines in others.

---

[8] Ibid., pp. 23-24.
[9] Ibid., pp. 24-26, D-3. Bolivia also exports small amounts of wood products under ATPA.

ATPA PROGRAM EFFECTS: ANDEAN AND U.S. RESPONSES

An evaluation of ATPA should indicate how any changes in trade patterns are affecting the economies of the Andean countries and the United States. Two studies required by the ATPA legislation tackle these questions. First, the U.S. International Trade Commission ATPA report evaluates both the Andean and U.S. responses to ATPA. The U.S. Department of Labor produces a separate targeted evaluation of ATPA's effects on U.S. workers. Both point to the marginal effects of ATPA on the economies of participating countries and the United States.

ATPA's Economic Effects on the Andean Countries

Although the trade effects of ATPA have been relatively small, there is some indication that the composition of trade has changed and that, with a few products, a case can be made that ATPA has contributed to this change. It is possible that the altered composition of U.S. imports from ATPA countries reflects broader change in what Andean countries are producing and that this in turn points to some indirect evidence that ATPA-eligible products are being substituted for illicit coca.[10]

It is difficult to gauge the effects of ATPA on national economies because the program has a small effect relative to other variables. National macroeconomic policies, particularly in countries undergoing long-term economic reform, have a much larger effect on economic trends. Domestic Andean government policies also support crop substitution, the effects of which are not easily distinguishable from those of ATPA. In effect, they work together. External shocks to the region's economies, such as repeated el Ninos and other natural phenomena, have devastating effects on the agricultural sector that easily overshadow incremental policy shifts like ATPA. Isolating the marginal effects of ATPA, therefore, is an imprecise exercise.[11]

Bolivia and Peru

In its 2000 report, the USITC used Bolivia and Peru as case studies to explore the possibility of a link between ATPA program effects and changes in economic production. Bolivia showed some diversification in exports to the United States that coincided with ATPA. In the mid-1990s, there was a marked expansion of jewelry and, to a lesser extent, leather and wood product exports that may be related to ATPA, but other domestic policy changes (e.g. the tax code) also affected production incentives for these goods. After 1996, however, this export growth trend slowed. In Peru, a broader array of export growth was discernable over the past decade, with a noticeable increase in copper cathodes and agricultural products, especially asparagus, all of which benefit from ATPA. Asparagus also stands out because it is grown near traditional coca cultivation areas and is presumed to be an alternative cash crop, at least in part encouraged by ATPA provisions.[12]

---

[10] The USITC also points out that the benefits of ATPA to eligible countries is declining as the "margin of preference" declines for various reasons, such as the continuing phase-in of other trade agreement tariff rate cuts from the Uruguay Round, as well as sectoral and regional agreements. For details, see: ibid., pp. 33.

[11] Ibid., pp. 53 and 55.

[12] Ibid., pp. 55 and 62.

Colombia and Ecuador

In its 1999 report, the USITC evaluated ATPA's impact on Colombia and Ecuador. Of the ATPA-eligible products from Colombia over the past decade, cut flowers have increased the most as a proportion of U.S. imports, but overall, the composition of Colombia's exports to the United States has not changed dramatically since ATPA began, in part because of the dominance of petroleum. Other nontraditional products, such as asparagus, do present some potential for increased benefits from ATPA, but overall its benefits are considered small. Ecuador has a similar profile, with little change in the composition of exports to the United States, but some credit significant increases in the production of cut flowers and seafood, both of which benefit from ATPA, with encouraging export diversification. The overall effect is still small given the myriad variables that affect production capabilities and decisions.[13]

Coca Eradication and Crop Substitution

Alternative crop production is a critical component of the coca eradication effort underway in the Andes. Although there is some indirect evidence to suggest that crop substitution is occurring, it is small overall and the effect of ATPA on this process is marginal at best. Whereas larger substitution effects may be linked to the cut flower industry in Colombia, there are many factors that allowed such alternatives to exist before ATPA was even conceived. All the evidence points to ATPA's supportive, but relatively small effect, particularly given the magnitude of the problem and the comprehensive effort needed to address the drug trade. For example, numerous obstacles impede the alternative development strategy including the high profitability of coca production, lack of physical infrastructure required to support alternative cash crops, and overt, often violent, guerrilla pressure to reject the program.[14]

ATPA's Economic Effects on the United States

Although ATPA was created to influence the economic landscape of the Andean region, Congress also requested analysis of how changes in trade patterns related to ATPA might affect the United States. The USITC looks at three basic issues: 1) consumer welfare gains from lower-priced imports; 2) the offsetting tariff revenue losses; and 3) producer welfare losses (production displacement). The U.S. Department of Labor produces a separate report dealing solely with ATPA's effects on the domestic labor force.

Changes in Trade Composition

Given that only a very small share of U.S. imports are involved in the ATPA program, its effects on the aggregate U.S. economy are negligible. Therefore, measuring the gains and losses to the U.S. economy must be done at the product/industry level. In 1999, copper cathodes, cut flowers (roses and chrysanthemums), tuna, and gold compounds together accounted for 83% of total imports that benefited exclusively from the ATPA provisions. Copper cathodes and cut flowers each contributed to approximately one-third of the ATPA-

---

[13] U.S. International Trade commission. *Andean Trade Preference Act: Sixth Report 1998.* USITC publication 3234, September 1999, pp. 106, 11-14, 118, 120-22.

[14] Wilson, Scott. Colombia's Anti-Drug Plan Fuels Fight in Coca Country. *The Washington Post*, October 14, 2000, p. A14 and DeYoung, Karen. Colombia Plan Faces 'Crunch Time.' *The Washington Post*, December 22, 2000, p. A35.

exclusive imports. Hence, an analysis of the benefits and displacement costs related to these products covers most of the effects ATPA has on the U.S. economy.[15]

Consumer Welfare and Tariff Effects

USITC market share data showed that ATPA-imported copper cathodes, although growing briskly, still accounted for only 7.4% of the U.S. market in 1999 and imported gold compounds claimed only 6.7%. Cut flowers, by contrast, accounted for up to 75% of the U.S. market. Based on a partial equilibrium analysis, the USITC estimated that the consumer welfare effects in all three cases were, nonetheless, small. In the first two, market-penetration was simply too small, but even in the case of Colombia's dominance of the U.S. cut flower market, the USITC suggests that U.S. consumers would have paid only 5.5% more for flowers than they would have in the absence of ATPA. In addition, the consumer benefits were offset, in many cases, by reduced tariff revenues. The net welfare effects for the United States as a whole, therefore, were considered small.[16]

Producer Welfare Effects

Of greater concern to many are ATPA's effects on U.S. producers. To the extent that ATPA encourages a marginal increase in imports, those industries in the United States that produce competing products are potentially "displaced" from the market. Given market share figures, the USITC found that only cut flowers and asparagus caused "displacement" of over 5% of the market. Asparagus imports are small and enter during the late summer and fall months when domestic crop production is low and so have a clear benefit to U.S. consumers. Because they do not directly compete with the U.S. growing season, however, they are not a primary target for concern over displacement.[17]

Cut flower imports have been a greater concern, but as the USITC points out, Colombia, the major flower exporter, had established its market dominance before ATPA, and the U.S. growers had already responded by differentiating their products. The overall impact of ATPA flower imports is deemed small given domestic industry adjustment. One indication that U.S. flower growers are no longer seriously concerned with competition from Andean imports is their decision to discontinue pursuing antidumping and countervailing duty remedies as of May and October 1999, respectively. In short, should ATPA tariff preferences be eliminated, it appears there would be little effect on the domestic cut flower industry.[18]

The U.S. Department of Labor (DOL) reports targets ATPA's impact on the domestic work force. It concluded that the overall effects of ATPA in 1998 were negligible given the strong U.S. economy and employment picture, and the fact that ATPA-eligible imports were so small that their effect on aggregate U.S. employment was virtually unmeasurable.[19] Based on an analysis of products that entered the United States duty free exclusively from ATPA provisions, the Department of Labor argued that only the cut flower industry was likely to have presented any adjustment problem. U.S. cut flower production had fallen by 11% in 1998 as ATPA imports rose, perhaps suggesting that ATPA may have had some effect on the industry's contraction, but the Department of Labor report is quick to note that other factors

---

[15] U.S. International Trade Commission, *Andean Trade Preference Act*, September 2000, pp. 36-37.
[16] Ibid., pp. 38 and 45.
[17] Ibid., p. 38.
[18] Ibid., p. 43.
[19] U.S. Department of Labor. Bureau of International Labor Affairs. *Trade and Employment Effects of the Andean Trade Preference Act.* Sixth Annual Report to Congress, by Robert C. Shelburne. 1999. p. 14.

may have affected cost competitiveness of the U.S. cut flower industry, such as complying with worker protection standards, and that in any case, their estimates were not precise.[20]

Of the workers potentially affected by layoffs in the flower industry, the DOL noted that all were seasonal agricultural workers who experience periods of unemployment, have a very low wage level, and live predominantly in poverty. Some 43% were estimated to be of "illegal, temporary, or unknown legal status." DOL did not estimate the "degree of adjustment difficulty," but noted that the strong U.S. economy should be able to minimize any employment dislocation that might occur. Adjustment costs faced by other industries from increased import competition from ATPA were considered insignificant.[21]

OUTLOOK AND LEGISLATION IN THE 107TH CONGRESS

ATPA is only a small part of the larger Andean counternarcotics effort. Coca production is the primary target of these efforts and because it is a highly profitable undertaking and particularly enticing for poor areas of the world, a key element of the strategy is supporting the cultivation of alternative cash crops.[22] ATPA's supporters argue that reduced tariffs conceivably play a part of the "alternative development" strategy by providing an additional financial incentive to substitute legal crops for coca cultivation. The increase in non-agricultural exports (e.g. copper cathodes), it could be argued, may also reflect, in part, ATPA's preferential tariff treatment.

Testimony before congressional committees has expressed the desire by groups in the United States and the Andean countries to reauthorize ATPA and consider expanding the tariff preferences to more products and countries. These views have been summarized before Congress by the Bush Administration as well, which has represented ATPA as achieving its goal of promoting "export diversification and broad-based economic development that provides sustainable economic alternatives to drug-crop production in the Andean region."[23]

In considering the merits of ATPA, it is important to understand that the benefits it provides are quantitatively small. ATPA's influence should be visible in the changing composition of U.S. imports, which has so far been marginal. Because many imports are not eligible by law for duty-free treatment or enter the United States under other preferential trade arrangements, only 10% of ATPA country imports enter the United States exclusively under the ATPA provisions. This has not changed in recent years, suggesting that ATPA's effect on trade is unlikely to increase, unless the program's parameters are modified.

Because the trade response is small, so too are ATPA's likely effects on the Andean economies. Still, indirect evidence suggests that it may have supported economic diversification into products such as copper cathodes and asparagus. Asparagus, for example, is being cultivated in larger quantities near traditional coca producing regions. Although an encouraging sign, given the high profitability of coca and active resistance by both armed guerrilla groups and peasants, there are limits to what ATPA may be expected to accomplish

---

[20] Ibid., p. 10. The DOL report covers 1998 and so does not reflect the fact that in 1999 the cut flower industry representatives dropped interest in antidumping and countervailing duty investigations, suggesting doubt in their ability to make a strong case that the industry is being materially harmed by ATPA-eligible imports.

[21] Ibid., pp. 11-14.

[22] U.S. Department of State, *International Narcotics Control Strategy Report (INCSR)*, pp. IV-6, 18, 27, 37.

[23] Testimony of Ambassador Peter Allgeier, Deputy United States Trade Representative, before the Senate Committee on Finance, Subcommittee on International Trade. August 3, 2001. p. 1.

and it is not clear that there is a strong direct link between increased ATPA-eligible exports and any verifiable diminished drug-related activity.

In addition to the economic analysis, the debate over ATPA will likely consider more intangible policy benefits. For example, supporters argue that ATPA is an expression of direct U.S. support for the regional counternarcotics efforts with potentially positive side benefits in the area of economic development. They also note that it is a less expensive and invasive counter-drug option compared to the large financial and military commitment of Plan Colombia.

Supporters of ATPA have proposed at least three program initiatives. First, reauthorize ATPA for an extended period of time to reinforce the U.S. commitment to the alternative development counternarcotics strategy. Second, extend duty-free treatment to other Andean exports, such as textile and apparel products, to broaden the program effects, particularly in Colombia, which remains the most problematic country. Third, include Venezuela as a beneficiary country, which although not currently a major coca producer, is part of the larger drug trafficking problem.

Legislation in the 107th Congress

On December 4, 2001, ATPA expired and U.S. tariffs were reimposed on affected Andean exports. On February 15, 2002, the Bush Administration acted to defer the collection of these tariffs for 90 days in expectation that the 107th Congress would either reauthorize ATPA or provide a short-term extension of its trade preferences, presumably retroactively. In the meantime, ATPA reauthorizing legislation has moved in both the House and the Senate.

In the House, H.R. 3009, the Andean Trade Promotion and Drug Eradication Act was introduced on October 3, 2001 by Representative Crane (for himself and Ways and Means Chairman Thomas). Hearings were held by the House Ways and Means committee on October 5, 2001. Chairman Thomas offered an amendment in the nature of a substitute and the committee ordered the bill favorably reported, as amended, by voice vote. On November 14, 2001, the bill was reported to the House (H. Rept. 107-290). On November 16, 2001, the House Rules Committee reported (H. Rept. 107-293) the rule (H. Res. 289) for consideration of H.R. 3009 by a vote of 225 to 191. H.R. 3009 was passed by the House the same day by voice vote.

In the Senate, S. 525, the Andean Trade Preference Expansion Act (ATPEA) was introduced by Senator Graham on March 13, 2001 and referred to the Committee on Finance. The Subcommittee on International Trade held hearings on August 3, 2001. The amended House-passed version of H.R. 3009 was also sent to the Senate on November 16, 2001, where it was referred to the Committee on Finance. Full committee consideration and mark up occurred on November 29, 2001, and by voice vote, the language of S. 525, with some modifications, was offered in the nature of a substitute for H.R. 3009, which was adopted, along with three amendments, and reported to the full Senate (S. Rept. 107-126). The Senate is not expected to act on the bill before March 2002.

Both the House and Senate versions of H.R. 3009 express the findings of Congress that extending and expanding trade preferences to ATPA countries is part of an effective U.S. foreign policy to counter illicit drug trafficking from the Andean region. To enhance the effects of ATPA, both bills provide for an extension of trade preferences into 2006 and cover exports previously excluded, including certain textile and apparel articles, canned tuna, watches and parts, petroleum, footwear, and selected leather bags and goods (see discussion below). These provisions provide treatment similar to that received by Caribbean countries under the Caribbean Basin Trade Promotion Act (CBTPA). There is a new emphasis on giving preferential treatment to articles made from regional fabrics, an important provision for Peru, which produces much of its yarn locally from alpaca, llama, and vicuna. Both bills include a longer list of country eligibility requirements and expanded transshipment and safeguard provisions to address concerns of U.S. apparel manufacturers.

House-Passed Version

The House-passed version of H.R. 3009 would extend preferential treatment to articles from ATPA beneficiary countries through December 31, 2006. Duty-free treatment would be expanded to cover five of eight categories of articles previously excluded, provided the countries meet new enhanced eligibility standards and the President of the United States does not declare any of the products "import sensitive" for purposes of this act. New non-apparel articles to be made eligible include: 1) certain footwear not eligible under the Generalized System of Preferences (GSP); 2) petroleum products; 3) watches and watch parts; 4) selected leather goods (including certain handbags, gloves, flat goods, luggage); and 5) tuna preserved in any airtight container (canned). Three categories of articles will remain ineligible for preferential treatment: 1) textiles subject to textile agreements and apparel products not specifically mentioned below; 2) sugar and related products; and 3) rum and tafia.[24]

The number of apparel articles that would receive duty-free treatment would be expanded based on various product categories differentiated by origin of fabric, yarn, and components used. Specifically, this section includes articles sewn or otherwise assembled from materials from one or more beneficiary countries that fall into the following categories:[25]

1. fabric components formed, or components knit-to-shape, in the United States from yarns formed in the United States or one or more beneficiary countries;
2. fabrics or fabric components formed, or components knit-to-shape, in one or more beneficiary countries, from yarns formed in one or more beneficiary countries, if such fabrics are formed chief in weight of llama or alpaca;
3. fabrics or yarn not produced in the United States or a beneficiary country, but are eligible for preferential treatment under the North American Free Trade Agreement (NAFTA) short-supply provisions (Annex 401);
4. apparel articles sewn or otherwise assembled in one or more beneficiary countries from fabrics or fabric components formed or components knit-to-shape, in a beneficiary country from yarns formed in the United States or in one or more beneficiary countries, whether or not the apparel articles are also made from any of the fabrics, fabric components formed, or components knit-to-shape in the United

---

[24] The bill would also amend the Caribbean Basin Trade Promotion Act and the African Growth and Opportunity Act to clarify congressional intent regarding various draft Customs regulations and addressing duty-free and quota-free treatment of, among other products, knit-to-shape articles and apparel articles that are cut both in the United States and the beneficiary countries. These provisions are not included in the Senate bill. See: U.S. Congress. House of Representatives. *Andean Trade Promotion and Drug Eradication Act.* Report 107-290 to accompany H.R. 3009. November 14, 2001. pp. 6-8 and 18-21.

[25] In paragraphs 1, 3, and 4 below, fabrics eligible for duty-free treatment include fabrics not from yarns if classified under HTS 5602 and 5603, referring to felt. This provision does not appear in the Senate Version. Ibid., pp. 3 and 12-13.

States defined in paragraph 1 above. Imports of apparel made from regional fabric and yarn would be capped at 3% of U.S. imports, growing to 6% of U.S. imports in 2006.

In addition, this act allows for duty-free importation of handloomed, handmade, and folklore articles, clarifies and enhances penalties for transshipment of apparel goods through the Andean countries, and provides for NAFTA-equivalent safeguard protections related to apparel imports. It also expands requirem3ents for becoming eligible as a beneficiary country to include, in addition to previously defined requirements: undertaking obligations set out in the World Trade Organization (WTO); participating in negotiations to complete the Free Trade Area of the Americas (FTAA); providing protection of intellectual property rights; adhering to internationally recognized worker rights; committing to eliminating the worst forms of child labor; meeting counternarcotics certification criteria; becoming party to the Inter-American Convention Against Corruption; and applying transparent, nondiscriminatory, and competitive procedures to government procurement.

Senate Finance Committee-Passed Version
The Senate Finance Committee-passed version (the Andean Trade Preference Expansion Act – ATPEA) agrees in principal with much of the House-passed version, but is slightly more restrictive in some product categories. It would extend the program through February 28, 2006 or until the FTAA is enacted, whichever comes first, and would expand coverage to most of the same products identified in the House bill.

Non-apparel provisions vary slightly or are worded differently from the House version. Of the eight categories of goods not eligible for preferential treatment under current expired law, five would receive tariff treatment equal to that under NAFTA, or a zero tariff if the products are so treated under different trade laws (e.g. the GSP or CBTPA): 1) selected footwear; 2) petroleum products; 3) watches and watch parts; 4) selected leather goods; and 5) rum and tafia products. Except for rum products this is similar to the House provisions. One category, sugars, syrups, and molasses, remains ineligible for trade preferences as in the House version. A second category, tuna prepared in airtight containers, is given duty-free treatment like the House version, but the Senate places a cap on this type of tuna import equal to 20% of U.S. production in the previous year and requires tuna to be harvested by U.S. or ATPEA beneficiary country vessels.[26]

Finally, textile and apparel articles are treated separately and in detail, allowing certain goods into the United States duty-free based on the origin of fabric, yarn, or components used. Apparel provisions are similar to those in the House bill, with a few exceptions. There are six categories of apparel products that would qualify for duty-free treatment. The first is similar to the House version and includes articles sewn or otherwise assembled from one or more beneficiary countries if so done with materials that fall into any of the following categories:

---

[26] This is one of three amendments made to the bill. The other two do not relate directly to ATPA. They include waiving restrictions on duty-free imports on fans from Thailand through July 30, 2002 and suspending from January 1, 2002 through December 31, 2006 duties imposed on selected steam or other vapor generating boilers used in nuclear facilities. See: U.S. Congress. Senate. *Andean Trade Preference Expansion Act.* Report 107-126 to Accompany H.R. 3009. December 14, 2001. pp. 6, 12, and 20.

1. U.S. fabric, or fabric components, or components knit-to-shape, from yarns wholly formed in the United States;
2. 2) a combination of both U.S. and ATPEA beneficiary country components knit-to-shape from yarns wholly formed in the United States;
3. 3) ATPEA beneficiary country fabric, fabric components, or knit-to-shape components, made from yarns wholly formed in one or more ATPEA beneficiary countries, if the constituent fibers are primarily llama, alpaca, or vicuna hair; and
4. fabrics or yarns regardless of origin, if such fabrics or yarns have been deemed, under NAFTA, not to be widely available in commercial quantities in the United States (short supply provisions).

The second duty-free category includes apparel articles knit-to-shape (except socks) in an ATPEA country from yarns wholly formed in the United States. The third category includes apparel articles wholly assembled in an ATPEA country from fabric or fabric components knit, or components knit-to-shape in an ATPEA country from yarns wholly formed in the United States, with an annual cap set on quantity imported and increased each year. The fourth category includes brassieres that are cut or sewn, or otherwise assembled, in the United States and/or one or more ATPEA country. The fifth category captures "handloomed, handmade, and folklore" articles, to be defined jointly by the United States and the beneficiary countries. The sixth category includes textile luggage assembled in an ATPEA country from fabric and yarns formed in the United States.

Like the House version, the Senate language also includes stronger transshipment penalties for infractions related to apparel products, and adopts safeguard provisions on apparel goods similar to those found in NAFTA, both of which also are found in the CBTPA. Country eligibility requirements are also lengthened in similar fashion to those found in the House bill (see **Appendix 1** for current program requirements).

Discussion of Proposed Legislative Changes

Supporters of the apparel provisions would argue that they serve multiple purposes, they: 1) provide similar tariff treatment to ATPA, NAFTA, and CBTPA countries, thereby eliminating the relative competitive disadvantage of ATPA countries; 2) deepen coverage of the ATPA tariff program to include products that compose a larger portion of Andean exports and hence improve the chances for greater impact on their trade diversification, economic development, and counterdrug activity; 3) encourage increased U.S. investment in ATPA countries; and, 4) take into account possible negative repercussions to domestic apparel manufacturers.[27]

Although it is possible that the ATPA countries will respond to these additional incentives, countries will not benefit equally. In dollar terms, Colombia may benefit the most because it has the largest share of U.S. apparel imports from ATPA countries (49% in 2000). Peru, which constituted 46% of U.S. apparel imports from these countries, uses mostly non-U.S. materials and so has lobbied for removing restrictions on use of local fabrics and yarns. It would benefit significantly if such language remains in the final version of H.R. 3009. Ecuador and Bolivia have small apparel export industries, each accounting for only 2% of the

---

[27] For more details, see: U.S. International Trade Commission. Apparel: Andean Countries Seek Parity with Caribbean Basin Countries to Remain Competitive in U.S. Market. *Industry Trade and Technology Review*, march 2001. pp. 9-13.

ATPA country apparel exports to the United States.[28] (Ecuador is a major tuna exporter and so would benefit to extent that restrictions on canned tuna are reduced or eliminated.)

Some groups in the United States challenge the expansion of ATPA provisions, arguing that the benefits to Andean countries may come at a cost to domestic industries. Apparel is a high profile U.S. import commodity group from the region. The U.S. industry is also facing an increasingly competitive environment worldwide. Therefore, domestic U.S. producers have expressed opposition to these legislative changes.

Overall, however, apparel products accounted for only 7% of U.S. imports from ATPA countries in 2000, although this percentage has doubled since 1994 (see **figure 1**). Also, ATPA apparel imports accounted for less than 2% of the total sector's U.S. imports in 2000. Still, the United States is the primary market for Andean apparel, capturing 93% of the region's apparel exports.[29] Although ATPA may still be only a small part of a large and long-term counternarcotics effort, expanding duty-free provisions of ATPA to a larger portion of the region's exports, including its growth industries, may have a marginal positive effect on the program's effectiveness.

APPENDIX 1. ATPA PROGRAM DETAILS

The ATPA program has two major facets. First, each of the four Andean nations must be designated a "beneficiary country" by meeting legislated standards.[30] Beneficiary status can be denied if a country: 1) is a Communist country; 2) unfairly nationalizes or expropriates U.S. property, tangible or intellectual, without due recourse or commitment for compensation; 3) fails to act in good faith in recognizing arbitral awards in favor of U.S. citizens or companies; 4) affords preferential treatment to products from other developed countries that may have a significant impact on U.S. commerce; 5) has a government entity that fails to follow copyright agreements for broadcast materials; 6) is not a signatory to an agreement providing for the extradition of U.S. citizens; or 7) is not taking steps to afford internationally recognized workers rights as in the Trade Act of 1974. All conditions, except 4 and 6, may be waived by the President if conferring beneficiary status is deemed in the economic or security interests of the United States. The President is also required to consider other factors, among them the prospective beneficiary country's: 1) interest in ATPA; 2) economic conditions and development policies; 3) trade policies and practices complying with rules defined in the World Trade Organization (WTO) agreement; and 4) efforts to meet the narcotics cooperation certification criteria.

Second, eligible articles must be imported directly from a beneficiary country. The content of materials and processing costs originating in CBTPA or ATPA beneficiary countries, Puerto Rico, the Virgin Islands and up to 15 percentage points of U.S. origin value must sum to at least 35% of the value of the article when it enters the United States. Many products are denied duty-free treatment, including textile and apparel products subject to

---

[28] Ibid., pp. 2-7 and 9-10.
[29] Ibid, p. 2.
[30] P.L. 102-182, title II, sec. 203, as amended (19 U.S.C. 3202). Because these benefits would violate the U.S. WTO obligation to accord all WTO members equal (most-favored-nation) treatment, they require a temporary waiver by the WTO, which was in place, but expired with the ATPA program on December 4, 2001. See: WTO General Council. *United States-Andean Trade Preference Act-Decision of 14 October 1996.* WT/L/184.

textile agreements, crude and refined petroleum products, canned tuna, and certain footwear, watches, sugars, syrups, molasses, and rum products. Selected import sensitive products are eligible for only a 20-percent reduction in duties, including certain handbags, luggage, flat goods, work gloves, and leather wearing apparel. The President may suspend duty-free treatment under title II of the Trade Act of 1974 (safeguard actions) or the national security provision (sec. 232) of the Trade Expansion Act of 1962, as amended (19 U.S.C. 1862). Other trade regulations apply, such as quotas and food-safety requirements.[31]

ATPA operates in addition to the Generalized System of Preferences (GSP), a program in place since 1976 giving duty-free treatment to certain developing country imports to promote economic development. Where the two programs overlap, many Andean exporters prefer to use ATPA because it covers more tariff categories, tends to be more liberal and easier to qualify under, and has had a ten-year authorization and so until recently, has not expired as has the GSP multiple times in the 1990s.[32]

---

[31] Ibid., sec. 204 (19 U.S.C. 3203), including detailed provisions for "perishable products."
[32] See: CRS Report 97-389 E, *Generalized System of Preferences,* by William H. Cooper.

APPENDIX 2. U.S.-ATPA COUNTRY MERCHANDISE TRADE, 1990-2000 ($ MILLIONS)

U.S. Exports							
Country	1990	1992	1994	1996	1998	2000	% Change 90-00
Bolivia	138	222	185	270	417	251	81.9%
Colombia	2,029	3,286	4,064	4,714	4,816	3,689	81.8%
Ecuador	678	999	1,195	1,259	1,683	1,037	53.0%
Peru	772	1,005	1,408	1,774	2,063	1,662	115.3%
Total ATPA	3,617	5,512	6,852	8,017	8,979	6,639	83.6%
Total World	393,592	448,164	512,627	625,075	682,138	780,419	98.3%
U.S. Imports							
Country	1990	1992	1994	1996	1998	2000	% Change 90-00
Bolivia	203	162	260	275	224	191	-5.9%
Colombia	3,168	2,837	3,171	4,424	4,656	6,969	120.0%
Ecuador	1,376	1,344	1,726	1,958	1,752	2,210	60.6%
Peru	802	738	841	1,261	1,975	1,996	148.9%
Total ATPA	5,549	5,081	5,998	7,918	8,607	11,366	104.8%
Total World	495,310	532,665	663,256	795,289	911,896	1,216,888	145.7%
U.S. Balance of Trade							
Country	1990	1992	1994	1996	1998	2000	% Change 90-00
Bolivia	-65	60	-75	-6	193	61	
Colombia	-1,139	449	893	291	160	-3,280	
Ecuador	-697	-345	-532	-700	-69	-1,173	
Peru	-29	266	566	513	87	-334	
Total ATPA	-1,930	430	852	98	371	-4,726	
Total World	-101,718	-84,501	-150,629	-170,214	-229,758	-436,469	
Data Source: U.S. Department of Commerce.							

Chapter 9

Caribbean Basin Interim Trade Program: CBI/NAFTA Parity

Vladmir N. Pregelj

Summary

The entry into force, on January 1, 1994, of the North American Free Trade Agreement (NAFTA) has eliminated the advantage that the beneficiaries of the Caribbean Basin Economic Recovery Act (CBERA) and related provisions of the Caribbean Basin Initiative (CBI) had enjoyed in trade with the United States relative to Mexico, and gave Mexico an increasingly significant competitive edge over the CBERA countries. The scheduled further implementation of the NAFTA would have resulted in a substantial advantage to Mexico over the CBERA countries and vitiate in part of the purpose of the CBERA.

Beginning with the 103rd Congress, Congress considered legislation to provide, temporarily, to CBI beneficiary countries tariff and quota treatment equivalent to that accorded to Mexico under the NAFTA. The legislation also would set up mechanisms for the accession of such countries to the NAFTA or an equivalent bilateral agreements with the United States. Due to its controversial nature, based on the perceived adverse consequences for the U.S. textile industry and substantial estimated negative effect on the U.S. budget, however the legislative process reached an impasse in mid-1995. Although favorably reported in several instances since then, the parity legislation was not enacted.

In the 105th Congress, parity provisions were added by the House to its budget reconciliation bill but omitted by the Senate and in conference. Parity provisions in a somewhat different language also were introduced in several other measures, of which a House and two Senate bills were reported favorably, but the House bill was defeated and the Senate measures did not come to vote.

Parity legislation was introduced again in both houses of the 106th Congress as free-standing measures or as part of broader legislation. Diverse versions of House and Senate parity legislation were eventually reconciled in the conference report on comprehensive trade legislation, passed by both houses and signed by the President May 18, 2000 (Caribbean

Basin Trade Partnership Act –CBTPA; Title II, P.L. 106-200). The parity program has been established with respect to 24 countries by Presidential proclamation and implemented with respect to 14 of them by a determination by the USTR of their compliance with the statutory requirements.

Legislation enhancing and broadening the scope of the CBTPA preferential treatment, included in broader legislation introduced in the 107th Congress, was passed by the House but stricken in the Senate.

MOST RECENT DEVELOPMENTS

In the 106th Congress, CBI/NAFTA parity measures were included in two instances in legislation of broader scope, providing enhanced trade preferences and assistance to Central American and Caribbean countries affected by the Hurricanes Mitch and Georges: the Central American and Caribbean Relief Act and the Caribbean and Central America Relief and Economic Stabilization Act; also introduced were two freestanding measures, one in either chamber, eventually resulting in a conference version passed on May 4, 2000, by the House and on May 11 by the Senate; it was signed by the President May 18, 2000 (Caribbean Basin Trade Partnership Act – CBTPA; Title II, P.L. 106-200). Twenty-four countries have been designated by Presidential proclamation as prospective beneficiaries of the program, 14 of which have been determined by the USTR to be in compliance with the statutory customs requirements for participation in the CBTPA program and are its actual beneficiaries.

In the 107th Congress, legislative language passed by the House to enhance and broaden the scope of the CBTPA preference (H.R. 3009) was stricken by the Senate Finance Committee report (S. Rept. 107-126) on H.R. 3009.

BACKGROUND AND ANALYSIS

Some Basics

In its fundamental elements, the U.S. trade and tariff policy has treated both the Caribbean Basin countries and Mexico, in many respects their competitor and a major U.S. trading partner, in an equal manner. Both are accorded most-favored-nation (nondiscriminatory) treatment, to both apply the general tariff advantages of the "production sharing" (also referred as "offshore assembly") provisions (and have been, in both cases, extensively used by U.S. firms), and, prior to the entry into force of the North American Free Trade Agreement (NAFTA), both were designated beneficiary countries (BDCs) of the U.S. generalized system of preferences (GSP). Until NAFTA, however, most Caribbean Basin countries had a significant advantage over Mexico because of their participation in the Caribbean Basin Initiative (CBI).

With the entry into force, on January 1, 1994, of the preferential tariff and quota provisions of the NAFTA, however, the earlier advantage of CBI countries over Mexico was totally eroded. Moreover, much of NAFTA's further staged implementation put CBI countries at a distinct competitive disadvantage compared to Mexico with respect to a substantial portion of U.S. imports from either area. The gap would become even wider with full implementation of NAFTA liberalization (by January 1, 2008). To mitigate, if not eliminate, the adverse effect of the advantages that Mexico already had gained and would continue to gain relative to CBI countries, legislation was introduced in the past three Congresses to authorize for imports from CBI countries tariff and quota treatment that is identical with or very similar to that accorded Mexico under NAFTA. This treatment would be of limited duration and, in some instances, with a specific view toward eventual accession of Caribbean Basin countries to the NAFTA or the proposed Free Trade Area of the Americas, or conclusion of an equivalent bilateral agreement with the United States.

To provide an idea of the nature and scope of changes in trade competitiveness between the CBERA countries and Mexico that have resulted from the implementation of the NAFTA, the relevant preferential or special tariff treatments, as applicable, are described below. The aspects of trade policy that apply generally to all (or most) U.S. trading partners (e.g., most-favored-nation/normal-trade-relations status, or production-sharing provisions) are not included in any detail.

Caribbean Basin Preference

The Caribbean Basin trade preference is the centerpiece of the Caribbean Basin Initiative (CBI), proposed in February 1982 by President Reagan as a comprehensive but temporary program "to promote economic revitalization and facilitate expansion of economic opportunity in the Caribbean Basin region." The preference and some other less comprehensive benefits were enacted in 1983 by the Caribbean Basin Economic Recovery Act (CBERA) and put into effect as of January 1, 1984. The CBERA has been amended several times, most substantively by the Caribbean Basin Economic Recovery Expansion Act of 1990 ("CBI II"), which added several improvements and made the program permanent.

In its key provisions, the CBERA authorizes unilateral preferential treatment (either duty-free, or at duty rates lower than those applicable generally) for most articles imported from 24 Caribbean Basin countries designated as its beneficiaries (Antigua and Barbuda, Aruba, Bahamas, Barbados, Belize, British Virgin Islands, Costa Rica, Dominica, Dominican Republic, El Salvador, Grenada, Guatemala, Guyana, Haiti, Honduras, Jamaica, Montserrat, Netherlands Antilles, Nicaragua, Panama, St. Christopher and Nevis, St. Lucia, St. Vincent and the Grenadines, and Trinidad and Tobago). Eligible for the duty-free preference under the CBERA are all otherwise dutiable products except import-sensitive articles: textiles and apparel subject to textile agreements, footwear ineligible for the GSP as of January 1, 1984, canned tuna, petroleum and its products, and watches and watch parts containing any material originating in countries denied the most-favored-nation status.

Certain import-sensitive leather articles, originally ineligible for duty-free treatment (handbags, luggage, flat goods, work gloves, and certain leather wearing apparel), have been accorded by the 1990 amendment preferential tariff treatment at reduced but still positive rates. This preference consists of a 20% cut in the regular (MFN) duty rates in effect at the end of 1991, phased-in through five stages beginning on January 1, 1992, and completed on January 1, 1996. The reduction, however, could not exceed 2.5% ad valorem or, for general rates reduced in the Uruguay Round, be 1% ad valorem greater than that reduction.

To be accorded the duty-free or reduced-rate preference, an eligible article must be a "product of" (as defined in the U.S. general rules of origin) a CBERA beneficiary country and imported directly from it, and at least 35% of the article's import value must have originated in one or more CBERA beneficiaries. In this context, Puerto Rico and the U.S. Virgin Islands are counted as CBERA beneficiaries, and up to 15% of the 35% of the article's qualifying import value may be accounted for by value originating in the U.S. customs territory (other than Puerto Rico).

Duty-free importation of sugar and beef products is subject to a special eligibility requirement that the beneficiary country submit and carry out a stable food production plan ensuring that increased production of sugar and beef will not adversely affect the overall food production of the country.

CBERA duty-free treatment may be suspended for any otherwise eligible article by Presidential proclamation implementing a remedial measure under the import-relief provision (Section 203) of the Trade Act of 1974 or the national-security provision (Section 232) of the Trade Expansion Act of 1962.

Not part of the CBERA but applicable only to CBERA beneficiaries is a provision under which any articles (other than textiles, apparel, and petroleum and its products) assembled or processed in a CBERA country entirely from components or ingredients made in the United States may be imported free of duty or quantitative restrictions.

Although textile apparel is ineligible under the CBERA for any type of tariff preference, a special access program (SAP) is in effect for apparel assembled in a CBERA country and imported under the "production sharing" tariff provision (i.e., with regular duty rates applied to a duty-base excluding the value of U.S. origin components) provided it is assembled from fabric formed as well as cut in the United States. Such apparel may be imported from CBERA countries in quantities above the regular import quotas up to the bilaterally agreed "guaranteed access levels" (GALs) (although with no reduction in the duty rate). GAL agreements are in force with Costa Rica, Dominican Republic, El Salvador, Guatemala, and Jamaica (but, in most instances, GAL imports have been replaced by those under the more favorable provisions of the parity legislation; see p. 9).

Most CBERA beneficiaries (except Aruba, Bahamas, Netherlands Antilles, and Nicaragua) also are beneficiaries of the GSP (described below), and may utilize its benefits alternatively to those of the Caribbean preference.

The overall statistical picture of U.S. imports from the 24 CBERA countries in the year 2000 (in parentheses, respectively, the year 2001) shows that out of the total value of $22,161.1 million ($20,678.9 million), $14,138.6 million; 63.8% ($15,089.2 million; 73.0%) was imported free of duty, of which $2,351.1 million; 10.6% (2,623.0 million; 17.4%) under the CBERA preference and $202.1 million; 0.9% ($178.9 million; 1.2%) under the GSP; the remaining $11,428.4 million ($7.147.8 million) (excluding duty-free imports under the CBTPA, for which see pp. 11 and 12) was duty-free under the regular rates or as the duty-free share of the production-sharing provisions. Including the value of imports subject to reduced rates, total U.S. imports under the CBERA program (duty-free and at reduced rates) amounted to $2,635.5 million ($2,706.3 million) (11.9%, resp. 13.1% of total U.S. imports from CBERA countries).

Pre-NAFTA Special Tariff Treatment of Mexico

Before the NAFTA entered into force, Mexico was a designated beneficiary developing country (BDC) of the GSP and, as such, enjoyed certain benefits that were similar to, if somewhat less generous than those of the CBERA beneficiaries. While the GSP authorizes duty-free importation (but has no provisions for imports at reduced rates), the range of articles eligible for the preference is narrower than that of the CBERA. Generally ineligible by law under the GSP are textile and apparel articles subject to textile agreements; watches, except those that the President determines will not cause injury to U.S. domestic watch or watch band, strap, or bracelet manufacturing or assembly industry; import-sensitive electronic articles; import-sensitive steel articles; import-sensitive semimanufactured and manufactured glass products; footwear, handbags, luggage, flat goods, work gloves and leather wearing apparel; and any other articles determined by the President as import sensitive in the GSP context. The GSP also is of temporary duration and must be renewed periodically by enactment. The most recent renewal remains in effect through September 30, 2001.

GSP eligibility can be suspended for individual articles imported from individual countries, usually following a review of the specific situation; it is also suspended when such imports exceed specified statutory levels, a criterion referred to as the "competitive need limit." The latter suspension may be waived under specified conditions. Under these provisions, suspension of GSP eligibility was in effect prior to NAFTA for imports from Mexico falling within some 90 tariff items, mostly fresh vegetables, copper ore and primary copper, and sundry auto parts.

In a rule of origin similar to that of the CBERA, an eligible import qualifies for the GSP preference if it is a product of a BDC and imported directly from it, and at least 35% of the article's import value has originated in the country of export or in two or more countries that are members of the same association of countries (Andean Group, Association of South East Asian Nations, Caribbean Common Market, Southern Africa Development Community, and West African Economic and Monetary Union), of none of which, however, Mexico is a member. Unlike the CBERA, the GSP does not allow the value of the components of U.S.-Puerto Rico-, or U.S. Virgin Islands-origin to count toward the required 35% BDC-origin value requirement.

A "special regime" arrangement for textile apparel, virtually identical to the CBI's special access program, also was in effect with Mexico prior to the entry into force of the NAFTA.

Total U.S. imports from Mexico in 1993, the last year before the onset of the implementation of NAFTA, amounted to (in millions) $38,667.7, of which $19,800.5 (51.2%) was duty free, further broken down into $4,498.1 (11.6%) under regular rates, $9,871.9 (25.5%) under the production sharing provisions and $5,430.5 (14%) under the GSP. Dutiable imports totaled (in millions) $18,867.2 (48.8%), of which $9,095.8 (23.5%) represented the dutiable portion of production-sharing products and $9,771.4 (25.3%) imports under regular duty rates.

A summary comparison of special trade benefits available to CBI countries with those available to Mexico before the entry into force of the NAFTA shows that CBI countries enjoyed a distinct advantage over Mexico because:

(a) The range of articles accorded preferential treatment under the CBERA is significantly broader than under the GSP because CBERA ineligibility applies only to those product categories specifically listed in the statute; under the GSP, however, not only is the range of articles excluded from the preference by statue broader, but additional discretionary and "competitive need" exclusions have been made.

(b) Under the "rule of origin" for the eligibility of a Mexican product for the GSP, its qualifying value could not include any value of U.S., Puerto Rican, or U.S. Virgin Islands origin, which is included under the CBERA.

(c) Import-sensitive articles eligible under CBERA for reduced-rate preference are excluded altogether from GSP eligibility.

(d) Duty- and quota-free treatment that applies to qualifying articles assembled or processed in a CBERA country entirely from components or ingredients originating on the United States did not apply to articles similarly processed in Mexico.

(e) The CBERA is a permanent program, whereas the GSP is authorized for a specific period of time and must be periodically reauthorized by legislation in order to remain in force.

Mexico's Benefits under the NAFTA and their Effect on CBERA Beneficiaries

When Mexico acceded to the NAFTA, its tariff position with the United States changed radically and improved substantially relative to that of the CBI countries as well as absolutely.

Although Mexico's GSP eligibility was revoked as of January 1, 1994 – the date NAFTA went into effect – the earlier duty-free status of articles imported from Mexico under the GSP was continued in force under the NAFTA on a permanent basis (rather than being contingent on extensions of the GSP authority), although under the somewhat less favorable NAFTA rules of origin. Moreover, duty-free status was accorded for the first time to many previously dutiable articles, including most of the articles subject to the GSP competitive need limits or discretionary suspensions, and to many articles duty free under the DBERA but ineligible for the GSP, including handmade or folklore textile and apparel articles. These actions equalized Mexico's duty-free preferential status with that of CBI countries, thus eliminating their earlier advantages over Mexico.

Also on January 1, 1994, the first stage of reductions that eventually (at the latest by January 1, 2008) are to eliminate the pre-NAFTA tariffs in a specified number of annual cuts was implemented. Further staged tariff reductions have taken place on January 1 of every year since. This process created an initially still marginal actual advantage for Mexico – which eventually would become substantial – with respect to articles ineligible for the Caribbean Basin duty-free preference (e.g., textiles and textile apparel), which, under the NAFTA, are in the phase-in process toward eventual duty-free and quota-free status. Similarly, the NAFTA staged reductions have already resulted in the elimination of CBERA's erstwhile advantage over Mexico with respect to import-sensitive articles eligible for the CBERA 20%-reduced duty rates. The phasing-in of these NAFTA's reductions (to zero) has been completed for most products as of January 1, 1999. By then, the duty rates subject to the longer of the two reduction schedules still being phased-in (to be completed by January 1,

2008) had been cut by 40% and those subject to the shorter schedule (to be completed by January 1, 2003) by 60%. At present, the respective cumulative cuts amount to 60% and

In the first 11 months of 2001, total U.S. imports from Mexico amounted to $121,221.2 million, $105,152.7 million (86.7%) of this free of duty, including %63,832.0 million (52.7%) under the NAFTA and the remainder under other tariff provisions. NAFTA imports of products whose duty rates are still in the process of being phased-out amounted to $11,486.1 million, for a total of imports under the NAFTA of $75,318.1 million (62.1% of all imports from Mexico).

Imports of articles ineligible for duty—free treatment under the CBERA in 2000 accounted for over one-half, by value, of all U.S. imports from the group (including the total value of partially nondutiable products of production sharing (see p. 3). The most crucial and potentially injurious to CBERA countries was the NAFTA treatment of textiles and apparel articles which, in addition to constituting the largest single category by far of U.S. imports from CBERA countries, do not qualify for that preference and are subject to relatively high duty rates. Some of the adverse effect of this NAFTA treatment on the CBERA countries was mitigated by the relatively long (6 or 10 annual stages, some even 15 stages) phasing-in period of the NAFTA duty elimination. Another mitigating factor was the extensive use by American firms in imports of apparel from CBERA countries of the production-sharing provision, where a portion of the value of the import already is duty free, which effectively reduces its duty cost to the U.S. importer. The same tariff treatment, however, is also available generally to similar imports from Mexico and that at decreasing duty rates.

Moreover, the NAFTA authorized eventual duty- and quota-free importation from Mexico of textile and apparel goods that had previously fallen under the "special regime" and of those that had not qualified for "special regime" (see p. 4) treatment because of additional processing, such as bleaching or dyeing, that was beyond mere assembly. In addition reduced rates were authorized under NAFTA within an overall quota for imports of textile apparel and other articles assembled in Mexico from components cut in the United States from fabrics imported from any third country. Reduced rates also were authorized, within separate quotas, for textile and apparel articles of wool, cotton and man-made fiber assembled in a NAFTA country from components cut or made from fabric or yarn originating outside the NAFTA area.

Less crucial for the CBERA countries was the NAFTA treatment of petroleum and its products. Its adverse effect on the competitiveness of CBERA-origin petroleum was likely to be limited: petroleum products accounted for a relatively small share (by value) of total U.S. imports from the group, U.S. regular duty rates on products in this category are very low (equivalent to a fraction of or slightly over 1%) and would take 10 years to be eliminated under the NAFTA. Moreover, this action affects directly only the three CBERA petroleum exporting countries: Bahamas, Netherlands Antilles, and Trinidad and Tobago.

The adverse effect of the NAFTA on U.S. imports of footwear from the CBERA countries also was less serious: footwear accounts for a relatively small share of imports from either source and much of it is imported into the United States under the production-sharing provision. The NAFTA duty elimination is being phased-in in ten stages, thus mitigating the severity of the change.

The CBERA ineligibility of watches and watch parts containing any material originating in non-MFN countries was, in practice, irrelevant since no imports of such watches were taking place.

To recapitulate: the implementation of the NAFTA not only eliminated all earlier tariff advantages of the CBI countries over Mexico, but created actual – and increasing – advantages for Mexico over the CBERA countries, specifically with respect to articles ineligible for the CBERA preference. With the further phasing-in of the NAFTA reductions, the CBERA competitive disadvantage vs. Mexico would be increasing and eventually become quite serious.

On the other hand, although not directly related to the NAFTA problem, the overall advantages of the CBERA (as well as of the NAFTA) are being diluted in any event by the phasing-in of the implementation of concessions agreed to by the United States in the Uruguay Round of multilateral negotiations and applied to imports from virtually all countries.

Parity Legislation and Action

Legislation intended to remedy the perceived most serious aspects of the NAFTA's adverse consequences for the CBERA countries – the actual advantages that Mexico had already gained, would continue to gain, over the CBERA countries – was introduced in the 103rd and the 104th Congress, but saw no action beyond committee hearings.

The legislation was held back primarily because of its in practice inevitable focus on textiles and apparel, and that in two aspects: (1) textiles and apparel, the principal category of articles affected by the proposals, are considered highly import sensitive and there was concern that significant increases in their imports would be disruptive of the domestic textile industry, and (2) because of their relatively high import duty rates, their reduction and eventual elimination would entail a significant loss of customs (hence, budget) revenues.

The most important – and, in terms of affected trade, broadest – feature of CBI/NAFTA parity legislation would be the new preferential treatment of textiles or apparel imported from CBERA countries: articles that were subject to import quotas and were ineligible for the CBERA preference. In its main aspects, such treatment would consist of quota-free or at least increased-quota imports, subject to an identical progressive elimination of customs duties on imports from CBERA countries as would apply to such imports originating in Mexico; it would, however, also subject them to the somewhat stricter NAFTA-like rules of origin.

Opponents of parity legislation claimed early on that, since NAFTA's entry into force of January 1, 1994, imports from CBI countries of textiles and apparel, a product category that allegedly would be severely adversely affected by the implementation of the NAFTA, not only had not abated but had increased significantly. In view of the pay-as-you-go budget requirements, an additional important adverse consideration has been the projected decrease in customs revenues that gradual freeing of the still dutiable articles (mostly textiles and textile apparel, which are dutied at relatively high rates) would bring about. Customs duty losses resulting from the CBI/NAFTA parity legislation were initially (1995) estimated variously at $1.1 billion over 5 years and $1.7 billion over 10 years.

105th Congress
The Congressional Budget Office (CBO), as cited in S. Rept. 105-280, estimated that the CBI/NAFTA parity legislation in the proposed Trade and Tariff Act of 1998 (S. 2400) would result in revenue losses (by fiscal year, in millions of dollars) of $98 in 1999, $138 in 2000,

$147 in 2001, and $26 in 2002; and an Administration estimate of the cost of its most recent proposal places it at $326 million in 2000 and $444 million in 2001. The latest projections by the CBO of reductions of federal revenues (S. Rept. 106-160) due to the CBI/NAFTA parity legislation estimate such losses (in millions) in FY2000 at $252, in FY2001 at $260, in FY2002 at $272, in FY2003 at $289, in FY2004 at $309, and in FY2005 at $83. In view of the projected termination of the program at the end of 2005, no losses have been projected for subsequent fiscal years.

Although several versions of CBI/NAFTA parity legislation were considered in the 105th Congress, none was enacted. The United States-Caribbean Trade Partnership Act, a subtitle of H.R. 2014 (Budget Reconciliation Act), was passed by the House, but omitted in its Senate, conference, and enacted versions. A freestanding measure with the same title and virtually identical operative provisions (H.R. 2644) was reported favorably in the House, but defeated in the floor vote. Two measures entitled United States-Caribbean Basin Trade Enhancement Act were reported favorably in the Senate but did not come to a vote: a freestanding bill (S. 1278), and a subtitle in the Trade and Tariff Act of 1998 (S. 2400), incorporating similar provisions.

106th Congress

In the 106th Congress, parity legislation was introduced in four different versions, of which only two received some legislative consideration. No action was taken on the **United States-Caribbean Basin Trade Enhancement Act** (Title I of the Central American and Caribbean Relief Act (**S. 371**) or the Administration proposal (**H.R. 1834**), also named **United States-Caribbean Basin Trade Enhancement Act** (CBTPA).

The other two bills, the **United States-Caribbean Trade Partnership Act** (Title I of the Caribbean and Central America Relief and Economic Stabilization Act (**H.R. 984**)) and the **United States-Caribbean Basin Trade Enhancement Act** (**S. 1389**), received some legislative action. H.R. 984 was reported favorably (H.Rept. 106-519, pt. 1) March 13, 2000, but not voted on. S. 1389 was reported favorably (S.Rept. 106-160) September 16, 1999, and its language was added to H.R. 434. The language of these two measures was used as the basis for the eventual compromise language agreed to in conference on the final version of H.R. 434.

The language of S. 1389 as reported has been included in its entirety as **Title II (Trade Benefits for Caribbean Basin)** in S.Amdt. 2325 to an expanded **H.R. 434**, passed by the Senate (76-19) November 3, 1999. Reconciliation of the parity provisions of the House and Senate versions of H.R. 434, focusing primarily on the preferential treatment of textile products, took place in protracted informal consultations between the two houses.

A formal conference report on **H.R. 434** (H.Rept. 106-606) was filed may 4, 2000, passed the House that same day (309-110) and the Senate on May 11, 2000 (77-19). It was signed by the President May 18, 2000 (P.L. 106-200) (Trade and Development Act of 2000), but not yet implemented. Its implementation was authorized by Presidential proclamation 7351 of October 2, 2000 (65 F.R. 59329; October 4, 2000), but the preferential treatment provided by it was to become effective with the respect to each of its individual beneficiary countries upon the determination by the U.S. Trade Representative, published in the *Federal Register*, that the country has satisfied the customs requirements for such treatment.

The key provisions of the **enacted version of the United States-Caribbean Basin Trade Partnership Act – CBTPA (Title II of P.L. 106-200)** reflect the policy, stated in the legislation, to offer the Caribbean Basin countries willing to prepare to become parties to a free-trade agreement with the United States treatment equivalent to that accorded to NAFTA countries, and to seek Caribbean Basin countries' participation in a free-trade agreement by 2005. The provisions focus primarily on the preferential treatment of textile products. The conference version has retained many provisions of the initial legislation and added others. It extended the transitional *period of preferential treatment* to run from October 1, 2000, through September 30, 2008, or, if earlier, the date a free-trade agreement between the United States and a CBTPA country enters into force.

Several *eligibility criteria* have been added (to those for the basic CBERA preference) specifically for a country's designation as a CBTPA beneficiary country for the transitional program with respect to the country's WTO obligations and accession to the FTAA, intellectual rights protection, worker rights, elimination of worst forms of child labor, counter-narcotics certification, participation in the Inter-American Convention Against Corruption, and government procurement.

With regard to *textile articles*, the enacted version has provided duty- and quota-free treatment as follows:

(1) Apparel assembled in a CBTPA beneficiary country from fabric made in the United States from U.S.-made yarn, and cut in the United States; or from fabric made in the United States from U.S.-made yarn, cut in the CBTPA country, and sewn together in a CBTPA country with U.S.-made thread.

(2) Apparel articles (except socks) knit-to-shape from U.S.-made yarn in a beneficiary country, or articles (other than non-underwear T-shirts) assembled from fabric knit in the United States or in a beneficiary country from U.S.-made yarn, and cut in a beneficiary country. Duty-free treatment of knit-to-shape articles applies to 250 million square meters equivalent (SME) for the year beginning October 1, 2000, with 16% annual increases through September 30, 2004, and, after that, through September 30, 2008, at the level for 2004, or in quantities set by law. The annual limit for non-underwear T-shirts has been set at 4.2 million dozen for the year beginning October 1, 2000, with 16% annual increases through September 30, 2004, and after that at the latter level, or in quantities set by law.

(3) Brassieres cut and assembled in the United States and/or one or more beneficiary countries during the six-year period beginning with October 1, 2001, if the cost of the U.S.-made fabric components used in their manufacture by their individual producer during the preceding year is at least 75% of their customs value; if the U.S.-component requirement is not met in any year, the producer will not be eligible for the preference until the year following the year in which the value of U.S.-made fabric components is at least 85% of the customs value of the brassieres produced by the individual producer.

(4) Apparel articles assembled in a beneficiary country from fibers, fabric, or yarn not formed in the United States or a beneficiary country, that are not widely available in commercial quantities (as described in Annex 401 of the NAFTA). The President is authorized to proclaim, upon request and under specified procedure, this preference for other fibers, fabric, or yarn.

(5) Certified handloomed, handmade, and folklore articles.

(6) Preferential treatment is not denied to articles containing limited quantities of foreign-origin findings or interlinings, or *de minimis* quantities of fibers or yarns of non-U.S. or non-CBTPA origin, or nylon filament yarn made in a country with which the United States has a pre-January 1, 1995 free-trade agreement (Canada, Mexico, and Israel).

(7) Textile luggage assembled in a CBTPA beneficiary country from fabric made in the United States from U.S.-made yarn, and cut in the United States; or from fabric made in the United States from U.S.-made yarn, and cut in a CBTPA country.

Penalties are provided for exporters transshipping textile articles ineligible for the preference, and for countries not taking transshipment prevention measures; and NAFTA-like emergency action is provided to remedy or prevent injury to a U.S. industry by surges in imports.

Other *import-sensitive articles* (ineligible for CBERA duty-free treatment, but some of which are dutied at CBERA preferential reduced rates) are to be dutied at NAFTA-Mexico rates (if lower than CBERA rates).

The measure contains definitions of concepts used and a variety of administrative provisions: customs procedures are to be identical to those under NAFTA, and the Customs Service is to study and prepare a report, to be submitted to Congress by the U.S. Trade Representative by October 1, 2001, on cooperation by CBTPA countries in preventing quota circumvention.

The President is authorized to withdraw or suspend the designation of any country as a CBTPA beneficiary or withdraw, suspend, or limit the preferential treatment under the CBTPA of any article of any country, if its performance under the specific eligibility criteria for CBTPA preferences is not satisfactory.

The measure changes several reporting requirements: beginning with December 31, 2001, the triennial USTR report on the overall operation of the CBERA is changed, for the duration of the transitional period, to a biennial report with added information on each CBTPA country's performance under the spec8ial eligibility criteria; and beginning with September 30, 2001, the annual report by the U.S. International Trade Commission to Congress and the President on the economic impact of the CBERA on U.S. industries and consumers (including those in Puerto Rico) is changed to a biennial report.

The measure provides, under specified conditions, CBERA-like duty-free treatment for spirituous beverages made in Canada with rum produced in the U.S. Virgin Islands or a CBERA beneficiary country.

The President is directed to convene a meeting of the USTR and trade ministers of the CBTPA countries for the purpose of reaching an agreement on initiating negotiations for CBTPA countries' entering into free-trade agreements with the United States.

- The *implementation* of the CBTPA was authorized by Presidential proclamation 7351 of October 2, 2000 (65 F.R. 59329; Oct. 4, 2000), designated 24 Caribbean Basin countries as beneficiaries of the program, and put into effect as of the same date with respect to 10 countries (Belize, Costa Rica, Dominican Republic, El Salvador, Guatemala, Haiti, Honduras, Jamaica, Nicaragua, and Panama) by a USTR determination of their compliance with the statutory customs requirements (65 F.R.

60236; Oct. 1, 2000); Guyana was added to the list effective November 9, 2000 (65 F.R. 69988; Nov. 21,2000).

- Because of its late implementation date, the year 2000 imports under the CBTPA program were minimal, all taking place in December 2000 and duty-free, and amounted to $157.0 million.

107th Congress

Legislation to enhance the benefits of the CBTPA was introduced October 3, 2001 in the House as Section 5 of the Andean Trade Promotion and Drug Eradication Act (H.R. 3009) and passed by it with some changes. Initially, it merely specifically declared knit-to-shape apparel components formed in the United States as equivalent to cut-fabric components as qualifying for the CBTPA for preferential treatment, when assembled in a CBTPA beneficiary country. This provision was intended to reverse the U.S. Customs Service's ruling excluding knit-to-shape components from the definition of cut-fabric components. The amended version of H.R. 3009, reported November 14, 2001 by the Ways and Means Committee (H.Rept. 107-290) and passed by the House November 16, 2001, made eligible for the preference also apparel assembled in CBTPA beneficiaries with U.S.-made thread from components cut from U.S.-made fabric, or knit-to-shape, either in the United States or a CBTPA beneficiary. It also significantly increased the annual ceilings for the preferential treatment of knit-to-shape apparel (other than socks) and non-underwear T-shirts.

H.R. 3009 was reported by the Senate Finance Committee December 14, 2001 (S.Rept. 107-126), but omitted by any CBTPA-related provisions, and was placed on the Senate calendar, with as yet no further action. The omission was primarily triggered by the controversy over the denial of preferential treatment to CBTPA –assembled components of fabric "fully formed" in the United States that were not also dyed and finished in the United States, which was strongly supported by certain sectors of the U.S. textile and apparel industry.

Legislation of limited scope also has been introduced, but not further considered: **S. 510**, introduced March 9, 2001, would provide CBTPA preferential treatment to certain cotton and man-made fiber bed linens, and **H.R. 1589**, introduced April 25, 2001, would do the same for socks and hosiery excluded by the present legislation.

During the 107th Congress, the President authorized the expansion of the CBTPA program to three more countries: Trinidad and Tobago effective February 6, 2001 (66 F.R. 9888), and Barbados, and Saint Lucia effective June 1, 2001 (66 F.R. 31272).

In 2001, the first full year of the CBTPA program, imports under its preference accounted for a substantial share (29.5%; $5,592.9 million) of total U.S. imports from its beneficiaries ($18,939.7 million) and for 35.6% ($5,139.6 million) of duty-free imports ($14,451.4 million), the largest share of which (45.8%; 6,618.9 million), however, entered under nonpreferential (regular) zero duties.

CHRONOLOGY

12/14/01 – H.R. 3009 reported by Senate Finance Committee (S.Rept. 107-126), omitting CBTPA provisions, and placed on the calendar.

11/16/01 – H.R. 3009, including enhanced CBTPA provisions, passed by the House by voice vote.

11/14/01 – H.R. 3009 reported favorably by Ways and Means Committee (H.Rept. 107-290).

10/03/01 – H.R. 3009, in Sec. 5 providing for enhanced benefits under the CBTPA program, introduced.

06/01/01 – Effective date for application of CBTPA benefits to Saint Lucia and Barbados upon USTR's determination of country's satisfactory compliance with statutory customs requirements (66 F.R. 31272; June 11, 2001).

04/25/01 – H.R. 1589 introduced to provide CBTPA preferential treatment to socks and hosiery.

03/09/01 – S. 510 introduced to provide CBTPA preferential treatment to certain cotton and man-made bed linens.

02/06/01 – Effective date for application of CBTPA parity benefits to Trinidad and Tobago upon USTR's determination of country's satisfactory compliance with statutory customs requirements (66 F.R. 9888; Feb. 12, 2001).

11/09/00 – Effective date for application of CBTPA benefits to Guyana upon USTR's determination of country's satisfactory compliance with statutory customs requirements (65 F.R. 69988; Nov. 20, 2000).

10/02/00 – In Presidential proclamation 7351, (65 F.R. 59329; October 10, 2000), President Clinton authorized the implementation of the CBTPA by designating 24 countries as beneficiaries of the program, but delaying its effect with respect to each of its individual beneficiary countries until a determination is made by the USTR that the country has satisfied the customs requirements for such treatment.

– Effective date for application of CBTPA benefits to Belize, Costa Rica, Dominican Republic, El Salvador, Guatemala, Haiti, Honduras, Jamaica, Nicaragua, and Panama upon USTR's determination of countries' compliance with customs requirements (65 F.R. 60236; Oct. 10, 2000).

5/18/00 – President Clinton signed H.R. 434 into law (Trade and Development Act of 2000), providing in Title II (United States-Caribbean Basin Trade Partnership Act –CBTPA) for Caribbean Basin countries preferential trade treatment in parity with that of NAFTA.

5/11/00 – Conference language of H.R. 434 passed by the Senate (77-19).

05/04/00 – Conference report on H.R. 434 (Trade and Development Act of 2000) (H.Rept. 106-606), containing Title II – Trade Benefits for Caribbean Basin, filed after protracted informal consultations, reconciling the versions of parity provisions of H.R. 984 as reported by the House and H.R. 434 as amended by the Senate.

– House passed conference version of H.R. 434 (309-110).

03/13/99 – H.R. 984 reported favorably by Ways and Means committee (H.Rept. 106-519, Pt. 1).

11/03/99 – H.R. 434, including Title II (United States-Caribbean Basin Trade Enhancement Act) as added by the Senate, passed by a vote of 76 ayes to 19 nays.

10/27/99 – Language of S. 1389 as reported included as Title II in substitute Senate amendment SP2325, proposed to an expanded H.R. 434, renamed the "Trade and Development Act of 1999."

09/16/99 – S. 1389 (United States-Caribbean Basin Trade enhancement Act), reported favorably with written report (S.Rept. 106-160).

07/16/99 – S. 1389 (United States-Caribbean Basin Trade Enhancement Act), an original Finance Committee bill, reported without written report.

06/10/99 – H.R. 984 ordered to be reported amended by the Ways and Means Committee.

05/18/99 – H.R. 1834 (United Stages-Caribbean Basin Trade Enhancement Act) introduced and referred to the Committee on Ways and Means.

03/23/99 – House Ways and Means Trade Subcommittee held a hearing on H.R. 984.

03/04/00 – H.R. 984, containing the "United Stages-Caribbean Trade Partnership Act" as Title I, introduced and referred to Committees on Ways and Means, International Relations, Banking and Finance Services, the Judiciary, and Armed Forces.

02/04/99 – S. 371, containing the "United States-Caribbean Trade Enhancement Act" as Title I, introduced and referred to the Committee on Finance.

CONGRESSIONAL HEARINGS, REPORTS, AND DOCUMENTS

U.S. Congress. Conference Committee. Trade and Development Act of 2000. Conference report (to accompany H.R. 434). Washington, U.S. Govt. Print, Off., May 4, 2000. 146 p. (At head of title: 106th Congress, 2d Session. H.Rept. 106-606).

U.S. Congress. House. Committee on Ways and Means. Andean Trade Promotion and Drug Eradication Act. Report together with additional and dissenting views (to accompany H.R. 3009). Washington, U.S. Govt. Print. Off., November 14, 2001. 43 p. (H.Rept. 107-290).

– Caribbean and Central America Relief and Economic Stabilization Act. Report together with additional and dissenting views (to accompany H.R. 984). Washington, U.S. Govt. Print. Off., March 13, 2000. 52 p. (H.Rept. 106-519, Part 1).

U.S. Congress. Senate. Committee on Finance. Andean Trade Preference Expansion Act. Report (to accompany H.R. 3009). Washington, U.S. Govt. Print. Off., December 14, 2001. 56 p. (S.Rept. 107-125).

– United States-Caribbean Basin Trade Enhancement Act; report (to accompany S. 1389). Washington, U.S. Govt. Print. Off., September 16, 1999. 29 p. (S.Rept. 106-160).

FOR ADDITIONAL READING

U.S. Office of the United States Trade Representative. Fourth Report to Congress on the Operation of the Caribbean Basin Economic Recovery Act. December 31, 2001. [http://www.ustr.gov/reports]

Chapter 10

WORLD TRADE ORGANIZATION: PROGRESS IN AGRICULTURAL TRADE NEGOTIATIONS MAY BE SLOW[*]

Susan S. Westin

This paper provides observations about the negotiations on agricultural trade being conducted by the World Trade Organization (WTO). Specifically, it will address (1) U.S. and other countries' objectives in the agricultural trade negotiations, (2) progress achieved during the 1999 WTO Seattle ministerial conference, and (3) prospects for future negotiations.

The observations are based on our past and ongoing work; our review of WTO and executive branch documents; related literature; discussions with experts on the WTO and international trade; and interviews with U.S. government, WTO, and foreign government officials from 15 countries. In addition, the author along with members her staff, attended the Seattle ministerial conference.[1]

SUMMARY

WTO member countries intended to launch a new round of multilateral trade negotiations covering agriculture and other issues at their biennial Ministerial Conference last December in Seattle. The principal objectives of the United States and several other agricultural exporting countries for liberalizing agricultural trade included (1) elimination of export subsidies, (2) a reduction in trade-distorting domestic agricultural support programs, and (3) an increase in market access for agricultural products in member countries. On the other hand, the European Union and other countries opposed any attempt to eliminate export subsidies.

Trade ministers meeting in Seattle intended to conclude the ministerial conference with a ministerial declaration that would launch a new round and set the agenda for negotiations in

---

[*] Excerpted from the General Accounting Office Website: www.gao.gov.
[1] For our assessment of the overall outcome of the ministerial conference, see World Trade Organization, Seattle Ministerial: Outcomes and Lessons Learned (GAO/T-NSIAD-00-86, Feb.10, 2000) for more details.

each subject area, including agriculture. There is general agreement by conference participants that negotiations on agriculture made the most progress of any area at the Seattle conference. Countries had moved closer to reaching consensus on many of the issues to be addressed and on the time frames for completing agricultural negotiations in a new round. However, this progress was essentially lost when countries could not reach consensus on an agriculture text, and the conference was adjourned without launching a new round or issuing a ministerial declaration.

Despite the impasse in Seattle, agricultural trade negotiations will resume this year in Geneva as mandated by the Uruguay Round Agreement on Agriculture. However, it is unlikely that these talks will meet U.S. objectives for liberalizing agricultural trade any time soon, for several reasons. First, the failure to issue a ministerial declaration may make it difficult for negotiators in Geneva to build on the progress made in Seattle. Second, there is some concern whether countries will be willing to make concessions on agriculture without trade-offs in other areas, as would have been the case in a trade round with a broader negotiating agenda. Third, not much progress should be expected this year, since groundwork must be laid before substantive negotiations can begin. For example, WTO members have yet to submit proposals as to what should be on the negotiating agenda for agriculture.

BACKGROUND

The United States is one of the largest importers and exporters of agricultural products in the world. Although accounting for only about 5 percent of overall U.S. exports, agricultural exports were about $48 billion in 1999. Furthermore, agricultural trade had nearly an $11 billion surplus compared with an overall U.S. trade deficit of about $271 billion in 1999. Also, U.S. markets for agricultural commodities are relatively open, with average tariffs on most agricultural products very low compared to those of many other WTO members. Consequently, the United States has pursued trade liberalization in the agricultural sector and has sought to include agriculture in previous rounds of multilateral trade negotiations.

The conclusion of the Uruguay Round in 1994 represented the first time that the multilateral trading system undertook to substantially reform agricultural trade. The Uruguay Round created the WTO, which provides the institutional framework for the multilateral trading system. WTO administers rules for international trade, provides a mechanism for settling disputes, and provides a forum for conducting trade negotiations. There are two agreements from the Uruguay Round that specifically address agricultural issues—the Agreement on Agriculture and the Agreement on the Application of Sanitary and Phytosanitary Measures (the SPS agreement).

The Agreement on Agriculture covers barriers to market access, such as tariffs and quotas, subsidies for exporters, and support for domestic agricultural producers. WTO members agreed to a 36 percent reduction in average tariffs of agricultural products by developed countries by 2000, and a 24 percent reduction by developing countries by 2004. In addition, the Agreement on Agriculture required that WTO members' spending on export subsidies be cut by 36 percent and that quantities subsidized be cut by 21 percent for developed countries by 2001.[2] The agreement also required cuts in certain types of domestic farm supports that could include price supports or subsidies for fertilizer and irrigation. Article 20 of the Agreement on Agriculture calls for renewed agricultural trade negotiations in the year 2000 to continue the long term objective of agricultural trade reform through substantial progressive reduction in support and protection. This is referred to as the "built-in agenda."

The SPS agreement sets out the basic rules for food safety and animal and plant health standards that affect international trade. It allows countries to set their own standards, but specifies that regulations must be based on sufficient scientific evidence, and it restricts the use of unjustified measures for trade protection.

In December 1999, trade ministers held their third biennial WTO ministerial conference to launch a new round of multilateral trade negotiations covering at least agriculture and services[3] but potentially including other areas such as industrial market access and government procurement. However, the December ministerial conference failed to achieve its goal. After 4 days of intensive talks, the conference was suspended on December 3 without agreeing on a round or issuing a ministerial declaration or any other formal documentation of its deliberations. As a result of the inconclusive nature of the Seattle meeting, the status of the ministerial conference and the prospects for a new round remain unclear. However, WTO members are scheduled to renew agricultural trade negotiations this year, as mandated by article 20 of the Agreement on Agriculture.

COUNTRIES' OBJECTIVES ON AGRICULTURAL TRADE

In efforts to launch a new round of trade negotiations in Seattle, the United States and other agricultural exporters sought to include additional disciplines on export subsidies and domestic farm supports, as well as market access issues, within the framework of agricultural negotiations. The European Union (EU) and Japan, on the other hand, had reservations regarding some of these issues and were more interested in making sure that certain agriculture-related nontrade concerns, such as food safety and food security, were addressed in the negotiations. Moreover, the EU and Japan were not satisfied with negotiations limited to the "built-in agenda" issues of agriculture and services. Rather, they called for a broad framework for negotiations to bring many new areas, such as investment and competition policy, under international disciplines.

The United States insisted that negotiations on agriculture address a number of tough issues, including the elimination of export subsidies, the imposition of substantial cuts in trade-distorting farm supports, and a call for reductions in tariffs. Other major agricultural exporting countries, known as the "Cairns Group," supported these goals. In addition, the United States wanted the agriculture negotiations to introduce stronger disciplines on the

---

[2] For more information on implementation of the Agreement on Agriculture, see The General Agreement on Tariffs and Trade: Uruguay Round Final Act Should Produce Overall U.S. Economic Gains (GAO/GGD-94-83b, July 29,1994), and Commitments by the European Union and the United States to Reduce Agricultural Export Subsidies (GAO/NSIAD-99-198R, June 18, 1999) for more details.

[3] As part of the built-in agenda, the Uruguay Round Agreement on Trade in Services, like the Agreement on Agriculture, called for negotiations in the services sector to begin in 2000.

activities of state trading enterprises,[4] and guarantees that decisions on imports of new technologies, such as biotechnology, would be based on scientific grounds and transparent (open) regulatory processes. At the same time, the United States sought to limit the introduction of nontrade issues, which the EU, Japan, and certain other countries wanted to be considered in the agriculture negotiations. The United States also opposed efforts to include U.S. export credit guarantee programs in the negotiations.[5] Finally, the United States wanted to avoid opening the SPS agreement to renegotiation, because of the possibility that such a move would undermine the principle that SPS measures must be based on scientific principles.

The efforts by the United States and the Cairns group to seek to eliminate agricultural export subsidies were difficult for the EU to accept. In particular, European officials noted that they simply could not support language calling for the "elimination" of all export subsidies as the starting point of negotiations. Although the EU has been reducing subsidies to agriculture since the Uruguay Round, it remains by far the world's largest user of agricultural export subsidies. Export subsidies are a key mechanism in the EU's Common Agricultural Policy, which is intended to preserve farm incomes and rural economies by supporting high domestic prices for a wide variety of agricultural commodities and products. EU member states have taken a very strong position on maintaining the Common Agricultural Policy, a central element in the EU's institutional system and regarded as essential to its cohesiveness. Moreover, the EU and Japan proposed that agriculture negotiations take into account the "multi-functionality" of the agricultural sector and address issues such as food security, food safety, environmental protection, animal welfare, and the economic viability of rural areas.

The EU and Japan also viewed the prospect of launching a new round as an opportunity to establish international rules in other areas of the global trading system. In addition to agriculture and services, they proposed including investment, competition policy, government procurement, and other issues in a broad framework for negotiations. According to an EU official, the EU expected that compromises on agriculture would be compensated by concessions in these other areas. Although U.S. negotiators indicated support for continued study of investment and competition policy by WTO working groups, the United States and many other WTO members were unwilling to include these issues in the negotiating agenda for a new round.

PROGRESS ACHIEVED AT SEATTLE MINISTERIAL CONFERENCE

There is general agreement by participants at the ministerial conference in Seattle that negotiations on agriculture made the most progress of any area. Many officials indicated that consensus was close on a draft text setting forth issues to be addressed and on time frames for completing agricultural sector negotiations in a new round. However, this progress in the agricultural area was essentially lost when countries could not reach final consensus on the

---

[4] State trading enterprises are generally considered to be governmental or nongovernmental enterprises that are authorized to engage in trade and are owned, sanctioned or otherwise supported by the government.

[5] U.S. export credit guarantee programs allow foreign buyers to purchase U.S. agricultural commodities from private U.S. exporters, with U.S. banks providing the financing.

text, and the ministerial conference ended without agreement on a final declaration to set the agenda for a new round of trade negotiations.

In an effort to give all WTO members an opportunity to take part in the negotiations at Seattle, five large working groups, open to all member delegations, were set up to address major issues, including agriculture. U.S. and foreign officials agreed that the working group on agriculture made the most progress in Seattle. Although many working groups were hampered by the late selection of their chairs, the agriculture working group chair was named 2 days before the conference officially began and was able to begin work immediately on a draft agriculture text. In addition to two formal working group meetings, the chair held over a dozen smaller meetings with key delegations where most of the progress was made on developing a text. The chair completed a draft text on agriculture on the next to the last day of the conference, which contained only few areas of disagreement among interested WTO members.

The negotiations proceeded in a "green room" process on Friday, the last day of the conference.[6] In the green room, negotiators worked with the draft agriculture text; the negotiations on agriculture lasted 6 hours. By mid-afternoon, the parties appeared to be close to reaching consensus, and a draft text was issued that represented considerable compromise among the interested countries.

The draft agriculture text included many provisions favored by the United States. For example, it called for negotiations to cover, "substantial reductions" in subsidies in the "direction of progressive elimination of all forms of export subsidization." Similarly, the text called for negotiations to cover, "substantial progressive reductions" in domestic supports to agriculture. However, the United States was unable to get any specific reference to state trading enterprises in the text, as it had sought. Some non-trade concerns that the EU and Japan had wanted to introduce into the negotiations were included, but they were to be addressed through WTO transparent and non-trade distorting measures. Furthermore, these measures were to be in compliance with WTO principles, in general, and with the existing SPS agreement, specifically.

However, at the end of the conference, neither an overall agreement nor an agreement on agriculture was reached, and no ministerial declaration was issued. Thus, no agenda was set for a new round of negotiations. Several factors led to the failure to reach consensus, including differences among key players on certain issues, including agriculture. Although the participants we interviewed generally agreed that progress had been made in the agriculture talks, they noted that differences on some controversial issues remained. For example, the EU still had difficulties with language in the agriculture text that called for the elimination of export subsidies, while Japan and Korea opposed wording on market access that might have ruled out maintaining high tariffs on certain imports, notably rice. Ultimately, the EU said it would not agree to the draft text on agriculture without reaching consensus on the other issues in the negotiations, including investment and competition policy.

It is impossible to determine whether an agreement on agriculture could have been reached in Seattle because of the number of other factors that led to the breakdown of the talks, particularly the intense disagreement on the scope of the new round. According to U.S.

---

[6] As opposed to the working groups that were open to all member delegations, traditionally negotiations have taken place among a smaller number of key WTO members to work out privately some of the more difficult compromises. This smaller group negotiation of 20-30 members is known as the "green room" process.

government officials, failure to reach consensus at Seattle was partly due to the unwillingness of the EU and Japan to compromise on certain key aspects of the agriculture negotiations. Some European officials told us they probably could have made concessions on agriculture if the rest of the negotiations had been successful. However, other European delegations told us they would not have been able to accept the term "elimination" of subsidies in the text, and they would have pushed for it to be deleted if the negotiations had continued.

PROGRESS IN THE MANDATED NEGOTIATIONS MAY BE SLOW

Despite the failure to launch a trade round in Seattle, agricultural trade negotiations will resume in late March, under article 20 of the Uruguay Round Agreement on Agriculture. However, progress in achieving substantive trade liberalization may have been impeded for several reasons. For example, the failure to launch a new round may make it difficult for negotiators in Geneva to continue where they left off in Seattle. Furthermore, negotiating agriculture in isolation without the possibility of trade-offs in other areas may be problematic. Finally, much groundwork must be laid before substantive negotiations can begin.

First, the inconclusive outcome of the ministerial conference will make it difficult for negotiators in Geneva to start where they left off in Seattle and thus take advantage of any forward movement on the issues that occurred. The draft agricultural text from Seattle will not be used as a starting point for renewed negotiations; rather, article 20 will be the basis for the negotiations. The draft text was more definitive than article 20 regarding the specific issues on the negotiating agenda and time frames for the negotiations. For example, article 20 only calls for the continuation of the reform process with a stated long-term objective of making substantial and progressive reductions in agricultural support. In contrast, as previously noted, the draft Seattle text specifically called for, among other things, negotiations to cover "substantial reductions" in subsidies in the "direction of progressive elimination of all forms of export subsidization." Additionally, the draft Seattle text contains interim benchmarks and a deadline for the negotiations of December 15, 2002. Article 20, however, does not set a final deadline or such interim benchmarks. Specifically, it does not state when members must reach agreement on how the negotiations will be conducted or when members must submit their negotiating offers.

The U.S. Trade Representative has maintained that the expiration of the "peace clause"[7] at the end of 2003 may be an incentive to negotiate on agricultural subsidies by that date; after expiration of the peace clause, for the first time WTO members will be able to challenge certain agricultural export subsidies and domestic support measures of other members. However, one senior European official did not believe that the expiration date would act as an incentive to complete the negotiations.

Second, there is some concern about whether countries will be willing to make concessions in agriculture without obtaining trade-offs in other areas, as would have been the case in a round with a broader negotiating agenda. As demonstrated in Seattle, trading partners with politically sensitive agricultural sectors, such as the EU, want to show their constituents that they have gained concessions in other areas in order to agree to reduce

---

[7] The "peace clause" is a provision in the WTO Agriculture Agreement that protects WTO members from some challenges to their agricultural support programs and subsidies.

agricultural protection and support. One EU trade minister recently stated that, for this very reason, the mandated article 20 negotiations are unlikely to move forward in the absence of a comprehensive new trade round.

Finally, several U.S. government officials told us that not much progress should be expected during the first year of the built-in agenda negotiations because many decisions about how to proceed have yet to be made. Negotiations under the built-in agenda for agriculture will be conducted under the auspices of special sessions of the Committee on Agriculture, a standing committee within the WTO. The first special session of the Committee on Agriculture will meet the week of March 20th. Although the committee chair has yet to be named, U.S. and WTO officials told us that they expect this to occur before the first special session. The first meeting may cover procedural matters, such as agreeing on a work program for the remainder of 2000, and setting a deadline for WTO members to submit proposals on what should be on the negotiating agenda. A WTO official told us that the deadline for submitting proposals will likely be sometime this fall, or early next year.

Chapter 11

TRADE: AFRICA

Lenore Sek

ISSUE

Major legislation to improve economic relations between the United States and sub-Saharan Africa was enacted during the 106th Congress. The "African Growth and Opportunity Act" (AGOA), Title I of the "Trade and Development Act of 2000" (P.L. 106-200), provides trade benefits to countries of sub-Saharan Africa that meet certain criteria. Benefits include participation in a high-level U.S.-sub-Saharan African economic forum and increased market entry under the Generalized System of Preferences. The legislation had been opposed by U.S. textile and apparel producers, who warned of illegal imports from other regions. So far, beneficiary countries have been identified, additional products have been added to the list for duty-free treatment, and countries are applying for benefits as apparel exporters. The 107th Congress might consider implementation issues.

BACKGROUND

In 2000, trade with sub-Saharan Africa was 2% of total U.S. exports and 1% of total U.S. imports. Three-fourths of total U.S. trade with sub-Saharan Africa is with just three countries: Nigeria, South Africa, and Angola (see table). Most U.S. exports to sub-Saharan Africa are machinery and transport equipment, and most U.S. imports are petroleum and other basic commodities.

Major U.S. Trading Partners in Sub-Saharan Africa, 2000

U.S. Exports			U.S. Imports		
Country	$ millions	%	Country	$ millions	%
S. Africa	3,085	52	Nigeria	10,549	45
Nigeria	718	12	S. Africa	4,204	18
Angola	226	4	Angola	3,557	15
Subtotal	*4,029*	*68*	*Subtotal*	*18,310*	*78*
Other 45	*1,897*	*32*	*Other 45*	*5,170*	*22*
Total, Region	5,926	100	Total, Region	23,480	100

U.S. foreign direct investment in Africa (including northern Africa) at the end of 1999 was 1% of all U.S. foreign direct investment. Most U.S. foreign direct investment has been in the petroleum industry.

Several federal programs support U.S. trade and foreign investment. (Although these programs include sub-Saharan Africa, a major share of the programs' activities are not carried on with the region.) The Generalized System of Preferences grants selective duty-free treatment to imports from developing countries. The Export-Import (Ex-Im) Bank encourages U.S. exports through loans, loan guarantees, and credit insurance programs. The U.S. and Foreign Commercial Service in the Department of Commerce offers an array of services to U.S. exporters. The Overseas Private Investment Corporation (OPIC) assists U.S. businesses to invest overseas.

LEGISLATION

The 106th Congress approved legislation to extend trade and investment benefits to sub-Saharan Africa as part of a larger trade bill, *P.L. 106-200* ("Trade and Development Act of 2000"). The law was enacted on May 18, 2000, and includes provisions on sub-Saharan Africa, the Caribbean Basin, and other trade programs

The provisions on sub-Saharan Africa are in Title I ("African Growth and Opportunity Act," or AGOA). The AGOA focuses on countries committed to economic reform and emphasizes expanded trade and investment between the United States and the countries of sub-Saharan Africa. It establishes annual high-level meetings between senior U.S. and African officials to discuss wide-ranging economic issues. It directs the President to report on possible negotiation of a free-trade agreement with countries of sub-Saharan Africa. It also directs the Ex-Im Bank, the OPIC, and the Foreign Commercial Service to give more resources to programs in sub-Saharan Africa.

A major provision of the AGOA pertains to the expansion of products that may enter the United States duty-free under the Generalized System of Preferences. Under the AGOA, additional products may enter the United States duty-free if the President, with advice from the International Trade Commission, finds the products are not import-sensitive. Apparel products must meet strict rule-of-origin requirements to qualify for duty-free and quota-free treatment. The AGOA includes provisions intended to deter illegal shipments of textiles and apparel through sub-Saharan Africa. Two current legislative issues related to apparel are (1) whether to change a statutory cap on apparel imports made with regional fabric and yarn (cap is currently 1.5% of total U.S. apparel imports and grows to 3.5% over 8 years); and (2) how to address a Customs Service legal interpretation that denies duty-free treatment to "knit-to-shape" articles.

In May 2001, President Bush submitted a report to Congress on the U.S. trade and investment policy for sub-Saharan Africa and on implementation of AGOA. This is the first of eight reports required under Section 106 of AGOA. President Bush also has set an October date for the first annual meeting of the U.S.-Sub-Saharan Africa Trade and Economic Cooperation Forum, a ministerial meeting among high-level U.S. and sub-Saharan African officials of sub-Saharan Africa. As the provisions of the AGOA are implemented, the 107th Congress may consider oversight hearings.

Chapter 12

DEFENSE TRADE: INFORMATION ON U.S. WEAPONS DELIVERIES TO THE MIDDLE EAST

Katherine V. Schinasi

The U.S. government provides military equipment, services, and training to countries in the Middle East region[1] through a variety of military assistance programs.[2] You asked us to identify (1) the amounts and types of military equipment, services, and training the U.S. government has delivered to the Middle East from fiscal year 1991 through fiscal year 2000, and (2) the conditions placed on the use of selected U.S. weapon systems delivered to the Middle East.

RESULTS IN BRIEF

From fiscal year 1991 through fiscal year 2000, the U.S. government delivered about $74 billion in military equipment, services, and training to countries in the Middle East. This included military items purchased by these countries through the Foreign Military Sales program, as well as those financed with grant funds provided through the Foreign Military Financing program. In addition, military equipment, services, and training is provided on a grant basis through the International Military Education and Training program and under the Excess Defense Articles and Emergency Drawdown authorities. The Foreign Military Sales and Foreign Military Financing programs account for about 96 percent of the value of military items the United States delivered to the region. The U.S. weapon systems delivered

---

[1] We included the following countries in the Middle East region in our review: Bahrain, Egypt, Israel, Jordan, Kuwait, Lebanon, Oman, Qatar, Saudi Arabia, Syria, United Arab Emirates, and Yemen. In addition, we included the Palestinian Authority in our review due to its location in the Middle East.

[2] For the purposes of this report, military assistance programs refers to security assistance programs administered by the Department of Defense.

include F-16 and F/A-18 fighter aircraft, Apache and Cobra helicopters, M1A1 tanks, and AMRAAM,[3] ATACMS,[4] and Stinger missiles.

State and Defense Department officials told us that conditions on the use of U.S. military equipment, services, and training delivered to countries in the Middle East, with few exceptions, are limited to standard conditions that the U.S. government places on all transfers of U.S. military items. By law, the United States may provide military items to foreign governments only for internal security, legitimate self-defense, participation in collective arrangements that are consistent with the United Nations' charter, or civic action.[5] Use conditions are contained in general mutual defense treaties and other international agreements, and sales agreements for military equipment, services, and training sold to foreign governments. In addition to the standard use conditions, we identified a limited number of cases where the U.S. government applied specific use conditions to weapon systems delivered to the Middle East. For example, U.S. manportable air defense systems (such as Stinger missiles) may not be assembled for training or testing by the foreign government without prior notice to U.S. military personnel located in overseas offices.[6]

BACKGROUND

The U.S. government provides military equipment, services, and training to countries in the Middle East through several military assistance programs, including the Foreign Military Sales program, Foreign Military Financing program, International Military Education and Training program, Excess Defense Articles authority, and Emergency Drawdown authority. These programs are generally governed by the Arms Export Control Act, as amended,[7] and the Foreign Assistance Act of 1961, as amended.[8]

Through the Foreign Military Sales program, the U.S. government sells military equipment, services, and training to foreign governments under sales agreements managed by the Defense Department. Although the Arms Export Control Act generally requires the U.S. government to recover the full estimated costs from the foreign government purchaser, U.S. grant funds provided under the Foreign Military Financing program can be used to purchase military items through the Foreign Military Sales program.

Through the Foreign Military Financing program, the U.S. government provides selected countries with grant funds to purchase military equipment, services, and training. As stated above, these funds can be used to purchase military items through the Foreign Military Sales program, or in some cases can be used to purchase such items directly from U.S. companies. In addition, Israel may use a portion of these grant funds to purchase military items directly from its indigenous companies. Purchases made directly from companies are generally referred to as direct commercial sales.

---

[3] Advanced Medium Range Air-to-Air Missile.
[4] Army Tactical Missile System.
[5] Military equipment and training may be used in developing countries to assist foreign military forces to construct public works or to engage in other activities helpful to the economic and social development of a country.
[6] The U.S. government requires that this condition be applied to all deliveries of manportable air defense systems, except for transfers to Australia, Japan, New Zealand, andNorth Atlantic Treaty Organization countries.
[7] 22 U.S.C. § 2751 et seq.
[8] 22 U.S.C. § 2151 et seq.

The U.S. government funds military training for foreign governments through the International Military Education and Training program. In addition, it provides military equipment, services, and training to foreign governments, on a grant basis, under the Excess Defense Articles[9] and Emergency Drawdown[10] authorities. Under these authorities, the U.S. provides military items directly from Defense Department stocks.

Through these military assistance programs, the U.S. government places conditions on deliveries of U.S. military equipment, services, and training to foreign governments. These conditions restrict the use of such equipment to certain authorized purposes and restrict the transfer of the equipment to third parties. Conditions may also specify security measures to be taken to protect the equipment or require special inventory checks by U.S. personnel. For the purpose of this review, we focused on use restrictions.

AMOUNTS AND TYPES OF U.S. MILITARY ASSISTANCE DELIVERED TO THE MIDDLE EAST

The U.S. government delivered about $74 billion in military equipment, services, and training to countries in the Middle East from fiscal year 1991 through fiscal year 2000. Table 1 shows the total value of U.S. military assistance that was delivered, by country, for the 10-year period. The data is arranged by each of the five military assistance programs we included in our review.[11] The amounts shown for the Foreign Military Financing program represent only the portion that was used for direct commercial sales.[12] The remainder of the Foreign Military Financing funds are included as part of the Foreign Military Sales totals since these funds were used to purchase items through that program. Table 1 shows the value of deliveries of military items purchased by countries in the Middle East through the Foreign Military Sales program or purchased as direct commercial sales using funds provided through the Foreign Military Financing program, as well as military items provided on a grant basis through the International Military Education and Training program and under the Excess Defense Articles and Emergency Drawdown authorities. Over the last 10 years, the Foreign Military Sales and Foreign Military Financing programs have accounted for about 96 percent of the value of military items the United States has delivered to the Middle East. The four largest recipients of military items in the Middle East have been Saudi Arabia, Israel, Egypt, and Kuwait. Syria and the Palestinian Authority did not receive U.S. military assistance during this period.[13]

---

[9] 22 U.S.C. § 2321j.

[10] 22 U.S.C. § 2318.

[11] The five programs we reviewed account for the majority of military assistance dollars to the Middle East, although the U.S. government has other means of delivering military assistance to foreign governments. For example, military equipment, services, and training can also be provided through Peacekeeping Operations, International Narcotics Control and Law Enforcement, and Nonproliferation, Anti-terrorism, Demining, and Related Programs.

[12] The total value of Foreign Military Financing grant funds appropriated to the Middle East during fiscal years 1991 to 2000 is over $33 billion, including $19 billion to Israel, $13 billionto Egypt, and $567 million to Jordan. However, these appropriated amounts have not allbeen disbursed as of August 2001.

[13] While the Palestinian Authority did not directly receive U.S. military assistance, the U.S. government indirectly provided the Palestine Police with $4 million in fiscal year 1994 and $5 million in fiscal year 1995 for non-lethal assistance. This assistance consisted of trucks, jeeps, uniforms, and medical equipment obtained from Defense Department stocks under Emergency Drawdown authority for Israel and then provided to the Palestine Police.

Table 1: Value of U.S. Military Assistance Deliveries to the Middle East, Fiscal Years 1991-2000.

Dollars in millions

Country	Foreign Military Sales	Foreign Military Financing-Commercial Sales	Excess Defense Articles	Emergency Drawdown	International Military Education & Training	Total
Saudi Arabia	$33,526.7	0	0	0	0	$33,526.7
Israel	6,365.6	$10,812.4	$767.4	$818.0	0	18,763.4
Egypt	10,030.9	2,097.9	539.4	13.5	$12.3	12,694.1
Kuwait	5,520.0	0	0	0	0	5,520.0
United Arab Emirates	1,380.0	0	0	0	0	1,380.0
Jordan	351.6	57.6	386.4	139.3	11.9	946.9
Bahrain	615.7	0	402.8	0	1.3	1,019.7
Lebanon	135.7	0	58.8	0	4.0	198.5
Oman	95.1	0	56.4	0	1.5	153.1
Yemen	5.8	0	0	0	0.5	6.3
Qatar	4.8	0	0	0	0	4.8
Total	**$58,031.8**	**$12,967.9**	**$2,211.3**	**$970.8**	**$31.6**	**$74,213.4**

[a]Totals may not add due to rounding.
Source: GAO analysis of Defense Department data.

Figure 1: Selected U.S. Weapon Systems Delivered to the Middle East[a]

	Bahrain	Egypt	Israel	Jordan	Kuwait	Oman	Saudi Arabia	UAE	Yemen
Aircraft									
F-15			•				•		
F-16	•	•	•	•					
F/A-18					•				
E-2C		•	•						
E-3A							•		
Helicopters									
Apache		•	•				•	•	
Apache Longbow		•							
Cobra	•		•	•					
Missiles									
AMRAAM	•		•						
Harpoon	•	•	•		•		•	•	
Hellfire		•	•				•	•	
Maverick	•	•	•	•	•		•		
Patriot		•			•		•		
Sidewinder	•	•	•	•	•	•	•		
Sparrow	•	•	•		•		•		
Stinger	•	•	•				•		
TOW	•	•	•	•	•	•	•	•	•
ATACMS	•								
MLRS	•		•						
Tanks									
M1A1		•							
M1A2					•		•		
Cluster bombs		•	•				•	•	

[a]Lebanon, Qatar, Syria, and the Palestinian Authority have not received any of the above U.S. weapon systems from fiscal years 1991 through 2000.
Source: GAO's analysis of the Defense Department's data.

The weapon systems that the U.S. government has delivered to countries in the Middle East include fighter aircraft, helicopters, tanks, missiles, and cluster bombs. Figure 1 identifies some of the weapon systems that have been delivered to specific countries.

CONDITIONS ON THE USE OF U.S. MILITARY EQUIPMENT DELIVERED TO THE MIDDLE EAST

State and Defense Department officials told us that conditions on the use of U.S. military equipment, services, and training delivered to countries in the Middle East, with few exceptions, are limited to standard conditions that the U.S. government places on all transfers of military items. According to these officials, the U.S. government carefully reviews each proposed military transfer to prevent sensitive military items from going to countries that would misuse them or to limit the military technology provided.[14] For example, Army officials told us that the TOW[15] 2B missile is sold to only a few countries, because it has more capability than the TOW 2A. Of the countries identified in figure 1, only Kuwait has received the TOW 2B missile. Several State and Defense Department officials cited this review process as the reason the U.S. government generally does not place specific use restrictions, in addition to standard use conditions, on military items transferred to foreign governments.

U.S. laws governing military assistance include conditions on the transfer of U.S. military equipment, services, and training. Both the Arms Export Control Act[16] and the Foreign Assistance Act[17] define the purposes for which U.S. military items can be transferred. These purposes are internal security, legitimate self-defense, participation in collective arrangements that are consistent with the United Nations' charter, or construction of public works or other economic and social development activities.

The U.S. government signed mutual defense treaties and other international military assistance agreements with foreign governments in the Middle East when military assistance was first provided to those countries. These treaties and international agreements include, by reference, the use conditions found in the Arms Export Control or Foreign Assistance Acts, or in some cases, include similar language to the use conditions provided by these acts. For example, a 1988 memorandum of understanding between the United States and Egypt for the coproduction of the M1A1 tank states that defense articles, services, and technology transferred to Egypt must be used in accordance with the Arms Export Control Act. In another example, a 1952 mutual defense assistance agreement states that Israel may use U.S. military equipment only to maintain its internal security, for legitimate self-defense, or to participate in United Nations collective security arrangements. This is similar to the language contained in the Arms Export Control and Foreign Assistance Acts.

The Defense Department uses sales agreements when it sells U.S. military equipment, services, and training to foreign governments through the Foreign Military Sales program. These sales agreements contain a number of standard terms and conditions, including

---

[14] See *Foreign Military Sales: Review Process for Controlled Missile Technology Needs Improvement* (GAO/NSIAD-99-231, Sept. 29, 1999) for information on the review process for military transfers.
[15] Tube-launched, Optically-tracked, Wire-guided.
[16] 22 U.S.C. § 2754.
[17] 22 U.S.C. § 2302.

conditions similar to those found in the Arms Export Control and Foreign Assistance Acts or in military assistance agreements. The standard use conditions require the purchaser to use the defense articles sold only for the purposes specified in any mutual defense assistance agreement, bilateral treaty, or regional defense treaty. If no such agreements or treaties exist, then defense articles are only to be used for internal security, individual self-defense, or civic action.

We reviewed over 80 sales agreements for weapon systems sold to the Middle East and found that those for man-portable air defense systems (such as Stinger missiles) contained use conditions in addition to the standard use conditions. The sales agreements require foreign governments to notify U.S. military personnel located in overseas offices prior to assembling the components of the man-portable air defense systems for training or testing. In addition, these components may not be assembled except in the event of hostilities or imminent hostilities, as part of regularly scheduled training, for testing, or to defend high-priority installations or activities.

We also identified a limited number of instances where additional use conditions were placed on a particular weapon system delivered to specific countries in the Middle East. These conditions were not included in the sales agreements, but were conveyed to the foreign governments through memoranda of understanding or formal discussions. For example, prior to selling fighter aircraft to one country in the Middle East, the U.S. government received assurances from the foreign government, through formal discussions, that the aircraft would not be based near one of the country's borders. In another example, the U.S. government signed a memorandum of understanding by which the foreign government agreed to use the U.S. weapon system only within that country's borders.

AGENCY COMMENTS

Copies of this report were provided to the Departments of Defense and State. Neither department provided written comments. However, both had technical suggestions, which we incorporated as appropriate.

SCOPE AND METHODOLOGY

To identify the amounts and types of U.S. military equipment, services, and training provided to countries in the Middle East from fiscal year 1991 through fiscal year 2000, we reviewed data on Foreign Military Sales, Foreign Military Financing, and International Military Education and Training programs. In addition, we reviewed data on military items provided under Excess Defense Articles and Emergency Drawdown authority. We excluded data on military items sold directly to the Middle East by U.S. companies, except for those paid for with Foreign Military Financing grant funds. To aggregate the military assistance data, we used delivery values for all but one of the programs we reviewed. For the delivery value of military items that foreign governments purchased directly from companies using Foreign Military Financing grant funds, we used the amounts obligated by those countries for each fiscal year because that information was not available for deliveries. Defense Department officials told us that the amounts obligated would most closely correspond with military item deliveries. Defense Department officials also told us that under the Foreign Military Sales program, the term delivered indicates that a sales agreement has been signed and implemented, but due to production lead-time or other factors, physical delivery of the items may take place at a later date.

To identify the conditions the U.S. government places on the use of military equipment, services, and training, we reviewed the Arms Export Control Act, the Foreign Assistance Act, key mutual defense treaties and other international military assistance agreements, Defense Department guidance, and over 80 sales agreements for selected weapon systems. We also interviewed State and Defense Department officials responsible for U.S. military assistance programs to discuss use conditions on military items.

INDEX

U

V

W